Eat My Flesh
And
Drink My Blood

Eat My Flesh
And
Drink My Blood

PAUL C. JONG

Hephzibah Publishing House
A Ministry of THE NEW LIFE MISSION
SEOUL, KOREA

Sermons on the Gospel of John (III)
Eat My Flesh And Drink My Blood

ISBN 89-8314-692-3
Cover Art by Min-soo Kim
Illustration by Young-ae Kim
Printed in Korea

Hephzibah Publishing House
A Ministry of THE NEW LIFE MISSION
48 Bon-dong, Dongjack-gu
Seoul, Korea 156-060

♠ Website: http://www.nlmission.com
          http://www.bjnewlife.org
♠ E-mail: newlife@bjnewlife.org
♠ Phone: 82(Korea)-11-1788-2954
♠ Fax: 82-33-637-4440

Table of Contents

Preface

In the history of Christianity, the Eucharist controversy that was triggered over the interpretation of Holy Communion still has not seen a clear settlement. In other words, depending on how one looks at the bread and wine used in Communion, there are several competing arguments as follows:

1) Transubstantiation—a position held by the Catholic Church, this view argues that the bread and wine of Holy Communion are actually transformed into the flesh and blood of Jesus Christ.

2) Coexistentialism—a view advocated by Martin Luther, this position argues that Jesus Christ is actually present in the bread and wine of Communion.

3) Symbolism—argued by Ulrich Zwingli of Swiss, it views Communion as a symbolic commemoration for the death of Jesus Christ.

4) Calvin's Doctrine of the Spiritual Presence of Jesus Christ—this position believes that Christ is spiritually present in the bread and wine of Communion.

To this day, Christians believe in one of the above views without any hesitation according to their own thoughts. However, of the four positions outlined above, except for Transubstantiation advocated by the Catholic Church, all three remaining positions are actually little more than partial modifications of Transubstantiation. In fact, all these arguments are nothing more than hypothetical notions made according to human thoughts, as their advocates completely failed to understand what the Lord meant when He said, *"Most assuredly, I say to you, unless you eat the flesh of the Son of*

Man and drink His blood, you have no life in you" (John 6:53).

Put differently, all these contentions surfaced precisely because their supporters were completely ignorant of the reason why Jesus told us to eat His flesh and drink His blood. At the Last Supper, Jesus told His disciples to remember His flesh and blood with bread and wine, and this bread here signifies the fact that Jesus took upon all the sins of this world once for all through the baptism He received from John the Baptist, while the wine means that Christ bore the condemnation of our sins in our place by being crucified and shedding His blood to death.

We must never render the just love and salvation of Jesus manifested in Holy Communion in vain. All of us should now once again reflect on the Lord's intention in commanding us to eat His flesh and drink His blood, and partake in Communion by faith. When we take part in Holy Communion, which constitutes the witness of salvation, we must have the proper understanding of the righteousness of God that has blotted out all our sins with the gospel of the water and the Spirit, and believe in this righteousness.

To repeat, if you participate in Communion believing in such doctrines as Transubstantiation, then I have no choice but to point out that your faith is gravely wrong. Jesus said, *"Most assuredly, I say to you, unless you eat the flesh of the Son of Man and drink His blood, you have no life in you" (John 6:53),* but does this really mean that we should then perform Holy Communion to literally eat and drink Jesus' flesh and blood, which have somehow been mysteriously transformed from bread and wine? According to theologians, when we perform Communion, Jesus Christ is actually present in its bread and wine, and therefore by eating this bread and drinking the wine, we would be eating the flesh of Jesus and drinking His blood.

If this were the case, then it would also mean that unless we partake in Communion, we would not be able to eat the flesh of Jesus nor drink His blood. However, such a claim is absolute nonsense. It is a deviation from the Truth. Is this what Jesus said?

Did He say that we have to perform Communion in order to really eat His flesh and drink His blood? No, He never said this. It is by believing in the Word of God that we are saved from our sins and receive everlasting life as well. If indeed we are to eat the flesh of Jesus and drink His blood only when we perform Communion, and we cannot otherwise have His flesh and blood, then doesn't this mean that our faith would be constituted of our own deeds? Anyone who teaches fallaciously like this will be judged by Jesus.

For us to truly eat the flesh of Jesus and drink His blood, this is not achieved just by participating in Holy Communion. It is by believing in what Jesus did in His 33 years of life on this earth that we can eat His flesh and drink His blood. When Jesus came to this earth, He took upon Himself all our sins, who were under the Law, and all its curses for these sins once and for all. It was to thus shoulder our sins on His body (flesh) that God Himself, who knew no sin, came incarnated in the same flesh as ours, and that is how He could accept every sin of this world all at once by receiving baptism on His body in a form of the laying on of hands. This was the flesh of Jesus that was offered to fulfill the righteousness of God. By believing in the fact that our sins were passed onto the body of Jesus through His baptism, we must eat His flesh. It is by this faith that we eat the flesh of Jesus. And we drink His blood by believing that Jesus carried these sins to the Cross and was condemned in our place, precisely because He had taken upon the sins of the world by being baptized by John the Baptist.

Until now, most Christians have not known the Truth, but only inherited religious acts. From the gospel to Holy Communion, today's Christianity maintains its orthodoxy not through the knowledge of the Truth, but by emphasizing only formal procedures and consecrated rites. As a result, when today's Christians come across the bread and wine that signify the flesh and blood of Jesus during Communion, they are thankful only for the sacrifice of His blood, and they can't help but remain completely ignorant of the fact that Christ took upon Himself all their sins once and for all by being baptized by John the Baptist. Therefore, I admonish all Christians throughout the whole world to learn, even from now on, what the flesh and blood of Jesus mean within the gospel of the water and the Spirit, to believe in it, and to thereby receive their salvation and also partake in Holy Communion with the right faith.

I would like to make it clear here that I am not trying to undermine your faith, but to correct your mistakes and reestablish your faith properly. It is my sincerest hope and prayer that Protestants, Catholics, and everyone who will ever come to believe in Jesus throughout the whole world would all understand and believe in the flesh and blood of Jesus properly within the gospel Truth of the water and the Spirit, and thus enjoy everlasting life.

May God's blessings be with you all. ✉

Author

CHAPTER 6

What Use Are These Small Loaves and Fish to Many People?

< John 6:1-15 >

"After these things Jesus went over the Sea of Galilee, which is the Sea of Tiberias. Then a great multitude followed Him, because they saw His signs which He performed on those who were diseased. And Jesus went up on the mountain, and there He sat with His disciples. Now the Passover, a feast of the Jews, was near. Then Jesus lifted up His eyes, and seeing a great multitude coming toward Him, He said to Philip, 'Where shall we buy bread, that these may eat?' But this He said to test him, for He Himself knew what He would do. Philip answered Him, 'Two hundred denarii worth of bread is not sufficient for them, that every one of them may have a little.' One of His disciples, Andrew, Simon Peter's brother, said to Him, 'There is a lad here who has five barley loaves and two small fish, but what are they among so many?' Then Jesus said, 'Make the people sit down.' Now there was much grass in the place. So the men sat down, in number about five thousand. And Jesus took the loaves, and when He had given thanks He distributed them to the disciples, and the disciples to those sitting down; and likewise of the fish, as much as they wanted. So when they were filled, He said to His disciples, 'Gather up the fragments that remain, so that

nothing is lost.' Therefore they gathered them up, and filled twelve baskets with the fragments of the five barley loaves which were left over by those who had eaten. Then those men, when they had seen the sign that Jesus did, said, 'This is truly the Prophet who is to come into the world.' Therefore when Jesus perceived that they were about to come and take Him by force to make Him king, He departed again to the mountain by Himself alone."

John chapter six is all about the bread of life in its entirety.

It is written in today's Scripture passage that when Jesus went over to the other side of the Sea of Tiberias, a great multitude followed Him. The reason why so many people followed Jesus was because they had seen the signs that He performed on those who were diseased. As Jesus went up on the mountain and sat with His disciples, He saw this great multitude coming toward Him, and so He said to Philip, *"Where shall we buy bread, that these may eat?"* Philip then answered Him, *"Two hundred denarii worth of bread is not sufficient for them, that every one of them may have a little."*

Another disciple, Andrew, then said to Jesus, *"There is a lad here who has five barley loaves and two small fish, but what are they among so many?"* Both Philip and Andrew only told Jesus what the actual situation was at that time. But Jesus told His disciples to make all those people sit down on the grass. He then took the five loaves and two fish that the lad brought, blessed them, and distributed them to all those sitting there. There were over 5,000 men alone who ate these bread and fish at that time, not counting women and children (Matthew 14:21; Mark 6:44).

Because of this miracle, the people gathered there tried to

make Jesus their king. The people of Israel were living under the colonial rule of Rome at that time, and so even as they tilled the ground, they had very little to survive on, as most of their harvest was taken away to pay for the assessed taxes by the Roman Empire. So it was more than possible for them to try to make Jesus their king. Since they could hardly feed themselves to survive, they had no money to get any treatments when they fell ill, and that was why they were following Jesus so closely, who had healed their illnesses and fed them full.

The Bread Mentioned in John Chapter Six Signifies the Flesh of Jesus

The flesh of Jesus signifies that Jesus shouldered our sins on His body by receiving His baptism, gave up His body to be crucified, shed His blood to death, rose from the dead again, and has thereby become our true Savior. By taking our sins upon His own body all at once, and by bearing the condemnation of these sins once and for all, Jesus has saved us perfectly from all our sins. The body of Jesus is the bread of life.

And the blood of Jesus is the true drink. From a certain point of view, the Bible may seem nothing more than a historical record of the people of Israel, but in reality, it is the Word of God that writes about the flesh and blood of Jesus that God has given us to bring life to the entire human race. Each chapter of the Bible contains the Word of life that God wants to speak to us. So if anyone has the accurate knowledge of what the Word of God is saying to him, he can be saved from all his sins.

Andrew said to Jesus, *"There is a lad here who has five*

barley loaves and two small fish, but what are they among so many?" The two small fish here refer to God's Church. Like these fish, God's Church is also unimpressive in its outside appearance. Nonetheless, it is God's Church that is now preaching the gospel of the water and the Spirit to everyone living on this earth. Thanks to the gospel of the water and the Spirit that we are spreading now, many people in this age are able to eat the flesh of Jesus and drink His blood. Because we are sharing this genuine gospel with the entire population of the world, of the more than 6 billion people living in this world, those who believe in this gospel are receiving the remission of their sins. Right now, God's Church is a small gathering in number. Some people may question how much could possibly be achieved through such a small number of ministers and saints, and the few coworkers scattered around the world, but because the Lord holds God's Church steadfast and works through it, He is saving everyone in the world from its sins. Our Lord has given the bread of life to those of us who believe in the gospel of the water and the Spirit.

Jesus Said That the Flesh of His Body is the Bread of Life for Us

When we partake in Holy Communion, we eat bread and drink wine, and the bread here symbolizes the body of Jesus, while the wine signifies the blood Jesus shed on the Cross. Jesus told us to remember Him with the bread and wine of Communion (Luke 22:19). Why? Because our Lord took upon all the sins of this world by receiving baptism on His body, and shed His blood on the Cross for us. Because our Lord took our sins upon His body through His baptism, they were passed onto

Jesus Christ, and this is how our sins could be washed away. When Jesus told us to eat His flesh and drink His blood, He was telling us to believe in the Truth that He took upon Himself our sins by being baptized, gave up His body on the Cross to shed His blood, rose from the dead again, and has thereby blotted out all our sins once and for all. So considering this, what would have happened had Jesus not shouldered our sins by receiving baptism on His body? We could never have washed away ours sins. That is why we must receive the remission of our sins by faith, by eating the flesh of Jesus and drinking His blood.

When we are too busy with our own affairs, we tend to forget how thankful we should be that the Lord has saved us from sin. In other words, even though we should indeed be grateful beyond words that the Lord has saved us through His flesh and blood, when our souls are darkened, we can't feel this grace. And as a result, we lose our gratitude for God and His grace, just as the church of Ephesus was rebuked for losing the first love despite the fact that it had worked and labored tirelessly for God (Revelation 2:1-4). However, when we free ourselves for a while from the affairs that have gripped us, set aside everything, and ruminate on God, we can see just how thankful we should be for God's grace. When I think about how the Lord came to this earth, how He was baptized to take upon my sins once and for all, how He carried these sins to the Cross to be crucified and was condemned for them, how He died and rose from the dead again, and how He has thereby made me a sinless man, I am overwhelmed with gratitude. When I get immersed in my work, I am too busy with what's right in front of me that I have little time to be thankful. But, when I stand before God once again, I am so thankful that He has saved someone like me.

Spiritual thoughts and carnal thoughts are often all mixed up in our minds, throwing us into confusion. However, when we think about what God has done for us, our hearts are filled with thankfulness. We need to once again remember that we could never have become sinless before God all by ourselves, because we are too insufficient and weak.

Jesus Christ is the very God who made us. Jesus is the Creator who made us as well as the entire universe, and therefore He is the Master of the universe. Jesus is the Savior who, when mankind that was made in the image of God fell into sin and was destined to hell, was born on this earth incarnated in the flesh of man through the body of the Virgin Mary to save His people from their sins; took upon the sins of the world by receiving baptism on His body; was condemned for them on the Cross and died; rose from the dead again; and has thereby truly and completely saved us from sin. I cannot thank God enough when I think about the gospel of the water and the Spirit.

When people stand before their death and destruction, they become very honest. If I assume that I am about to die right now at this very hour, I would set aside all the affairs of this world and think only of my relationship with God. And even as I take in my last breath, I would be completely at peace and joyful for having eaten the flesh of Jesus and having drank His blood while alive.

Not long ago, on Easter Sunday, we thanked the Lord again for giving us everlasting life. After being baptized by John the Baptist and dying on the Cross, our Lord rose again from the dead and lived again. Because the Lord's resurrection is our own resurrection, of you and me who believe in His gospel, just as the Lord rose from the dead again, our bodies will be transformed and we will also be resurrected into new bodies that will never die. In other words, just as the Lord rose again from the dead, we the believers in the gospel of the water and the Spirit will also rise again from the dead. Indeed, we believe in the Lord's resurrection, and we believe that we, too, will be resurrected.

When Easter comes around, even the pastors who have not been born again preach, "Since Jesus died on the Cross and rose from the tomb again, you should also live with the hope of resurrection." The question, however, is whether or not they really believe in the resurrection of Jesus. Put differently, are they really sure that they themselves will be resurrected on the Lord's Day? They can't be sure. Even though they say with their lips, "Yes, I believe," they have doubts in their hearts, wondering, "Will this really happen?"

Before I was born again, my mind could not understand the meaning of resurrection either. I wondered, "How could Jesus rise again after death? How can a dead man ever rise again?" However, because the Lord who shouldered the sins of the world through His baptism is essentially the almighty God Himself, it was eminently possible for Him to rise again from the dead. The Lord said that just as He rose from the dead again, we, too, will live again. He said to us, "Those who eat My flesh and drink My blood, I will raise them on the last day. All who believe in Me will receive everlasting life."

That is indeed true. As Easter comes around, preachers who have not been born again speak of irrelevant things, but we should realize that the Lord has raised us to live again by giving us new life, believe in this, and give wholehearted thanks to Him. After carrying out the Lord's work, we will eventually go and stand before His presence.

What will happen to this body when we stand before God? Those who believe in the gospel of the water and the Spirit believe that they will live again. Those who don't believe in this gospel, however, will not be able to participate in the first resurrection (Revelation 20:5-6). How could they, who did not eat the flesh of Jesus and drink His blood by believing in the gospel of the water and the Spirit, have any hope and believe in the resurrection of Jesus and theirs? People find it impossible to believe with their hearts that they will be resurrected in the future precisely because they do not know that Jesus took the sins of the world upon His body by receiving baptism from John the Baptist, shed His blood unto death on the Cross, and rose again from the dead.

Because Jesus is fundamentally God Himself, He could truly save all of us by coming to this earth incarnated in the flesh of man, taking upon Himself your sins and mine once and for all by being baptized by John the Baptist, dying on the Cross, and rising from the dead again. If Jesus had been just a man, this would have been impossible, but He achieved this because He is God Himself. There is absolutely no human being, who is only one of God's many creatures, that was ever born without sin in this world. All human beings are born sinners.

However, because Jesus is the Son of God the Father, because He Himself is the One who created the entire universe with His Word, and because it is the will of God the Father to save us from sin, Christ came to this earth in obedience to this will of the Father, and has indeed saved us through the gospel of the water and the Spirit. Our Lord has resurrected us who believe in this Truth from both spiritual and bodily death. It's because Jesus is your Savior and my Savior that He has indeed done this for us. That is why in our hearts we have faith in God and a profound gratitude.

We have to grasp and believe that Jesus is God (1 John

5:20). If Jesus were just a creature, no one would be able to be saved. Let's assume here that someone virtuous and highly respected in this world shouldered your sins and mine and died for us. Could you and I then really be saved? No, we won't be saved. That's because there is no one who does not commit sin, and therefore even if this person were to shoulder our sins and die in our place, he cannot save any other sinners, for he himself is a sinner.

It's because only the almighty God alone can save us from sin that He Himself came to this earth to deliver us. That is why our Lord, who is God Himself, took the sins of the world upon His own body by being baptized, thereby cleansing away our sins. It's also because Jesus is God Himself that the Lord was able to be condemned for our sins and die on the Cross in our place, and it's because of His power that He could also rise from the dead again. That is how Jesus has truly saved you and me from sin. And that is why we give our thanks to God by believing in this Jesus.

There are countless people in this world leading religious lives according to their thoughts. Their religious lives are obvious. Based on today's Scripture passage, they preach as the following: "How was it possible for the bread and fish to multiply so miraculously? Here, as a child offered his small lunch to Jesus without any hesitation, the grownups were moved by this and offered their lunch that they had stashed away, and as all this food was gathered together and shared equally, there was enough food to fill everyone and still have twelve baskets of food left over. So let us also offer even small sums and help the poor. Every little bit helps, and so we should all pool donations to help the poor." But this actually turns the Word of God into a lifeless ethical system of human norms.

The lunch that the child brought at that time only had five

barley loaves and two fish. He probably got his lunch from his parents, who apparently made sure to pack him with something to eat as he went off to see Jesus. But the child offered this small lunch to the Lord. The Lord then blessed this and performed the miracle of five loaves and two fish. Such a miracle does not arise no matter how human beings like us bless on this lunch. Anyone whose head is straight knows that this is impossible. Instead of just accepting it as a given since it's from the Bible, imagine you were doing this yourself, and think about it again. If you were to pray over this lunch and say, "May God bless it," would this lunch be multiplied all of a sudden to feed everyone gathered there and still have twelve baskets left over? Of course not! No such a miracle can arise out of our own power. Only Jesus can achieve this.

Right now, we are spreading the gospel of Truth all over the world. There are plenty of people in this world who are just preaching their own gospel. But those who preach the gospel of the water and the Spirit are few and far between. There is no other gospel of Truth but this gospel of the water and the Spirit. It is this gospel of the water and the Spirit that we believe in and preach, and this very gospel that you and I are spreading is the Word of God that is more than able to save everyone throughout the whole world. The gospel of the water and the Spirit is the blessed gospel and the bread of life that enables mankind to be washed clean from all its sins and receive new life. Some of us have only recently heard the gospel of the water and the Spirit, while for others, it's been a long time since they were born again by believing in this gospel. But all of us know equally well that this gospel of the water and the Spirit is the only gospel of the Truth.

The gospel of the water and the Spirit is the Truth that the Lord has cleansed away all our sins with His baptism and His blood on the Cross: By coming to this earth, taking upon the sins of the world through His baptism, shedding His blood and dying on the Cross, and rising from the dead again, our Lord has become our Savior. The five barley loaves in today's Scripture passage symbolize the salvation of grace that the Lord has bestowed on us, and this implies the very gospel of the water and the Spirit. In the Bible, the number five signifies God's grace and blessings.

My fellow believers, in the gospel of the water and the Spirit that we believe in, there are the blessing of salvation, the blessing of everlasting life, and the blessing of new life. It is a truly wonderful gospel. It is this gospel that we believe in, and it is this gospel that we are preaching throughout the whole world through our books. Even at this very moment, people all over the world are sending us their testimonies of salvation, telling us that they have received the remission of their sins by believing in this gospel of the water and the Spirit. There are many missionaries and pastors among them. My fellow believers, are these people then saying that they were born again only now because they had not believed in Jesus all this time, or believed in Him later than us? No. What happened is that they had believed in a false gospel all this time, and it was only now that they found the gospel of the water and the Spirit preached by God's Church and believed in it. That is why they have come to abide in God's grace only now.

Our Lord promised that He would bring down the former rain and the latter rain according to appropriate times (Joel 2:23). During the era of the Early Church, when the Apostles were preaching the gospel of the water and the Spirit, God had brought down the former rain, and now, He is covering the whole planet with the latter rain. This latter rain is coming down all over the world through our paper books and e-books, and through the Internet. In other words, by feeding on this gospel of the water and the Spirit, people are quenched from their spiritual hunger and thirst and receiving everlasting life. When our Lord came to this earth, He offered His body to us to take our sins upon this body through His baptism, washed away all our sins by being condemned on the Cross, and rose from the dead again. We must eat the bread of life that He has given us. To those who believe in this gospel that Jesus has given us, He has also given salvation and eternal life.

Our Lord said, "Whoever eats the bread that I give will never hunger again." He also said, *"Whoever drinks of the water that I shall give him will never thirst. But the water that I shall give him will become in him a fountain of water springing up into everlasting life" (John 4:14).* No matter how many things of the flesh people might have, they are still thirsty and hungry spiritually. They may drink, sing, and dance in this world, but their hearts are filled with only sadness. They may have all the fun to be had today, gorge themselves on the finest food, get drunk till they pass out, and enjoy the greatest pleasure on earth, but when tomorrow morning comes, their hearts will once again be empty. The reality of human existence is that its heart, passions, thoughts, and body all thirst after something endlessly. However, because the Lord Himself took upon all our sins by being baptized, died on the Cross, rose from the dead again, bore all the condemnation of our sins, and washed us from all our sins, those who believe in this Jesus as their Savior always have joy in their hearts. They are always bold, and they always thank God for their salvation.

My fellow believers, our Lord commanded us to preach the gospel of the water and the Spirit. Throughout the whole world, there aren't that many ministers or saints who are preaching this gospel. Their number is only as small as the child's lunch in today's Scripture passage. Yet this lunch alone was enough to feed all those people and still have leftovers. None other than this is God's power and blessing.

Right now, you and I are spreading the gospel of the water and the Spirit to everyone all over the world. It's because God's Church believes in this gospel and preaches it throughout the whole world that God's blessings are added to this. No matter how far away someone might be from us, if he only believes in this gospel of the water and the Spirit with his heart, then he can be washed from all his sins and become a truly sinless child of God. And he will receive all the spiritual blessings of Heaven, solving not only the problem of his soul, but also the problem of his flesh. We believe that God will bless us as our faith grows. Such a wondrous work described in today's Scripture passage is unfolding at this very moment. Therefore, a minister who preaches the gospel of the water and the Spirit is a truly competent minister before God. The saints who are gathered in God's Church that preaches the gospel of the water and the Spirit are truly holy saints. And this Church that proclaims the gospel of the water and the Spirit is God's true Church.

Although there are many self-titled churches of God in this world, the real question is whether or not they are really preaching the gospel of the water and the Spirit. Those who boast about the size of their church buildings, the number of their congregations, or the fame of their pastors are holding fast onto something useless. No matter how famous and renowned their pastors might be, all that these pastors are doing is just getting paid more and acclaiming their own names. That is the only purpose of these pastors. No matter how many different titles they may carry around with them, they have absolutely no spiritual power.

What about you then? Do you believe in this gospel of the water and the Spirit? This gospel of the water and the Spirit is hidden as a mystery, so that those whose hearts are not upright many not see it even as they see it, and not hear it even as they hear it. However, for those who are seeking the Truth, the Bible reveals this gospel in each chapter, so that they may find it. In other words, although Christian sinners speak of the gospel of only the blood of the Cross, God is continually speaking of the gospel of the water and the Spirit. This gospel of the water and the Spirit consists of both the baptism that Jesus received and the blood that He shed on the Cross. Had Jesus not been baptized by John the Baptist, He could not have taken upon our sins, nor would it have been necessary for Him to be crucified.

If there are only the blood of the Cross and the resurrection of Jesus in the gospel of today's Christianity, how could we receive the remission of our sins? It is because the Lord came to this earth, took upon all the sins of the world by being baptized by John the Baptist, carried them to the Cross, and was condemned for them that we have been washed from all our sins. Had the Lord Himself not been baptized by John the Baptist, He could never have shouldered the sins of the world.

Today, except for the gospel of the water and the Spirit, any other gospel composed of only the blood of the Cross is a corrupted gospel. How corrupt is it? You may think that it doesn't make that much difference to leave out the baptism of Jesus from the gospel of the water and the Spirit, but depending on which gospel you believe in, the consequences are enormously different.

During the times of the Early Church, the Apostles preached the gospel of the water and the Spirit. The Apostle

Peter said, *"There is also an antitype which now saves us— baptism" (1 Peter 3:21).* Paul, too, preached the gospel of the water and the Spirit. He said, *"For as many of you as were baptized into Christ have put on Christ" (Galatians 3:27).* The Apostle John also bore witness of the gospel of the water and the Spirit in 1 John chapter five. Every Apostle believed as the following: "When Jesus was baptized by John the Baptist, He shouldered all my sins, and by shedding His blood to death on the Cross, He paid off all the wages of every sin that He had borne." Therefore, anyone who believes only in the blood of the Cross rather than in the gospel of the water and the Spirit actually believes in Christianity only as a religion. If this is the case, then he still remains a sinner even as he believes in Jesus as his Savior.

How can you then wash away the sins that are in your heart? When Jesus was baptized by John the Baptist, He said to him, *"Permit it to be so now, for thus it is fitting for us to fulfill all righteousness" (Matthew 3:15).* "All righteousness" here is the result that the Lord achieved by being baptized, and thus taking upon all the sins of this world and blotting them out once and for all. Jesus came to achieve this work that fulfills all the righteousness of God, and He completed this work by being baptized by John the Baptist.

What does it mean for us that Jesus received baptism from John the Baptist? It means that by being baptized by John the Baptist, Jesus accepted all our sins all at once and washed them all away once and for all. If there is sin in your heart, and you want to wash it away, what should you do to achieve this? You must believe that Jesus washed away all your sins by being baptized by John the Baptist. You must realize and believe without fail that at the very moment Jesus was baptized by John the Baptist, all your sins were passed onto the body of

Jesus. Otherwise you will never be able to wash away your sins.

How could we wash away our sins by ourselves? Could we wash them away through our own prayers of repentance? Could we clean them away if we live as virtuous Christians doing many good deeds? Could you go to the Kingdom of Heaven if you were to sacrifice yourself to preach the gospel of Jesus?

As a hymn sings, "♬Weeping will not save me! ♪ Though my face were bathed in tears, ♬That could not allay my fears, ♪ Could not wash the sins of years," your sins do not disappear no matter how much you cry. The true remission of sin is attained only if we believe in what Jesus has done for us. It is not attained by doing something on our own, but rather, we are saved from all our sins when we believe in the gospel of the water and the Spirit—that Jesus, out of His love for us, came to this earth to blot out all our sins; that to achieve this He took upon our sins by being baptized by John the Baptist; that He died on the Cross and rose from the dead again, and that He has thereby saved us. In other words, we are saved by hearing the gospel of the water and the Spirit with our ears and believing in it with our hearts. There is no one who can be saved through his own good deeds.

If anyone would just recognize himself properly before the Word of God, he can easily realize that he is bound to commit sin throughout his life, from his very birth to the day he dies. If someone thinks otherwise, that's only because he is getting defensive and overrating himself. Every human life is a constant series of one sin after another, from the very beginning to the end. As Jesus said, *"Whoever looks at a woman to lust for her has already committed adultery with her in his heart" (Matthew 5:28),* just how many sins does mankind commit with its thoughts, words, eyes, and acts?

From the very moment everyone is born, he says, "Give me this, and give me that." And it is precisely because everyone is born with sin in his heart that he practices evil in his life. But does this mean that people would improve when they get older? No, on the contrary, they get worse when they get older. They commit even more sins, and they curse even more. No one actually learns how to commit sin, but everyone is so skilled at it.

When I was young, I, too, used to think of myself as a good kid, obedient to my parents and well behaved. The neighbors also thought highly of me, worthy of an award for my display of filial piety. So I myself thought, "I must be really virtuous!" However, once I grew older and reached puberty, I began to commit sin according to my age. I committed so many sins that I even heard people say to me, "Did your mom teach you like this?" I was deceiving myself, thinking, "I am not someone who would commit such a sin, and yet I've sinned! It was a mistake! I am not that kind of person, never!" As I grew older and began to commit sin, I was surprised at myself first, and then others were surprised at me. And I, too, was shocked at the other people's sins.

After a while, as I got older and became a young man, I realized, "Mankind is such a brood of sin by nature." After this, I came down with a serious illness that almost killed me, and this near-death experience led me to believe in Jesus. However, my heart's sins did not disappear, but they continued to torment me. Seeing how I was so helpless to commit sin even though I believed in Jesus, I was so disappointed in myself that I even tried to commit suicide once.

Nonetheless, the Lord came to meet me with the gospel of the water and the Spirit. At that time, as I believed in this genuine gospel, so many sins that had been in my heart all disappeared completely. Before I found the gospel of the water and the Sprit, I had many sins in my heart even though I believed in Jesus. Although in those days I was saying to people, "Believe in Jesus and be washed from your sins. And offer prayers of repentance to wash away your personal sins," I myself had many sins. At that time, I was studying theology and ministering as well, but my sins were written in my heart. Mankind's sins are written in the tablet of its conscience (Jeremiah 17:1). That is how one realizes the sins that he committed before God.

Do you then think that you can live virtuously if you just try hard and be more careful? That's very difficult. In fact, it's impossible. While you can pretend to be good, it is impossible for anyone to live a perfectly virtuous life before God. Everyone commits sin until the day of his death. That is precisely why Jesus came to this earth and took upon your sins and mine by being baptized, all in order to wash them away. It's because our Lord took away our sins through His baptism that the sins of our hearts were washed away. The problem, however, is that most people are completely oblivious to this fact. For us to believe in Jesus as the Savior is to believe that Jesus has saved us by coming to this earth, taking upon our sins by being baptized, being crucified to death, and rising from the dead again.

That is why the Bible says that one can see the Kingdom of God and enter it only if he is born again of water and the Spirit (John 3:3-5). God could save you and me only if He came to this earth incarnated in the flesh of man, take upon Himself all our sins by being baptized by John the Baptist, wash them all away by being condemned for them, and rise from the dead again. That is why our Lord has saved us in this way. It is by realizing this fact and believing in it that you and I have been saved.

"Even though I am such a sinful person, and even though I can't help but commit sin all my life, to save such a person like me from sin, the Lord came to this earth, was baptized, died on the Cross, rose from the dead again, and has thereby saved me indeed. He is my Savior. Because all my sins were also passed onto the Lord when He was baptized, I have no sin. Because the Lord was condemned for my sins on the Cross and shed His blood to death, now there is no more condemnation of sin for me. That's because the Lord was baptized and already condemned for me." The right faith is for us to grasp the gospel of the water and the Spirit and believe in it like this.

Just because we attend every church meeting without missing any, volunteer ourselves to do Christian charity works and other such good deeds, faithfully offer our tithes, and propagate the gospel diligently, this does not mean that our faith is good. Whoever comes to the Church must first be remitted from his sins by believing in the gospel of the water and the Spirit. To instead front his own devotion and merits without even receiving the remission of his sins, as if he were helping the Church, is not the right faith. If anyone has sin in his heart, he will be cast into hell. So, someone who still has not received the remission of his sins must first believe in the gospel of the water and the Spirit given by Jesus and be redeemed from his sins.

What could such a person possibly do to help God? Who is helping whom, when he himself is in such a dire quagmire? The very first thing that one must do before God is to receive his salvation from God and be remitted from his sins, and thus attain new life. It is only after then that he should try to solve his spiritual and physical problems with the help of the Lord. It makes no sense for someone who hasn't even solved his most fundamental problem to try to volunteer his service or do good deeds in God's Church.

The problem with today's Christians is that they just keep trying to help God on their own. That is why so many churches are only building bigger church buildings and raising higher church towers, rather than leading people to their redemption from sin. There are so many palace-like churches in this world. Such a phenomenon is extremely wrong.

My fellow believers, what kind of church is God's real Church? A church is not just a chapel building. The gathering of the saints who believe in the gospel of the water and the Spirit and spread this gospel is the real Church of God. Even though they may be gathered together and worshipping in a rundown building, if the people there really know and believe in the gospel of the water and the Spirit, then this place is indeed God's beautiful Church.

When you come to God's Church, the Church offers its fellowship to you, solves the various problems that are in your mind with the Word, leads you, and prays for you. It thus saves your soul first. Also, God's Church sometimes counsels the saints with their carnal problems, as well as leading them in everyday life. Is it God's Church, if it does not have the gospel of the water and the Spirit? No, of course not.

God's Church enables you to eat the flesh of Jesus and drink His blood through the gospel of the water and the Spirit, and it thereby leads you to the blessed way that washes you from all your sins. May God's great blessings be with each and every one of you who has eaten the flesh of Jesus and drunk His blood. ✉

To Believe in Him Whom God Appointed Is The Work of God

< John 6:16-29 >

"Now when evening came, His disciples went down to the sea, got into the boat, and went over the sea toward Capernaum. And it was already dark, and Jesus had not come to them. Then the sea arose because a great wind was blowing. So when they had rowed about three or four miles, they saw Jesus walking on the sea and drawing near the boat; and they were afraid. But He said to them, 'It is I; do not be afraid.' Then they willingly received Him into the boat, and immediately the boat was at the land where they were going. On the following day, when the people who were standing on the other side of the sea saw that there was no other boat there, except that one which His disciples had entered, and that Jesus had not entered the boat with His disciples, but His disciples had gone away alone— however, other boats came from Tiberias, near the place where they ate bread after the Lord had given thanks— when the people therefore saw that Jesus was not there, nor His disciples, they also got into boats and came to Capernaum, seeking Jesus. And when they found Him on the other side of the sea, they said to Him, 'Rabbi, when did You come here?' Jesus answered them and said, 'Most assuredly, I say to you, you seek Me, not because you saw

the signs, but because you ate of the loaves and were filled. Do not labor for the food which perishes, but for the food which endures to everlasting life, which the Son of Man will give you, because God the Father has set His seal on Him.' Then they said to Him, 'What shall we do, that we may work the works of God?' Jesus answered and said to them, 'This is the work of God, that you believe in Him whom He sent.'"

Greetings to all my brothers and sisters! I am so thankful to God that we are able to worship Him on this beautiful spring day, when His beauty is manifested in all its glory with the flowers blossoming everywhere.

Today's Scripture passage also comes from John chapter six. As the people asked Jesus, *"What shall we do, that we may do the works of God?"* Jesus answered, *"This is the work of God, that you believe in Him whom He sent."* In other words, God is pleased when we believe in Him whom God Himself sent. This is the core message of today's Scripture passage.

By blessing five barley loaves and two fish, Jesus had fed countless starving Israelites. So the crowd who ate the bread followed Jesus around. Jesus, knowing that they were about to take Him by force to make Him their king, once again left for the mountain alone, and the disciples got into the boat first and were sailing toward Capernaum by themselves. By the time they reached the middle of the sea, it was getting dark, and Jesus had not come to them yet.

Then the sea arose in a great storm. Water began to pour into the boat. As the disciples were scrambling to bail out the water and trembling in fear, the Lord walked toward them on the water in the middle of the storm. Thinking that it was a ghost that was approaching them, the disciples got even more afraid, but Jesus said to them, "It is I; do not be afraid" (Mark 6:50). As soon as Jesus got into the boat with the disciples, the boat reached its destination right away.

When Jesus and His disciples had crossed the sea to Capernaum, a great multitude came over the sea and found Him there. Jesus then said to them, "Did you follow me because you ate the bread, or because you saw the miracle that I performed for you? It's good if you followed me because you understood the meaning of My miracle, but it's wrong and meaningless if you followed me to eat more bread for your flesh." He said this because the bread of the flesh is all gone once it's eaten and digested. So Jesus said, *"Do not labor for the food which perishes, but for the food which endures to everlasting life."* The people then asked Him, *"What shall we do, that we may work the works of God?"* and Jesus said to them, *"This is the work of God, that you believe in Him whom He sent."*

There are times when we, too, follow the Lord to eat the bread of the flesh. However, the Lord told us to labor for the food that does not perish. Even after being saved from all the sins of the world, we still find ourselves at a loss sometimes, not knowing what we should do to do God's righteous work. But the Lord said, *"This is the work of God, that you believe in Him whom He sent."*

Who is He whom God sent to us? It is Jesus Christ. God the Father loved this world so much that He sent His only begotten Son. God the Father sent Jesus Christ to this earth. Our Lord said, "God the Father has set His seal on the Son of Man." God the Father has saved us through the gospel of the water and the Spirit, so that the entire human race may receive the remission of sin and become God's children through Jesus

Christ. Our Father sent Jesus Christ as the only Savior of mankind.

People often wonder, "We really want to do God's work, but what should we do to do His work?" To believe in Him whom God sent is God's work. In other words, to believe in Jesus Christ is the very work of God. As the Bible says, *"Nor is there salvation in any other, for there is no other name under heaven given among men by which we must be saved" (Acts 4:12),* there is no other Savior of mankind but Jesus Christ. By sending His own Son to this world, God the Father has made it possible for everyone to be saved and enter the Kingdom of Heaven.

For Us to Believe in Him Whom God Sent Is to Do God's Work

Jesus Christ came to this earth incarnated in human flesh as a man, and by receiving baptism at the Jordan River from John the Baptist, He took upon all the sins of every mankind once and for all. Because our flesh is weak, we commit sin constantly until the day we die, but Jesus Christ shouldered all these sins of the flesh once and for all when He was baptized by John the Baptist. And by being crucified and shedding His blood, He ended all our sins and saved us forever. He then rose from the dead again in three days, ascended to Heaven to sit at the right hand of the throne of God the Father, and has thus become the Savior of all mankind.

Now, for us to do God's work is to believe in Him whom God sent as our Savior—that is, in Jesus Christ. And it is God's work to believe with our hearts in the gospel of the water and the Spirit through which Jesus has saved us. This is the will of

God and our salvation. How should we do God's work? We should believe in Jesus Christ as our Savior—this is to carry out the work of God. What about you then? Haven't you been working hard on your own, trying to do something for God? Just because you work hard on everything and anything for God, this does not mean you are actually doing God's work. Rather, to believe in the amazing miracle of God, in His salvation that has made us perfectly sinless, is God's work. That is why it is we the believers—that is, those of us who have received the remission of sin by believing in Jesus Christ—who are doing God's work.

Even before I was born again, I was already leading a church. At that time, my plan was to rake in a lot of money and build several big buildings, one to be used as a place of worship, another one for educational center, and yet another building for a recreational facility. I thought this was what I should do to carry out a great ministry, even as I myself was sinful. But this was nothing more than my own greed.

However, as I turned to the Bible after receiving the remission of my sins, I saw what Jesus said here, that to believe in Him whom God sent is do God's work, and so I changed my mind. That's because the Bible says that for us to believe in Jesus Christ is God's work.

God the Father sent Jesus Christ and John the Baptist to this earth. We know very well that God the Father sent Jesus to us. But did God really send John the Baptist as well? We need to confirm this from the Bible.

John 1:6-7 say, *"There was a man sent from God, whose name was John. This man came for a witness, to bear witness of the Light, that all through him might believe."* In other words, God the Father sent His Son and John the Baptist to this earth for a special purpose. So, God's work is to believe in what these two did. God does not want us to do just anything arbitrarily, but He wants us to be saved by believing in Him whom God sent. That is why God said, "To believe in Him whom I sent is to do My work." Put differently, rather than believing on our own without even understanding God's desire and instead of letting our own zealousness overtake us into volunteering, evangelizing, and sacrificing ourselves, to believe in Jesus Christ and John the Baptist, those whom God sent, is to do God's work.

God said the following about John the Baptist: *"There was a man sent from God, whose name was John. This man came for a witness, to bear witness of the Light, that all through him might believe" (John 1:6-7).* Whom did God send? They are Jesus Christ and John the Baptist. John the Baptist was sent to this earth to bear witness of the Light, Jesus Christ, and as the representative of mankind and the last prophet of the Old Testament. Referring to John the Baptist, the Bible says that he was the greatest of all those born of women (Matthew 11:11).

John the Baptist baptized Jesus in the Jordan River. This was to pass the sins of the world to Jesus. And the following day, John the Baptist bore witness of Jesus, saying, *"Behold! The Lamb of God who takes away the sin of the world" (John 1:29).* By this, John the Baptist meant, "He is the Son of God, the very Savior of mankind. When I laid my hands on His head and baptized Him yesterday, all the sins of the world were passed onto Him." John the Baptist thus testified here that he had baptized Jesus, and that all the sins of the world were now passed onto Him, so that many would believe in Jesus as their Savior.

Those whom God sent to this earth are two; the first one is Jesus, and second one is John the Baptist. Therefore, to do

God's work is to believe that God the Father sent Jesus and John the Baptist, and to believe in what they did. Is this how you believe? Today, many Christians do not believe that God sent John the Baptist to pass the sins of the world to Jesus, and instead believe only in Jesus' blood on the Cross. This kind of faith is not the faith that is based on the gospel of the water and the Spirit. The adherents of this faith do not believe in those whom God the Father sent. If anyone believes only in Jesus' blood without believing in what John the Baptist had done together with Christ, then he is not doing the work of God. So when we preach the gospel, we must preach what Jesus Christ and John the Baptist did as those whom God sent. Therefore, those who believe in the true gospel must preach, along with Jesus' death on the Cross, how He took upon the sins of the world through the baptism that John the Baptist gave Him. To preach like this is to preach none other than the gospel of the water and the Spirit.

Thirdly, those whom God sent are His servants. To believe in the servants of God is to do His work. In the Old Testament, God sent many servants. There were countless servants in the times of the Old Testament, from Abraham to Isaac, Jacob, Moses, Joshua, Isaiah, Ezekiel, Jeremiah, Daniel, Habakkuk, Nehemiah, Malachi, and so forth. In the New Testament, there were the twelve disciples of Jesus, and there also were other servants under them. We call the disciples of Jesus "the Apostles." The word "Apostle," which is *"Apostolos"* in Greek, means "a delegate, messenger, one sent forth with orders." Therefore, to believe in the Apostles whom Jesus sent is to do God's work. To believe in God's servants of this age sent by Him is also God's work. In other words, if we can't believe in the servants whom God raised, then this means we don't believe in God Himself.

Do you believe that I am a servant appointed by God? In human terms, I can't ask you to believe in me. Yet when people like Sun-Myung Moon or Paul Yong-ki Cho tell others to believe in them, many actually do trust them. But unlike them, I have no confidence to say, "Believe in me." I am a man of many shortcomings. I also have many selfish desires. I'm such a man that when I sit around the table with my brothers of faith and I see something tasteful, I want to get it before my brethren, and when there is something good, I want to make it mine.

When I went to Chuncheon City for the first time, I wanted to have some sea squirts. I remembered how I had enjoyed sea squirts when I used to live near the sea long ago. So I bought some sea squirts with the brethren, but there weren't that many to go around. Wondering to myself how to share such a little amount with them, I asked one of the brethren, "Have you had sea squirts before?" When he told me that he never had them before, I told him that I was going to teach him how to eat them. I said to him, "This sea squirt tastes better the longer you chew on the shell. So you should eat the shell first." While I ate several pieces of the flesh, he kept chewing on the shell. When there weren't that many pieces of the flesh left, I felt bad in my conscience, and so I told him to spit out the shell and eat the flesh. After he had a couple of bites, they were all gone.

Later on, we had another chance to eat sea squirts, but this time I broke into laughter at the table remembering the episode. I said to him, "Actually, I told you before to eat the shell first so that you wouldn't eat too much. Are you going to eat the shell first this time again?" And from then on we shared the flesh of the sea squirts together.

As you can see from this little episode, there is really no

ground for me to actually ask you to believe in me. In human terms, I am not trustworthy, but the one thing that I ask you to believe is that I am a servant of God. While I may not be believable when I am kidding around with food, you have to believe that I am someone who believes in Jesus and His messengers, and preaches the Truth. And if you believe in what I am saying, you will attain eternal life, receive the remission of your sins, and prosper in both body and spirit. While it is I who speak, it is not my own words that I preach, but I believe in Jesus Christ and preach His wisdom, understanding, and faith. That is why I ask you to believe in the servants whom God has appointed. And it is God's work to believe in them like this.

To believe in the servants of God is to do His work. It is when you obey the servants of God that you can receive the remission of your sins, and be led with their guidance in your everyday life. And you can carry on with your life of faith properly and will be blessed for your faith. However, what happens when you don't believe in the servants whom God has raised? You end up departing from God's Church unable to believe in God either. When God wants to do something, He does not work unless it's through the servants whom He has established. God first teaches His servants the gospel that brings salvation and how to live by faith, and then He speaks these to all His believers through those servants. That is why you must trust in God's servants.

My fellow believers, do you believe in God's servants? To believe in those whom God sent is God's work. Some people do not believe in God's servants even though they have been saved from sin by believing in the gospel of the water and the Spirit. Such people say that they can lead their lives of faith quite well without the servants of God, but that is not actually the case. In other words, unless you hear the Word through the servants of God, you cannot lead your life of faith properly. If you don't believe in the servants raised by God, and if you are not led by them, then no matter how you might have received the remission of your sins, you will just turn into a couch potato, carrying out the works of the flesh that you shouldn't, and get into fights with others. In contrast, when you really listen to the Word through the servants of God, you can believe in God Himself and carry out His work faithfully.

The same principle applies to me as well. If I am a saint, then there must be someone who preaches the Word to me also. Without someone preaching the Word to me, I cannot carry on with my life of faith properly. I've done everything. I've served the Lord as a layman, and I've also held a secular job. I've done pretty much everything there is to do. So I know your mind very well. I know very well how you should serve the Lord. I am sure that God has trained me in every aspect so far to establish me as one of His servants.

God Has Raised His Servants for Us

To trust in the servants appointed by God and be led by them is to do God's work. We must understand and believe so. If you can't recognize the servants of God whom He sent, then you cannot recognize Jesus Christ either. If you don't recognize John the Baptist whom God sent, then you cannot understand the gospel of the water and the Spirit. And therefore you cannot be saved from your sins and receive God's blessings. How can we be led by God? We can be led by Him when we believe in the servants whom He has raised.

Yet some people do not trust in the God-established

servants. Such people's faith will wither away soon. The very foundation of their faith is wrong. They say to God's servants to listen to their own words. So when there are too many self-claimed instructors in the Church, God's order begins to break down and the spiritual power of the Church disappears. This may sound a bit exaggerating, but the Bible says that there were ten thousand instructors in the Corinthian church (1 Corinthians 4:15). This means that there were that many people who tried to teach on their own while ignoring Paul, a servant raised by God. How was this church of Corinth then? It was an utterly disorderly and licentious church.

To those who do not believe in the servants raised by God even as they come to God's Church, and instead think in their minds, "Are you the only servant of God? I am also a servant of God," I have the following words to say: "You are out of your mind. You are so reckless that you are asking for your own death." Korah conspired with 250 leaders of other tribes and rebelled against Moses and Aaron, whom God had raised (Numbers 16:1-3). What happened as a result? The earth opened its mouth and swallowed them up, with their households and all the men with Korah, and with all their goods. (Numbers 16:32).

The Bible says, "What shall we do, that we may work the works of God? This is the work of God, that you believe in Him whom He sent." Even though this is what is written in the Bible, are you still not going to believe in those whom God sent? If so, then it can only mean that you are out of your mind. You will then face spiritual death.

When one first believes in the gospel of the water and the Spirit and receives the remission of his sins, he is healed from his spiritual and bodily illnesses as a matter of course, as he finds peace of mind and overflows with joy. Most illnesses of the body and the mind are healed on their own. When one really believes in the Lord's gospel with his heart, then this is actually what happens. Those who are physically weak become strong. They become much healthier. It is by listening to the Word of God from His servants and feeding on the spiritual milk in God's Church that your faith grows and you can enjoy God's grace and blessings. This is the normal life for anyone who has come into the Church.

Yet despite this, some people still stubbornly refuse to listen to the servants of God. If you do this, your life of faith in His Church will be all over in no time. No matter how great your individual faith might be, God has raised His servants so that you would hear His Word through them and be led by their guidance, and so those who ignore this and try to do God's work all on their own come before God's presence with a legalistic faith that's oriented toward their own works. They are satisfied when the result of their diligent service is good, but when this is not the case, they get all sulky, falling into the merit-oriented life of faith. In other words, they once again fall into legalistic faith even after being saved. In the Book of James, of course, there is a passage that says that faith without works is dead. But, this means that true faith is followed by practice.

To believe in those whom God sent is His work. It is when we first believe in what was accomplished together by those whom God sent, Jesus and John the Baptist, that we are saved from sin and also receive the blessing of everlasting life. Because we have been saved and blessed by believing in the gospel of the water and the Spirit, it is from here that our works of faith springs forth. You believe that Jesus took upon the sins of this world and follow this Truth precisely because you have come to believe in what was done by John the Baptist, a servant of God, and his witness. That is how you do the works of faith, showing that you have indeed been saved. This is what the passage in James really means.

However, many people don't believe in God's servants. Instead of believing in the servants of God, they actually scorn them inside.

My fellow believers, to believe in the role of John the Baptism and that he is a servant of God is to do God's work. If you want to mature spiritually, grow in faith, be led by God, and live the rest of your life blessed by Him, then you must believe in John the Baptist, a man sent by God. There are others whom God sent as well. God sent His servants to sinners. The people of God must believe in the witnesses of the gospel of the water and the Spirit. Sinners should trust in the words of the righteous. That is doing God's work. Jesus told us to labor for the food that endures. It is when sinners listen to the gospel from the servants of God that they obtain incorruptible, everlasting life.

I admonish you to mature in your life of faith. You have been saved by believing in Jesus Christ and what was done by John the Baptist. After this, you must believe in the servants whom God has raised. Whether a servant falls or rises all depends on God. During the reign of King David, a man named Uzaah drove a cart with the Ark of Jehovah on it, and when the oxen stumbled and the Ark seemed to teeter, Uzaah put his hand on the Ark and was killed right at the spot (2 Samuel 6:3-7). God killed him instantly. Uzaah had grabbed the Ark of Jehovah in panic because it was about to fall. Why was this so wrong? Should he have not held the Ark, even as he saw that it was falling? We may think in our human perspective that Uzaah didn't really deserve to die here, but breaking the statutes established by God cannot be tolerated.

God Himself made us, and to turn us into His people, He sent His Son Jesus Christ. And God also sent John the Baptist, and these two did the great work of salvation together, with one passing our sins and the other taking upon these sins. We cannot judge what was planned and achieved by God Himself.

Can God's servants do anything willfully? No, of course not. While I, too, sometimes go on my way, in the end, I subject myself to the will of God. You may think that I can do everything arbitrarily, but I cannot do anything on my own will to the end. God Himself speaks to His servants when they go against His will, saying, "I've told you time after time, and yet won't you still listen to me?" He doesn't actually say this to their ears, but He convicts their hearts. Once God controls the servants' hearts, they can't just do whatever they want to do.

God's servants do not just do everything according to their own wish. Do not think that the servants of God can do whatever they want to do, simply because they are not controlled by anyone else. They can't do this. As they are indwelt by the Holy Spirit, He speaks to them whenever they go astray. They are completely beholden to the Holy Spirit. God is absolute. God speaks His Word and does everything according to this Word. You have to realize that even His servants are not free to do whatever they wish. Once you realize the fact that God rules His servants, you will be able to trust in them.

How about you? Can you do whatever you want? No, absolutely not. Those who have received the remission of sin are indwelt by the Holy Spirit. That's why when they hear the Word of God, they are joyful, their hearts can believe in the Word, and they desire to follow it. Faith springs forth in them.

In contrast, try doing whatever you want to do, and see if you can get away with this. The Holy Spirit will discomfort your heart to suffer in pain and grief. Unless you listen to the Word of God and follow it, you can't live as your heart is too tormented. The Holy Spirit makes it impossible for you to do anything other than to follow the will of God. He leads you into the Church and makes you listen to the words of God's servants.

Do you really want to live faithfully before God? Do you want to do His work? Then believe in those whom God sent—none other than this to do the very work of God.

Some People Are Teaching That Jesus Saved Us from Our Sins by Dying on the Cross

Most Christians do not believe in John the Baptist, a man sent by God. In other words, they don't believe in his ministry and witness. And they only believe a half-gospel that claims Jesus has remitted away our sins just by shedding His blood and dying on the Cross. However, they can't really receive the remission of their sins by believing like this. Far from obtaining everlasting life, what results from this kind of faith is that they end up being bound by the Law. Such people cannot escape from the yoke of the Law, even though God has given them the Law so that they would realize their sins through it and receive the remission of their sins by believing in Jesus Christ, the Savior of mankind sent by God.

Some people, even after hearing the gospel of the water and the Spirit and receiving the remission of sin, go to their former churches that preach only the gospel of the blood of the Cross alone and continue to lead their lives of faith there. These people are not doing God's work. To believe in the Word of God is to do His work, even if we were playing soccer.

God's work is to believe in the servants raised by God, to also believe in John the Baptist whom God sent, and to believe in Jesus Christ as our Savior. In other words, it is by faith that we labor, not with our own toil.

Does this then mean that no work is needed once we are saved? No, that's not the case. We labor precisely because we believe. It's because we believe that we work voluntarily and joyfully. It's because we believe that we come to the Church. And it's because we believe that we serve the Lord.

What is doing God's work? It is to believe in those whom God sent. God has sent His servants to us on this earth. Believing in the Word of God preached by His servants is to do His work. It is when we believe in God's Word that He works in our lives and He is pleased. Do you think that it's God's work to live a godly life all by yourself and commit no sin? When you go out to the streets, you often come across people shouting out on the mike, "Believe in the Lord Jesus, and you will then be saved!" While these people think that they are doing God's work, they are not actually doing anything for God. God's work is to believe in those whom He sent.

Whom did God send? He sent Jesus and John the Baptist. God also sent His servants. Therefore, to trust in these servants raised by God, and to believe in His Word preached by them, is to do God's work. That is why when we read the Word of God, we must believe in what Jesus has done for us together with John the Baptist. It is when we believe in the gospel of the water and the Spirit preached by the servants of God that we do His work. When we believe in the role of John the Baptist sent by God, and in the fact that Jesus Christ has become our true Savior by taking upon our sins through His baptism, bearing our condemnation, and rising from the dead again—this is when we are doing Gods' work.

As such, we must turn to the Word and believe in it. We must listen to the Word. God said, *"Faith comes by hearing, and hearing by the word of God" (Romans 10:17)*. It's when we hear the Word that faith comes to us, and it's when we believe in the Word that we do God's work.

My fellow believers, have you been saved by faith? If you have indeed been saved by believing in the Word, then you should now trust in God's Church and be united with it. You must unite yourself with the Church, and you must unite yourself with the servants whom God has raised. You must trust in the words of the servants of God. You must accept the gospel preached by God's servants. You must share fellowship with your fellow saints. And you must follow the Word of God in obedience. This is doing God's work.

We should be rejoiced to do God's work. To carry out His work, we must believe in those whom He sent. Rather than trying to do God's work by ourselves, we must believe in those whom God sent. This is how we can obtain everlasting life, follow God, and receive His abundant blessings. To believe in the Word is to believe in God, and to do His Work.

I give my thanks to God. God said, "To believe in those whom I have sent is to believe in Me." Do you believe in God? Do you believe in those sent by God? Do you believe in His Word? Do you believe that the saints whom God has placed on this earth are His own people? I believe that God has raised His servants in His Church. I believe that the saints are righteous people. I believe that all of us are God's own people. It is God's work that we are now doing.

We are able to live a wonderfully blessed life by faith in God. By believing in what are we blessed? It's by believing in what Jesus Christ and John the Baptist did, and in the servants raised by God, that we receive all the blessings of Heaven.

When we believe, our illnesses will also be healed. We receive the remission of our sins by faith as well. When we believe, we will be made the servants of righteousness like Abraham. When we believe, we will prosper in both body and spirit. I admonish you all to follow by faith the servants whom God has raised.

I give all my thanks to God for giving us the faith to believe in those whom He sent. ✉

Work for the Food That Endures to Everlasting Life

< John 6:16-40 >

"Now when evening came, His disciples went down to the sea, got into the boat, and went over the sea toward Capernaum. And it was already dark, and Jesus had not come to them. Then the sea arose because a great wind was blowing. So when they had rowed about three or four miles, they saw Jesus walking on the sea and drawing near the boat; and they were afraid. But He said to them, 'It is I; do not be afraid.' Then they willingly received Him into the boat, and immediately the boat was at the land where they were going. On the following day, when the people who were standing on the other side of the sea saw that there was no other boat there, except that one which His disciples had entered, and that Jesus had not entered the boat with His disciples, but His disciples had gone away alone—however, other boats came from Tiberias, near the place where they ate bread after the Lord had given thanks—when the people therefore saw that Jesus was not there, nor His disciples, they also got into boats and came to Capernaum, seeking Jesus. And when they found Him on the other side of the sea, they said to Him, 'Rabbi, when did You come here?' Jesus answered them and said, 'Most assuredly, I say to you, you seek Me, not because you saw the signs, but because you ate of the loaves and were filled. Do not labor for the food which perishes, but for the food which endures to everlasting life, which the Son of Man will give you, because God the Father has set His seal on Him.' Then they said to Him, 'What shall we do, that we may work the works of God?' Jesus answered and said to them, 'This is the work of God, that you believe in Him whom He sent.' Therefore they said to Him, 'What sign will You perform then, that we may see it and believe You? What work will You do? Our fathers ate the manna in the desert; as it is written, 'He gave them bread from heaven to eat.'' Then Jesus said to them, 'Most assuredly, I say to you, Moses did not give you the bread from heaven, but My Father gives you the true bread from heaven. For the bread of God is He who comes down from heaven and gives life to the world.' Then they said to Him, 'Lord, give us this bread always.' And Jesus said to them, 'I am the bread of life. He who comes to Me shall never hunger, and he who believes in Me shall never thirst. But I said to you that you have seen Me and yet do not believe. All that the Father gives Me will come to Me, and the one who comes to Me I will by no means cast out. For I have come down from heaven, not to do My own will, but the will of Him who sent Me. This is the will of the Father who sent Me, that of all He has given Me I should lose nothing, but should raise it up at the last day. And this is the will of Him who sent Me, that everyone who sees the Son and believes in Him may have everlasting life; and I will raise him up at the last day.'"

Today, I would like to speak to you about the bread of life mentioned in John 6:16-40. It's written prior to today's

Scripture passage that our Lord fed more than 5,000 people by blessing five barley loaves and two fish, and that there were twelve baskets still remaining as a leftover. As our Lord had healed many sick people, a great multitude was following Him around. Men and women alike, and young and old, countless people were following Jesus to get their physical illnesses healed and their hunger solved. In today's parlance, Jesus now had a fan club.

Labor for the Food That Endures to Everlasting Life

After performing the miracle of feeding over 5,000 people, Jesus sought to go across the sea to a town called Capernaum. As the people tried to make Him their secular king, Jesus went to the mountain alone to pray, and meanwhile His disciples sailed across to Capernaum by themselves. After the disciples had rowed for about three or four miles, a fierce storm arose. However, as Jesus walked on the water toward the boat and got onboard with His disciples, they were able to reach their destination safely.

The next day, the people at the other side of the sea saw that there was no boat there but just one, and so they hurriedly got into the boat looking for Jesus, thinking, "Jesus must have gone somewhere by boat." When they reached the other shore and found Jesus, they said to Him, "Rabbi, were you here? When did You come here?" Jesus then said to them: *"Most assuredly, I say to you, you seek Me, not because you saw the signs, but because you ate of the loaves and were filled. Do not labor for the food which perishes, but for the food which endures to everlasting life, which the Son of Man will give you, because God the Father has set His seal on Him" (John 6:26-27).*

Jesus knew that they came to Him again because they had eaten the bread of the flesh, and that is why He said to them, *"Do not labor for the food which perishes, but for the food which endures to everlasting life, which the Son of Man will give you."* The Son of God came to this earth incarnated in the flesh and said that He Himself will give the bread of everlasting life to people. That's why He said, "Don't work for the food that perishes. Far from it, you should labor for the food that will make you live forever, and I Myself will give this food to you." As well, referring to Himself, Jesus said, *"God the Father has set His seal on the Son of Man."* This means that God the Father has decided to give the bread of life to everyone through no one else but Jesus.

The people who came looking for Jesus were puzzled by what He said, because all that they were interested in was just their own carnal affairs. They had thought that the Lord would once again bless and feed them with tasteful fish and bread, but instead, Jesus rebuked them, saying, "You are just looking for the food that perishes! Labor for the bread of everlasting life." He then said to them that He Himself would give this bread. So the people who had followed Him couldn't help but ask Him for more detail. They said to Jesus, "You told us to labor for the bread that endures to everlasting life, but what shall we do to do the works of God?" Jesus then answered and said to them, *"This is the work of God, that you believe in Him whom He sent."*

My fellow believers, you have to keep in mind that to believe in Him whom God sent is to do God's work. Because Jesus Himself is the One whom God the Father sent, the One who has blotted out all the sins of the world, and the One who gives everlasting life, it is God's work to believe in Him whom God sent. To believe in Jesus is to do God's work, and this is the way to everlasting life. In contrast, for you to do good deeds blindly, to pray a lot, or to serve others in any way do not necessarily mean that you are doing God's work. Yet the people there didn't know this, and so when the Lord told them to labor for the food that endures to everlasting life, they asked Him, "What shall we do? We do also want to do the work of God." They then heard from the Lord, *"This is the work of God, that you believe in Him whom He sent."* In other words, our Lord wanted them to really receive the bread of eternal life by believing in Him. So, Jesus said explicitly, "If you believe in Me, you will receive everlasting life. I have come to give you the bread of everlasting life."

The multitude then asked again: "What sign will You perform then, that we may see it and believe You? What work will You do? On what basis should we believe You? What miraculous work will You perform? As we know, our fathers ate the manna in the desert; as it is written, 'He gave them bread from heaven to eat.' Can you really perform such a miracle?" In other words, when Jesus said to them, *"This is the work of God, that you believe in Him whom He sent,"* they asked Him in return, "Can you then perform such a sign?" So our Lord said to them, "Most assuredly, I say to you, Moses did not give you the bread from heaven, but My Father gives you the true bread from heaven. For the bread of God is He who comes down from heaven and gives life to the world." Put differently, this is what Jesus said: "It's not Moses that gave you the bread from Heaven, but it was God. As Moses prayed, God brought down the manna, and this was the bread of the flesh. However, only My Father gives you the true bread from Heaven, and the bread of God is He who comes down from

Heaven and gives life to the world." So this passage means that Jesus Himself is the bread from Heaven, the true bread of everlasting that God the Father sent down to give life to mankind.

The people then said to Jesus, "Then give us this bread always," to which the Lord said, *"I am the bread of life. He who comes to Me shall never hunger, and he who believes in Me shall never thirst."*

Here, I would like to share the Word with you about the bread of life. Referring to Himself, the Lord said, *"I am the bread of life."* Since the Lord Himself is the bread of life, when one eats this bread of life by faith, then he will receive everlasting life. As Jesus said, *"He who comes to Me shall never hunger, and he who believes in Me shall never thirst,"* what we can realize here is that Jesus Himself is the bread of life for us. Our Lord Himself is the true bread that came down to this world. He is the true bread which, when people eat it, enables them to receive eternal life. The Lord spoke of Himself by drawing an analogy to the bread to explain that He came to this earth to give eternal life to all human beings. To do so, He was incarnated in the flesh of man, was baptized by John the Baptist to accept the sins of mankind onto His own body, washed away all our sins through this baptism, and carried the sins of the world to the Cross to bear all their condemnation.

Jesus Is the Bread of Life

Those who ate the manna all died, just as everyone in this world who ever ate the elixir of life also died. However, those who really believe in the Lord with their hearts will receive everlasting life. God the Father bestows eternal life on whoever believes in the Lord who came to this earth incarnated in the flesh, was baptized to take upon Himself our sins and thus accepted them all and washed them away, was crucified and shed His blood unto death to be condemned for these sins, and rose from the dead again. In other words, our Lord says here that those who truthfully believe in Him with their hearts, who has given true life to you and me, will attain new and everlasting life, and drink the water of eternal life to never thirst again forever.

By performing the miracle of five loaves and two fish, the Lord fed over 5,000 people. They were full, but only in body for a short while. Now, they had to receive everlasting life by wholeheartedly believing in Jesus Christ who proclaimed Himself as the true bread of life. It was completely wrong for them to follow the Lord for any other purpose, only to obtain the food that would perish—that is, to see signs and miracles, to be healed from illnesses, or to prosper materially. Our Lord said, *"All that the Father gives Me will come to Me, and the one who comes to Me I will by no means cast out" (John 6:37).* Who are those whom the Father gives to the Lord? They are not those who seek the things of the flesh, but those who want their souls to be saved from sin and to become God's children—that is, those who yearn for eternal life.

Even though our Lord came to this world as the true bread of life, countless people remain unable to obtain true life, as they do not know Jesus properly nor believe in Him properly. In other words, there are many people who, even though they believe in Jesus fervently, are nonetheless unable to receive eternal life, for they believe in Him mistakenly. They believe in and follow Jesus only to become rich, to drive a nice car, or to find fame, but we should not follow the Lord for such purposes. It is completely wrong to believe in Jesus and follow Him only as a matter of religion.

The people whom God the Father sends to the Lord are those whose spirits are truly poor and who seek spiritual things. They are not those who cling to the wealth of this world, its fame, or its power, but they are those who know that they are bound to hell for their sins, and who truly yearn to be remitted from their sins. It is these people whom God the Father sends to the Lord to receive the remission of their sins through the gospel of the water and the Spirit.

My fellow believers, soon destruction will come to this world. Regardless of whether people believe this or not, God's promise will be fulfilled without fail. You will see the world crumbling down with your own eyes if you live just a bit longer. Truly, this world will all disappear without a trace. And only the Kingdom of God will stand forever. So I am only too thankful that I've come to live by believing in the gospel Truth of the water and the Spirit, and that the Lord has blotted out all my sins.

To blot out our sins, the Lord shouldered them by being baptized and paid off all their wages by shedding His blood on the Cross, thus making us sinless. It's because God has made us, who have received the remission of sin, into His workers and enabled us to enter and live in His Kingdom that I am so thankful and so joyous. The Lord has indeed given us the bread that truly does not perish. Because the Lord has given us not the bread that will disappear, but the bread that will never disappear for eternity, I cannot help but give thanks to God for the true salvation from sin that He has given us.

Everything in This World Is Actually Nothing

It is written, *"Do not love the world or the things in the world. If anyone loves the world, the love of the Father is not in him. For all that is in the world—the lust of the flesh, the lust of the eyes, and the pride of life—is not of the Father but is of the world" (1 John 2:15-16).* Which one among these things in this world, such as fame, wealth, power, pleasures, or knowledge is more precious than everlasting life? Far more important than such things is everlasting life. This eternal life is a gift of God that one can receive only if he is cleansed from all the sins of his heart. Just as God the Father promised that He would wash away our sins through His Son, and just as the Son said that He would become the bread of life, Jesus Christ, the true bread sent from Heaven, took upon Himself all your sins and mine by being baptized, was condemned for our sins by being crucified, and has given us true life by rising from the dead again.

When I say that everything in this world is nothing, countless people may think that this is complete nonsense. Even so, compared to such heavenly blessings that enable us to wash away all our sins from our hearts, become God's children without sin, and enter and live in His Kingdom, the things of this world are indeed nothing.

What is life? Everyone is born from dust only to return to dust—this is what life is. Life is nothing but a short journey. In other words, life does not amount to anything even when it seems to be successful. Just as a traveler returns back home at the end of his journey, life does not stay here forever. We live on this earth only for a short while as travelers, and we must return to our eternal home. Our real home is elsewhere. The destination of our lives lies somewhere else.

Therefore, those who think that they would live forever on this earth and cling to what's on this earth are actually seeking the food that will only perish. When such people hear Jesus saying to them, "I will give you the bread of life," they just think, "What is He talking about? Bread is just bread; so what's this bread of life?"

My fellow believers, you must grasp that the bread of life is none other than Jesus. Jesus is the true bread of everlasting life, the bread of the remission of sin, and the bread of salvation. That is why Jesus said, "I am the bread of life. I will give you this bread of life. I came down from Heaven not to do My own will, but the will of Him who sent Me." It was to teach this that Jesus had performed the miracle of five loaves and two fish, and fed countless people with the bread of their flesh first.

Jesus is the bread of life. Therefore, those who profess to believe in Jesus even as they do not know exactly how He has become our bread of life are completely foolish, for they are seeking before the presence of Jesus not the true bread that's from Heaven, but they are just asking for the bread of the earth. In other words, countless Christians are still asking for this perishable bread that the crowd in John 6 had tasted only for a short while through the miracle of five loaves and two fish.

My fellow believers, we must know and believe in Jesus as our Savior to receive the remission of our sins, become God's children, and enter His Kingdom to enjoy everlasting life and live forever. At the very least, those who want to believe in Jesus as their Savior must confess the sins of their hearts, believe in Jesus, and be cleansed from all their sins first. They must believe in Jesus to thus become God's children and enter His Kingdom to live forever. In contrast, it's completely foolish and fallacious to believe in Jesus only as a matter of religious life.

Jesus Said, "All That the Father Gives Me Will Come to Me"

Who are those whom the Father sent to Jesus Christ? They are those who seek the things of Heaven. God never sends anyone who seeks the things of the earth.

We are now holding our revival meeting. Even though we have opened the way for those who seek the things of Heaven to come to this gathering, few have actually come. This shows how everyone has put off the things of Heaven behind to seek only the things of the earth. In other words, people look for Jesus wishing to become rich, to be healed from their illnesses, to buy a house, or to find a good spouse. Such people simply cannot come to our Church no matter what. Nor does the Father send such people to Jesus, who gives eternal life that is in the gospel of Truth. God sends them to the churches where Christian sinners are gathered.

Everyone knows whether or not there is sin in his heart, and whether he himself is bound to hell or not. You know yourself whether you want to believe in Jesus for the spiritual purpose of receiving the remission of your sins, or for the carnal purpose of prospering in this world. If you would just give some insight into your heart, you can realize whether you are after what is spiritual or what is carnal. Yet despite this, many people still continue to deceive their own consciences and make a mockery out of God. God is now grinding His ax against these people. He is saying, "For all of you who seek only the bread of the flesh, I am waiting with the furnace ready. Don't worry about the fire; I will keep it burning, for I am very patient."

Those who have not been born again seek the things of the flesh, and they are more than capable of justifying this. However, what is clear is that the motivation to become a Christian must be spiritual. Jesus came to this world as the Savior who would deliver us from our sins (Matthew 1:21). This means that Jesus is the One who has saved us from all our sins, not someone who makes us rich, prosperous, or healthy. We believe in Jesus in order to receive the remission of our sins, to be made righteous, to become God's children, and to enter and live in His Kingdom. You must not believe in Jesus only to receive the blessings of the earth, regarding Christianity merely as one of the many religions of the world. If this were why you believe in Jesus, then it would be better for you not to believe in Him at all and just believe in something else.

The Bible says that it is appointed by God for mankind to be born once and die once, and that after this there will be judgment (Hebrews 9:27). My fellow believers, our Lord knows us all too well. In general, human beings are to live in this world for 80 years at most, and then go to stand before the presence of God. Soon, all of you will also end your journey on this earth and return to your eternal home. I am sure that you all really want to find and receive the food that never perishes while you are still living on this earth, and to thereby enter the Kingdom of God. To do so—that is, to be washed from your heart's sins—you must really look for the Truth. If you have sin, then to find the exact answer to the question, "How can I wash away my sins?" you must come out to God in all honesty. In other words, you must come out to God purely for the salvation of your soul, without interjecting anything else into your relationship with God. A sinner must exclude all his carnal desires such as the desire for fame or money, and instead think only of what he should do to break down the wall of sin that's standing between him and God.

There is only one way for you to be approved by God as a perfect person: You must be washed from your sins to be accounted for righteousness. How, then, can you be washed from your sins? Could you be remitted from your sins just by living virtuously on your own and trying hard to stay away from sin? No, this is not possible. What should you do then? Just as our Lord said in today's Scripture passage, the remission of sin is something given by the Lord Himself. Because it is Jesus Christ the Son of God who grants us the true remission of sin, gives us everlasting life, and blesses us to become God's own children, we must believe in Jesus, the God-given true bread that came down from Heaven.

Do you believe that the bread of life from Heaven is Jesus Christ? Do you now realize and believe in what Jesus Christ did for you and me when He came to this earth? It was to become our true bread that Jesus received baptism for us on His body from John the Baptist. Jesus took upon our sins by receiving this baptism, carried the sins of the world to be crucified, and shed His blood to death. And it was to give everlasting life to mankind that the Lord rose from the dead again. All this was planned in Heaven even before the creation. We must partake in the providence of God by believing in this Jesus Christ. We must believe in this Truth of salvation without fail. It is those who believe like this that receive the remission of their sins, attain everlasting life, and eat the true bread that came down from Heaven. None other than this is the very miracle that God showed when He came to this earth.

The people asked Jesus, "As it is written, Moses brought down the manna from Heaven, and so we ate. What is Your sign then that will make us believe in You?" The greatest miracle in this world is the Lord's power that has blotted out our scarlet sins once and for all. The very fact that the Lord was born on this earth incarnated in the flesh of man, was baptized at the age of 30, was crucified, rose from the dead again, and has thereby saved us—none other than this is the greatest miracle and sign.

When the Truth of salvation is so clearly shown, how could you not believe in it? Was our Lord simply crucified to death when He came to this earth? Didn't He also take upon your sins and mine by being baptized? Indeed, it's because Jesus received baptism that our sins have disappeared. Even though Jesus Himself has shown this fact, people still do not know it and do not believe in it. Even as they believe only in the blood of the Cross, they are so clamorous to claim that they believe in Jesus. Trying to wash away their daily sins by offering prayers of repentance is akin to asking Jesus to continue to blot out their sins, even though Jesus has already blotted out their every sin.

You and I should never do this, but instead, we must eat the bread that came down from Heaven by faith. Only when we eat this bread from Heaven by faith do we no longer be such insufficient believers who keep asking for more and more. When the bread from Heaven comes down, we should just eat it by faith, and yet despite this, many people are trying to reach their salvation by making their own bread and offering it to God. The bread of the earth gets mildewed in just a day or two, rotting away with maggots and filling the room with the stench of decay. In contrast, the true bread that came down from Heaven is the genuine bread of everlasting life that never goes stale or mildewed.

Jesus, who has given us the bread of everlasting life, lives forever. And He has blotted out all our endless sins and given us true life. We must eat the bread that came down from Heaven with our hearts by believing in it with our hearts. We must indeed eat and believe in the bread given by the Lord with our hearts; if we otherwise eat the bread of our own making, this will not turn into the bread of life.

What do sinners really need? Do they not need to get their hearts washed from their sins, become sinless people and God's children, and prepare for the next world? Everyone needs the kind of faith that will prepare him for the next world. It doesn't matter how people live in this present world. After all, life on this earth is ephemeral. Whether people live well or not, all their lives are short. Everything of this earth is only momentary.

Mankind must eat the bread that came down from Heaven. This bread must be eaten with the heart, not through one's own good deeds and acts of sacrifice. Nor should anyone try to buy it with money. This bread that came down from heaven is the bread that does not perish forever, washes away every sin, and makes everyone live forever if he would only eat it by faith. So why would anyone try to buy this bread with money or obtain it through his own virtuous deeds? Yet despite this, those who are ignorant of the gospel Truth of the water and the Spirit and do not appreciate its value still try to do so.

Matthew chapter 13 says that the Kingdom of Heaven is like a merchant seeking beautiful pearls. It says that when a pearl merchant came across one pearl of great price, he went and sold all that he had and bought this pearl (Matthew 13:45-46). My fellow believers, even if you have to give up your everything, you must believe in and follow Jesus Christ, the true bread that came down from Heaven. Don't you find this Word worthy of believing, this amazing Truth of salvation that the Lord has saved us from all our sins by coming to this earth, being baptized, dying on the Cross, and rising from the dead again? Isn't it really worthy of holding onto, to believe and defend, and to spread and live for it?

The gospel of the water and the Spirit is the bread that came down from Heaven. It is the most precious bread, the bread that never perishes nor disappears. So because of this bread, we can always laugh in joy, thank God all the time, and live a spiritual life at all times. My fellow believers, that we are able to find comfort even in our sufferings and find true satisfaction even in our poverty is all because we have eaten the everlasting bread of Heaven and obtained eternal life. The gospel of the water and the Spirit brings true joy and real satisfaction to us.

As such, those who have found the Truth of everlasting life buy this Truth even if they have to give up everything they have. There is no one who has ever met Jesus without sacrificing his everything. If you want to believe in the gospel of the water and the Spirit and receive the remission of your sins, you have to cast aside everything that you had known before. You must grasp that everything apart from the gospel of the water and the Spirit is actually nothing, akin to garbage. Can you even compare the gospel Truth of the water and the Spirit to anything that you had known until now? The things of this world are nothing more than garbage when compared to the gospel of the water and the Spirit. What things of the world can you possibly compare to the things of the Lord? Everything of the world will be corrupted in time, for it will all perish and disappear.

The Lord came to this earth to give us the bread of life that will never perish nor be corrupted. He is the true bread of life that came down from Heaven. By becoming the true bread of life, the Lord has indeed blotted out all your sins and mine.

By being baptized, He took upon the sins of the world and cleansed away all our sins. Because the Lord bore the sins of the world through His baptism, everyone who believes in this has washed away all his sins. How about you then? Have you washed away all your sins from your heart? I know that you have now cleansed away all the sins of your heart by believing in the gospel of the water and the Spirit.

My fellow believers, do you think that just about anyone can believe in Jesus Christ, the bread of life? No, we can believe in the Lord only if He meets us first. Then what kind of people does the Lord meet? He meets those whose hearts are fitting in God's sight. These people, whom God finds worthy to grant His permission and say, "You deserve to believe in My Son. You are qualified to believe in My Son," are none other than those whose spirits are poor, who hunger for righteousness, and who mourn over their sins. God judges the rest to only say, "You are not qualified to believe in My Son."

To give everlasting life to none other than you and me, Jesus has saved us through the gospel of the water and the Spirit. Our Lord said, *"Whoever eats My flesh and drinks My blood has eternal life, and I will raise him up at the last day" (John 6:54)*. What will raise us on the last day is also this very faith in the gospel of the water and the Spirit.

My fellow believers, that you believe in the Lord as your Savior is indeed a marvelous blessing. You have accepted the gospel of the water and the Sprit to believe in the Lord as your Savior. Do you think that you can change this faith with something else? Do you think there is something else that's more precious than this? The Lord Himself has become the bread of life for us and told us to come and eat of Him. He said, "If you eat Me by faith, you will receive the remission of your sins and attain everlasting life. Your eternal life will be guaranteed. I have prepared everything for you." We must truly understand Jesus Christ as the bread of life. Believing in Him truthfully, we must eat this true bread of life.

In this age, there are many Christians professing to believe in Jesus. But how many of them really believe in Jesus as the true bread of life? How many people come to church to believe in Jesus Christ as their Savior and their true bread? It's very few. The problem is that almost all Christians believe in Jesus in their own way, without knowing what they should really seek. What's most important for any Christian is the remission of sin. Faith starts from the remission of sin, and only when faith begins properly like this can you attain every blessing from Heaven. Are you really filled spiritually when you are just licking on the surface of the Word leaving out what is most indispensable?

The first button to your life of faith is properly put on when you know and believe in the Truth that the Lord has become the true bread of salvation for you and me. To blot out your sins and mine, the Lord bore our sins by being baptized, shed His blood on the Cross, and rose from the dead again. Because the Lord has completely fulfilled our salvation, He has enabled us to obtain our salvation if only we would truly believe in Him. This is the core message that our Lord is delivering to us through today's Scripture passage.

And the Lord said, *"The one who comes to Me I will by no means cast out" (John 6:37).* All those who come out to the Lord seeking the remission of their sins will find the gospel of the water and the Spirit, and by believing in this gospel with their hearts, they will all be redeemed from their sins. When we come and stand before the presence of the Lord, we must do so for a spiritual purpose. We must come to God for the salvation our souls and their benefits. Anyone who comes out to the Lord for any other purpose will drop out of the march of everlasting life, for he does not believe in the gospel of Truth with his heart. Even though it may seem similar in outside appearance whether one follows the Lord for a spiritual purpose or for a carnal purpose, the consequences are starkly different.

Jesus Christ, the true bread from Heaven, has saved us from all our sins through His baptism and His blood on the Cross. In dong so, the Lord has given us new life, and He has enabled us to live with Him forever, to never taste death again. Now, believing in the fact that whoever believes in this gospel of Truth has received the remission of his sins, and believing that we will live again on the last day, we must fulfill everything that God has entrusted to us. In this present age when great tribulations are truly imminent, we must have hope, and we must believe in this true gospel with our hearts.

Let us all live by faith and then go to our Lord to meet Him face to face. ✉

Living According To the Spirit

< John 6:26-40 >

"Jesus answered them and said, 'Most assuredly, I say to you, you seek Me, not because you saw the signs, but because you ate of the loaves and were filled. Do not labor for the food which perishes, but for the food which endures to everlasting life, which the Son of Man will give you, because God the Father has set His seal on Him.' Then they said to Him, 'What shall we do, that we may work the works of God?' Jesus answered and said to them, 'This is the work of God, that you believe in Him whom He sent.' Therefore they said to Him, 'What sign will You perform then, that we may see it and believe You? What work will You do? Our fathers ate the manna in the desert; as it is written, 'He gave them bread from heaven to eat.'' Then Jesus said to them, 'Most assuredly, I say to you, Moses did not give you the bread from heaven, but My Father gives you the true bread from heaven. For the bread of God is He who comes down from heaven and gives life to the world.' Then they said to Him, 'Lord, give us this bread always.' And Jesus said to them, 'I am the bread of life. He who comes to Me shall never hunger, and he who believes in Me shall never thirst. But I said to you that you have seen Me and yet do not believe. All that the Father gives Me will come to Me, and the one who comes to Me I will by no means cast out. For I have come down from heaven, not to do My own will, but the will of Him who sent Me. This is

the will of the Father who sent Me, that of all He has given Me I should lose nothing, but should raise it up at the last day. And this is the will of Him who sent Me, that everyone who sees the Son and believes in Him may have everlasting life; and I will raise him up at the last day.'"

The Truth That We Must Know

Before we begin, let us turn to a couple of passages from elsewhere in the Bible. Romans 8:5 states, *"For those who live according to the flesh set their minds on the things of the flesh, but those who live according to the Spirit, the things of the Spirit."* Further down, Romans 8:12-14 say, *"Therefore, brethren, we are debtors—not to the flesh, to live according to the flesh. For if you live according to the flesh you will die; but if by the Spirit you put to death the deeds of the body, you will live. For as many as are led by the Spirit of God, these are sons of God."*

Our Lord has saved us from all our sins. Our God came to this earth as our Savior and has saved us from all our sins. Knowing very well just how truly weak we are, our Lord came to this earth and took upon the entire sins of all human beings by being baptized at the age of 30. And He carried the sins of the world to the Cross, was crucified and shed His blood, and was thereby accursed and condemned for our sins. Like this, as Jesus has saved us from sin through the gospel of the water and the Spirit, He has become our true Savior. As we live on in this world, we have so many insufficiencies and weaknesses, and yet our Lord came to this earth to become our Savior, was baptized, died on the Cross, rose from the dead again, and has thereby saved us all.

We humans must live by trusting in God. While living on this earth, we cannot help but stumble constantly and abandon ourselves to despair, for we are too weak. That is why we must live by our faith in God. That we can carry on with our lives in this world is all made possible by our faith in God. If we do not trust in Him, we simply cannot survive. It is by placing our faith in God that we can succeed in our businesses and live our daily lives uprightly until the day the Lord calls us home. And it is by our faith in God that we have been freed from all our sins, saved, blessed, and protected by God in our lives.

It is written, *"But without faith it is impossible to please Him" (Hebrews 11:6)*. Just as God said so, anyone without faith cannot really please Him, but whoever knows that he is weak and insufficient, and who holds onto the gospel of the water and the blood, thanks for it and believes in it, can attain peace. Furthermore, grace is bestowed by God on such righteous people who know the limits of their human strength, admit their powerlessness, rely on God asking for His help, trust in Him, and follow Him. Such a person is to live a life that is filled with the grace of God.

We human beings are to live by believing in God. Put differently, we human beings cannot be sustained unless we believe in God. That is why God came to this earth to become our true Savior. It is to become our Shepherd that the Lord came to this earth and has saved us the lost souls. When we were wandering in the desert, God Himself came to us and led us to green pastures beside the still waters. We must therefore believe in God. And it is by placing our faith in Him that we can carry on with our lives in this desolate world.

Some Christians think that believing in Jesus is one thing, but living in society is another. They think that their social lives are best led by their own strength. Such thoughts, however, are nothing more than a product of sheer ignorance. It is only by faith that we receive the remission of our sins and also become God's children. Just as we are saved by faith, it is also by faith that we should live in society.

My Fellow Believers, Take a Look at This Psalm

As shown in the Psalms, after David became king, he waged countless wars. He was someone who believed in God. As it is written, *"For by You I can run against a troop; By my God I can leap over a wall" (2 Samuel 22:30),* it was by his faith in God that he ran over the walls and waged his wars. By his faith in God he prayed to Him and asked Him, and then he got answers to his prayers from God and followed them accordingly. Whenever God's prophets instructed him, David believed in their words as the Word of God, and he waged his wars, conquered all the nations around Israel, and secured tributes from them all. From his Psalms in the Bible, we can see that David had indeed lived by faith.

Likewise, for us to abide in the Spirit while living in this world is also made possible by trusting in God. All of us must always live by believing in God, never losing our faith in Him. I admonish you all to live by faith without fail. It is my sincerest hope for all of you to really have faith in God just like king David.

We must live with faith, though it may be as small as a mustard seed. Even if you don't even have this faith as small as a mustard seed, I still admonish you to trust in God, hold onto His Word by faith, and accept the advice of the servants of God, His Church, and your predecessors of faith. You should hold onto the Word of God with your hearts ready to say, "Though I have no faith, if the Word of God says so, then it is right." Then this will enable your faith to grow into a mustard seed, there will be works of life arising in you, and the power of the Word of God will come to you. This is how faith grows.

My fellow believers, let us live by faith in God. Our Lord said in Romans 8:5, *"For those who live according to the flesh set their minds on the things of the flesh, but those who live according to the Spirit, the things of the Spirit."* The Lord is teaching us the lesson that those who live for the flesh seek just the things that please the flesh. And He is also teaching us and making it clear to us that those who live according to the Spirit set their minds on the salvation of the other souls.

All of us are debtors to God for His love. That's why we have to repay God's love. We are truly indebted to the love of God and His grace of salvation. Had God not saved us through the gospel of the water and the Spirit, we would have had no choice before Him but to be cast into hell. Yet through the gospel of the water and the Spirit, our Lord has saved us, whom had been all bound to hell. By coming to this earth, being baptized, and shedding His blood on the Cross, our Lord has saved you and me from all our sins. Jesus took upon all the sins of the world through His baptism, so that we may be redeemed from all our sins. He died on the Cross so that we may be delivered from all condemnation, and in doing so He has saved us from all sins.

We are all indebted to God's love and His salvation. Of course, we are not capable of repaying all our debts to Him for His love, but we should at least live according to how He wants us to live. Although we are born-again people, because we still have the flesh, we sometimes commit carnal acts. However, our status still remains as God's born-again children. If you believe that Jesus came to this earth and blotted out all the sins that you would commit until the day you die, then you should realize that you are God's born-again people led by the Spirit.

It is written in Romans 7:5-6, *"For when we were in the flesh, the sinful passions which were aroused by the law were at work in our members to bear fruit to death. But now we have been delivered from the law, having died to what we were held by, so that we should serve in the newness of the Spirit and not in the oldness of the letter."* Before we were born again, sinful passions were at work in our bodies. And they made us bear the fruit of death, as God is teaching us here. However, the Apostle Paul also says that now we have come to serve the work of saving souls through the Holy Spirit, since we died to the Law and the flesh, and he tells us to realize this.

Those who follow God must know that their flesh as well as the Law has already died with Jesus. They must grasp this, believe in it, and follow it. What, then, does it mean that our flesh has already died? It means this: We all sin until the day we die, but as our Lord was baptized, He took upon all the sins of the world committed with our flesh, and when He carried these sins to the Cross and was crucified vicariously in our place and instead of everyone all over the world, our flesh also died. Jesus' death is none other than your death and mine. When Jesus was crucified and His flesh died, our flesh also died.

Therefore, all Christians must believe in Jesus' baptism, His death on the Cross, and His resurrection. You must believe that when Jesus was baptized, all your sins were passed onto Him. Jesus shouldered all the sins of the world, including even all your future sins that you will ever commit until the day you die, and was crucified and died on the Cross for you. This is what you must believe. It is by faith that we are not overcome by the flesh, nor perish for it, but are instead saved.

We have died to the Law of God also. We are dead to the Law in His Truth. However, what does the Law demand? As it is written, *"The wages of sin is death,"* the judgment that the Law demands from us is none other than death. Through His baptism our Lord took upon all the sins that we commit by offending the Law. That is why Jesus had to be crucified to death. Now, as much as we are dead to the Law, we are also dead to our flesh, but alive to God—this is what we must believe. We must all believe that our souls have been saved by faith, and that our bodies will also be resurrected.

Today, We Read John 6

In today's Scripture passage, Jesus said, *"Do not labor for the food which perishes, but for the food which endures to everlasting life, which the Son of Man will give you, because God the Father has set His seal on Him" (John 6:27).* Our Lord taught us not to labor for the perishable food, but to do what brings everlasting life.

This Scripture passage continues on in verses 28 and 29 to say, *"Then they said to Him, 'What shall we do, that we may work the works of God?' Jesus answered and said to them, 'This is the work of God, that you believe in Him whom He sent.'"* Essentially, in this passage Jesus said that to believe in the Lord is to do God's works. People labor for two different things. They work for the food that perishes, and they also work for the bread of everlasting life. It is for these two things that they labor. And He made it clear that we should labor not for the food that perishes, but for life.

When our Lord performed the miracle of five loaves and two fish on the other side of the Sea of Tiberias, with this small amount of food that was enough for only a single lunch, He fed so many people that the Bible says, *"The men sat down, in number about five thousand" (John 6:10).* So multitudes followed Jesus, but their purpose in following Him was to obtain only the bread of the flesh. They followed Jesus, in other words, so that they may be fed again with dinner, now that they were fed with lunch.

Of course, we all need the bread of the flesh also. However, what our Lord said is this: *"Do not labor for the food which perishes, but for the food which endures to everlasting life" (John 6:27).* What happens when we really believe in our Lord? We will receive life then. Our Lord said, *"I am the bread of life" (John 6:35).* Indeed, by giving up His body, our Lord has given us everlasting life.

It is written, *"This is the work of God, that you believe in Him whom He sent" (John 6:29).* While we should all work, we should do what brings us salvation, and what shares salvation with others. How, then, can we do this work of salvation and share it with others? We can do this by eating and sharing the bread of the Spirit, believing that Jesus is the bread of life.

And we must also realize that God does not spurn anyone who comes to Jesus. Our Lord said that He is the bread of life: "Believe in Me. I am the Son of God, the Creator who made the whole universe, and I bore all your sins on My own body. Believe that I am the Savior who took upon all your sins on My body. I shouldered the sins of the world by being baptized, and I was condemned on the Cross. I rose from the dead again, and I have saved you all. If you really believe that I am the very God who enables you to attain life, be saved, and receive the remission of your sins, then you will eat the bread of life, receive the food that does not perish, and reach eternal salvation." This is what our Lord was saying.

In fact, God our Father has saved us by sending His Son to this earth. To believe in Jesus, the Son of God the Father and our Savior, and thereby receive the remission of our sins and eternal life, is to have the food that does not perish forever. To receive everlasting life, the remission of sin, and this salvation is the will of God, that is, what the Father wants from us.

How did our Lord save us when He came to this earth? How did He become our bread of life? What kind of bread should we eat, so that we may attain life?

Yesterday I spoke about Emperor Qin Shi who tried to find the elixir of life. Nowadays, we hear that kids can grow taller when they are injected with new growth hormones, and we also hear about the development of new hormones that invigorate old people, but we haven't heard of any panacea that can bring eternal life. If there were some kind of bread that can make you live forever and never die, wouldn't you eat this bread? Of course you would. That's because everyone wants to live forever, just as Emperor Qin Shi searched for the elixir of immortality.

When Emperor Qin Shi heard that he would never get old and maintain his youth if he drank the extracts of certain herbs, he sent out his servants all over the world to look for them. So, many of his men traveled all over the world and brought back the best herbs they could find to him. The emperor continued to eat these herbs, but, in the end, he still died anyways.

However, there *is* the bread of true immortality on this earth. This bread is the body of Jesus. To eat the body of Jesus is to receive eternal life. To eat the flesh of Jesus is to obtain everlasting life.

Jesus gave up His body for us. During the Last Supper on the Passover night, Jesus gathered all His disciples, broke the bread, and gave it to them. And He said, "This is My body." Jesus said that His body was the bread of everlasting life. Why did Jesus say this? It was because He shouldered all the sins of this world on His body when He came to this earth. The Lord identified Himself as the Alpha and the Omega. This means that He created the entire universe and He will judge the world to open a new and everlasting world to come. To save us humans and to finish this world in His love and justice, He took upon all the sins of everyone on this planet on His body from the beginning to the end. That is why He could say that His body was the bread of life.

Let us turn to Matthew chapter three. We see here Jesus beginning His public life, and the very first thing that He did was to receive baptism on His body from John the Baptist. In Matthew 3:15-16, it is written, *"But Jesus answered and said to him, 'Permit it to be so now, for thus it is fitting for us to fulfill all righteousness.' Then he allowed Him."* Why then was the Lord baptized by John the Baptist? And why did He say, "Thus it is fitting for us to fulfill all righteousness"?

Throughout John in chapter six, Jesus said, "If anyone eats My flesh, he will never hunger. My flesh is food indeed, and My blood is drink indeed. Anyone who does not eat My flesh and drink My blood will not receive eternal life." Why did Jesus say this? Why did our Lord say that His body was the bread of life? That's because when Jesus came to this earth, He accepted all the sins of the world by being baptized by John the Baptist, the greatest of all those born of women. It's because Jesus had accepted the sins of the world by receiving baptism on His body that He said that all righteousness was fulfilled, and that His body had now become the bread of life.

The Lord Was Baptized to Bear Our Sins

Exactly when did Jesus take upon all the sins that you commit throughout your lifetime, all the sins of my entire lifetime, and all the sins committed by everyone else in this world? He took the sins of the world when He received baptism on His body. Just as He said, *"For thus it is fitting for us to fulfill all righteousness" (Matthew 3:15),* it was by being baptized by John the Baptist that Jesus made everyone sinless. John the Baptist fulfilled his duty as the High Priest by passing the sins of mankind onto Jesus through His baptism. Just as the High Priest had passed the yearly sins of the people of the Old Testament all at once by laying his hands on the head of the scapegoat, Jesus came to this earth as the sacrificial Lamb and was baptized to save sinners from sin. He fulfilled all righteousness by being baptized, saying, *"For thus it is fitting for us to fulfill all righteousness" (Matthew 3:15).*

Because of sin, no one can avoid death. Yet everyone wants to live long and keep his youth. Moreover, everyone wants to enter the Kingdom of God as a righteous person without sin. However, because of sin we are to die, because of sin we are to be condemned, because of sin we are to be accursed, because of sin nothing ever goes right for us, because of sin we can't approach God, and because of sin we can't avoid hell.

Yet to save such people like us, the Lord was baptized on His body. By accepting all the sins of the world through His baptism, Jesus fulfilled all righteousness. He accepted all sins onto His body by being baptized, and this body of Jesus became the bread of life for all of us. Therefore, the salvation that brings everlasting new life dwells in those who believe that all their sins were passed onto Jesus. The baptism of Jesus constitutes the salvation that brings life. It is by believing in the gospel of the water and the Spirit that we receive the remission of our sins.

How do we believe in God and Jesus to receive the remission of our sins? We have come to be remitted from our sins by believing that Jesus Himself came to this earth to save sinners, took upon Himself all our sins by being baptized, and was condemned as the Lamb of God that carried the sins of the world. It is by being baptized and dying on the Cross that Jesus has saved us, through His own body and blood. Therefore, whoever believes in this Jesus with the heart can attain new life, receive the remission of sin, be made righteous, become one of God's children, and enter the Kingdom of God.

My fellow believers, what is our Lord trying to tell us in John chapter six? He is telling us to work for the bread that enables us to live forever. What kind of work must we do? We must do what brings everlasting life to us. It is really to receive eternal life that we must believe in Jesus and follow Him.

And after receiving the remission of our sins, we must do the work of sharing everlasting life. God says that only those who have been born again through the gospel of the water and the Spirit can do the work of sharing this life. As Jesus said that to believe in Him whom God sent was to do the work of God, to believe is to work. Believing in Him is not insignificant. To believe is also a work.

My fellow believers, regardless of how the Lord has made it possible for you to be born again of the water and the blood, it is of no use if you do not believe in this Truth. Even though Jesus has saved you by coming to this earth, being baptized, shouldering the sins of the world, and dying on the Cross, if you do not hold onto this Truth by faith, then you cannot receive everlasting life. If you do not believe, the Word of God is all useless for you.

My fellow believers, if you just say with your words that you believe, but do not really believe with your hearts, then your faith is good for nothing. Indeed, the Bible says that with the heart one believes unto righteousness, and with the mouth confession is made unto salvation. The Word of God proclaims that you receive everlasting life by believing with the heart that Jesus took upon all your sins by being baptized. It is by believing in the gospel of the water and the Spirit according to God's Word that we are remitted from all ours sins. This is what Paul really meant by the passage, *"For with the heart one believes unto righteousness, and with the mouth confession is made unto salvation" (Romans 10:10).*

My fellow believers, why did Jesus come to this earth? He came to save you and me from sin. Why was Jesus baptized? He was baptized to accept all the sins of you and me. Why did Jesus go to the Cross and was crucified? He was crucified because He had taken upon all our sins. Why did Jesus have to rise from the dead again? It was to bring us, who had died because of sin, back to life again. By accepting all our sins through His baptism, dying on the Cross, and rising from the dead again, Jesus has given new life to those who believe in Him, bestowing them with everlasting life and the righteousness of eternal salvation. You must believe that it was to remit away all your sins before God that Jesus was resurrected. My fellow believers, you must understand this with the head and believe in this Truth with the heart.

Why was Jesus baptized? Because in the Old Testament sin was passed onto an unblemished sacrificial animal through the laying on of hands, Jesus came to this earth and was baptized in the same way as in the Old Testament. Our Lord Himself made it clear, that He would never cast out those who come to Him. The Lord will never spurn His believers.

The Lord is the bread of life. To those who believe that the Lord bore all the sins of the world on His body by being baptized, and that He died on the Cross and rose from the dead again to bring you back to life, our Lord is the bread of life. By believing with the heart in the baptism of Jesus and His blood on the Cross, we can eat this bread. And whoever eats this bread is saved and receives life.

We need to consider for what we should live our remaining lives. We need to think about how we should live; whether we should live according to the work of the Spirit that saves souls, or for our own flesh. Anyone who was born again from sin by believing in the gospel of the water and the Spirit must believe that he had died to the flesh and the Law, and that therefore he has now become a worker whose duty is to save souls. We all need to believe in this. By this faith, we must follow the Spirit, not the flesh. Since we who have received the remission of sin now have nothing to do with sin, we should work to save other souls. Rather than working for the food that perishes, we must do the work of the Spirit that makes others never thirst again and brings everlasting life to them. We must follow the Spirit.

Quite often, we are bound by ourselves even after receiving the remission of our sins, but how should we live? What is our Lord saying to us today? Is He telling us to follow the flesh? Or is He telling us to follow the Spirit? He is telling us to follow the Spirit. Even though we often follow the flesh, we are still God's born-again children. No matter how insufficient each of us might be individually, if we only have the faith that has saved us, and faith in the Word of God, then we are all still of those who follow the Spirit. So, let us be mindful of the fact that we are God's people, the ones who follow the Spirit, no matter how insufficient we might be.

Is it right for us to follow the flesh or the Spirit? Although we sometimes follow the flesh, it is right for us to follow the Spirit, enabling others to attain life. God is telling us every moment that despite our insufficiencies, we are not the people of the flesh, but the people of the Spirit. When we preach the gospel and follow the Spirit, others can receive the remission of sin and attain everlasting life. Herein lies the reason why we must follow the Spirit. But what will happen if we otherwise follow the flesh? If we end up following the flesh, no one can earn new life through us. People will not be saved, in other words. If we work according to the Spirit, others will receive life. That is why we must follow the Spirit.

Some souls have been saved through this revival meeting. Although you and I are in fact full of shortcomings, we've worked hard because we follow the Spirit. We've made many sacrifices to save souls, and we've endured through many insults to lead them. So as a result, many souls have been saved so far. Though you and I might have been insufficient, many souls have received the remission of sin by hearing the gospel from us.

My fellow believers, we must remember what our Lord said here, *"Do not labor for the food which perishes, but for the food which endures to everlasting life" (John 6:27)*. We must labor for the food that endures to everlasting life. Though we are insufficient, we must still follow the Spirit. We must follow the Spirit with all our strength. Each of us must say to oneself, "No matter how insufficient I might be, I am a righteous person who is capable of following the Spirit. I am someone who can save others. For the Lord put my flesh and the Law to death, and I have been raised back to life again, I am capable of following the Spirit." We need to say this to ourselves. And we need to tell ourselves, "I must follow the Spirit." No matter how insufficient we ourselves might be, we still need to set our goal at least. We need to make up our minds clearly.

Though you are insufficient, by no means does this mean that you are not the people of the Spirit and God's children. Because we believe in the gospel of the water and the Spirit, we are God's children despite our insufficiencies; what is important is whether or not we are capable of following the Spirit, and whether we are qualified to do so. In short, those who have been born again of the water and the Spirit are qualified to follow the Spirit. We are the children of God's righteousness who can follow Him by faith, and who can labor to save souls by faith. My fellow believers, I admonish all of you to have faith.

And I admonish you to follow the Spirit. Let us all set each of our hearts, and let us realize that though we are insufficient, God has blessed us to follow the Spirit. My fellow believers, no matter how insufficient you might be, know that you are capable of following the Spirit, and do follow Him with this faith. In doing so, God will bear many fruits through you.

Whenever we hold revival meetings, we see many souls being saved from sin. Would this have been possible if each of you had worked individually? Just how many shortcomings do you have on your own, when looked at individually? Would you be able to follow the Lord all on your own individual ability? No. But no matter how insufficient you might be, are you the Spirit's people or the people of sin? You are the people of the Spirit. Those who have the Holy Spirit are the people of the Spirit. When the people of the Spirit gather together and pool their strengths to follow the Spirit, the work of salvation is bound to unfold, no matter how insufficient each of them might be. This is the power that God has bestowed upon His Church. Knowing this, we must never fall into despair or be despondent because of our individual insufficiencies, and we must instead follow the Lord in faith united together in His Church.

My fellow believers, faith is not of theory: For us to receive the remission of our sins by believing in the gospel of the water and the Spirit, to follow the Lord after being born again of water and the Spirit, and to live by faith and bear the fruits of faith, faith cannot be merely hypothetical. All the aspects of our faith should be actual and real. What our Lord is actually saying to us is to follow the Spirit, not the flesh. We must follow the Spirit by faith. Although we often stumble and fall, we get up on our feet again, dust off ourselves, and follow the Lord again, which is something that only the righteous can do. No sinner can do this.

My fellow believers, I admonish you all to have genuine faith. Believe that God has saved you perfectly. Do you believe this, my fellow believers? And if you have indeed been saved through the gospel of the water and the Spirit, then believe that you are capable of following the Spirit. Believe that you can do God's work if you labor by believing in the gospel of the water and the Spirit. Anyone who is saved should follow the Spirit by faith with a united heart. ⊠

Work for the Food That Does Not Perish On This Earth

< John 6:26-59 >

"Jesus answered them and said, 'Most assuredly, I say to you, you seek Me, not because you saw the signs, but because you ate of the loaves and were filled. Do not labor for the food which perishes, but for the food which endures to everlasting life, which the Son of Man will give you, because God the Father has set His seal on Him.' Then they said to Him, 'What shall we do, that we may work the works of God?' Jesus answered and said to them, 'This is the work of God, that you believe in Him whom He sent.' Therefore they said to Him, 'What sign will You perform then, that we may see it and believe You? What work will You do? Our fathers ate the manna in the desert; as it is written, 'He gave them bread from heaven to eat.'' Then Jesus said to them, 'Most assuredly, I say to you, Moses did not give you the bread from heaven, but My Father gives you the true bread from heaven. For the bread of God is He who comes down from heaven and gives life to the world.' Then they said to Him, 'Lord, give us this bread always.' And Jesus said to them, 'I am the bread of life. He who comes to Me shall never hunger, and he who believes in Me shall never thirst. But I said to you that you have seen Me and yet do not believe. All that the Father gives Me will come to Me, and the one who comes to Me I will by no means cast out. For I have come down from heaven, not to do My own will, but the will of Him who sent Me. This is the will of the Father who sent Me, that of all He has given Me I should lose nothing, but should raise it up at the last day. And this is the will of Him who sent Me, that everyone who sees the Son and believes in Him may have everlasting life; and I will raise him up at the last day.' The Jews then complained about Him, because He said, 'I am the bread which came down from heaven.' And they said, 'Is not this Jesus, the son of Joseph, whose father and mother we know? How is it then that He says, 'I have come down from heaven'?' Jesus therefore answered and said to them, 'Do not murmur among yourselves. No one can come to Me unless the Father who sent Me draws him; and I will raise him up at the last day. It is written in the prophets, 'And they shall all be taught by God.' Therefore everyone who has heard and learned from the Father comes to Me. Not that anyone has seen the Father, except He who is from God; He has seen the Father. Most assuredly, I say to you, he who believes in Me has everlasting life. I am the bread of life. Your fathers ate the manna in the wilderness, and are dead. This is the bread which comes down from heaven, that one may eat of it and not die. I am the living bread which came down from heaven. If anyone eats of this bread, he will live forever; and the bread that I shall give is My flesh, which I shall give for the life of the world.' The Jews therefore quarreled among themselves, saying, 'How can this Man give us His flesh to eat?' Then Jesus said to them, 'Most assuredly, I say to you, unless you eat the flesh of the Son of Man and drink His blood, you have no life in you. Whoever eats My flesh and drinks My blood has eternal life,

and I will raise him up at the last day. For My flesh is food indeed, and My blood is drink indeed. He who eats My flesh and drinks My blood abides in Me, and I in him. As the living Father sent Me, and I live because of the Father, so he who feeds on Me will live because of Me. This is the bread which came down from heaven—not as your fathers ate the manna, and are dead. He who eats this bread will live forever.' These things He said in the synagogue as He taught in Capernaum."

When Jesus went up to the mountain and preached, multitudes were following Him. Then putting His hands on the small amount of food that was only enough for a single lunch, Jesus blessed it and performed the miracle of feeding more than 5,000 people with bread and fish, leaving twelve baskets of leftovers. So the people followed Jesus and sought to have Him as their king. They thought, "Wouldn't it be wonderful to have such a king?" So they sought to make the Lord their king, but Jesus departed and went over to the other side of the sea.

When the great multitude followed Him desperately wanting to attain another meal from Him, Jesus rebuked them, saying, *"Do not labor for the food that perishes, but for the food that endures to everlasting life" (John 6:27).* The multitude had followed Jesus for the food that perishes, to quench their hunger temporarily at that time, without realizing that the truly everlasting food was with Jesus. This is why Jesus rebuked them.

The lesson of this passage also applies to the born-again. Jesus also reiterated about how we should live after being born again. Our Lord said, *"For to be carnally minded is death, but to be spiritually minded is life and peace" (Romans 8:6).* The

Lord said that while our carnal thoughts bring death to us, spiritual thoughts bring everlasting life.

When We Do God's Work, for What Should We Labor?

We have been saved, but what kind of work should we do after being saved? Should we labor for what would perish? Or should we labor for the food that endures to everlasting life? Should we labor for what does not perish, enabling others to receive everlasting life, or should we labor for what perishes? This is what Jesus was addressing. He was telling us to labor for the food that does not perish, to do the kind of work that enables others to receive eternal life.

For us to preach the gospel of the water and the Spirit is to preach Jesus who identified Himself as the bread of life. We are of those who labor for the work of everlasting life that does not perish. We, who are spreading the gospel all over the world, are such people. When we preach the gospel of the water and the Spirit, people will hear this Truth, and when they believe in this Truth with the heart, they will surely receive the remission of their sins and attain everlasting life. What is important is what kind of work you and I would do after receiving the remission of sin. Would you labor for the food that perishes? Or would you labor for the food that does not perish? The food that perishes refers to completely useless work, while the work of everlasting life refers to the work of saving souls.

What, then, should we do? We can be both carnally and spiritually minded. While the right thing for us to do is to think of and do what is good for other souls, we all have a free choice. So we ourselves must think about this question of for what we should live, decide on one, engrave this in our hearts, hold onto it and follow it.

Although countless people were following Jesus, their purpose was just to feed themselves. They followed Him only to receive and eat the food of the flesh that would all be digested away in a day; they did not follow Him believing that the Lord had the real, everlasting food. In today's Scripture passage, we see the Lord warning those who were following Him for the perishable food. Jesus told the disciples and many others to labor for the food that endures to everlasting life, and to follow Him for this. That is why it is so important for us to set our minds on for what and how we should labor when we are working.

We can do both works, the spiritual and the carnal, but it is critically important to set our hearts on the right work. We need to realize clearly what spiritual work is, what it is that endures to everlasting life, from where and through what this work comes, and how we can do this work. We are prone to think highly of ourselves when we are actually nothing. So, Paul the Apostle warns us saying, *"For if anyone thinks himself to be something, when he is nothing, he deceives himself" (Galatians 6:3).* Therefore, we have to examine once again whether we are determined to labor for the food that does not perish and live our lives accordingly.

Of different types of Christians, there are those who follow Jesus for their own flesh, and others who follow Jesus to receive eternal life. Essentially, in other words, there are those who follow Jesus to do the work of the flesh, and there are those who do the work of Jesus to receive eternal life.

The critical problem is that 99.9 percent of today's Christians are attending church only to be fed with the food of the flesh. The Apostle John said, *"I pray that you may prosper in all things and be in health, just as your soul prospers" (3 John 1:2),* but we all know that there are many who believe in Jesus not for their souls, but for their carnal riches and fame. In other words, there are many Christians who believe in Jesus just to become rich, to prosper in business, and to live a healthy and lavish life. As a matter of fact, if Christians in the past 2,000 years of the history of Christianity were boiled down to 100 believers, 99 of them believed in Jesus for their own flesh.

In a survey of Christians in the United States, three types of sermons were identified as the sermons most frequently preached by American pastors. The first type was the notion one would become rich if he believes in Jesus; the second was the claim that one would attain fame if he believes in Jesus; and the third was the notion that one would be happy if he believes in Jesus. The pastors, in other words, were feeding their congregations with the food of the flesh. What was the result of such sermons that preached, "You'll be rich if you believe in Jesus. You'll be happy if you believe in Jesus. You'll be famous if you believe in Jesus"? As Christians became wealthy and content with their lives, and raised their social status in this world, they no longer believed in Jesus. Even worse, they ended up turning against Jesus.

In Korea also, far too many Christians say that they attend church so that they would be cured of their illnesses and become rich, so that their families would be in harmony, or so that some scumbag would turn into a good person, all from believing in Jesus. These Christians believe in Jesus only for their own flesh to prosper. Jesus said not to labor for the food that perishes, but for the food that does not perish and endures to everlasting life. Yet despite this, 99.9 percent of Christians believe in Jesus so that their flesh shall prosper.

Jesus rebuked such people in today's Scripture passage:

"Do not believe Me nor follow Me for such things. Labor for the food that does not perish, for the food that endures to everlasting life." So Jesus said, "In the times of the Old Testament, the manna came down from heaven. God brought the manna through Moses, but even those who ate it all died in the wilderness. But the Son of Man is the bread of life. I give you the bread of life. If you believe in Me, follow Me, and testify of Me, so that people will receive everlasting life. And they will not thirst forever. I am the bread of life, and this is the will of My Father, that whoever sees the Son of Man and believes in Him may have eternal life; and I will raise him that believes on the last day."

As it is written, *"I am the living bread which came down from heaven. If anyone eats of this bread, he will live forever; and the bread that I shall give is My flesh, which I shall give for the life of the world" (John 6:51),* none other than Jesus Himself is the bread of life. That is why Jesus said, "Eat of Me. And believe in Me. And Preach Me. If you want to labor, labor for the work of the Father. How can you do the work of God? To believe in Him whom God sent is to do His work."

Jesus said, *"Whoever eats My flesh and drinks My blood has eternal life, and I will raise him up at the last day. For My flesh is food indeed, and My blood is drink indeed. He who eats My flesh and drinks My blood abides in Me, and I in him" (John 6:54-56),* and, *"He who eats this bread will live forever" (John 6:58).* Jesus was talking about Himself. Here He told us to eat His flesh, but how can we eat Jesus' flesh? It is by believing that Jesus took upon all the sins of world by being baptized on His body that we can eat His flesh. In other words, Jesus was telling us to believe that He took all our sins upon Himself by being baptized to save us from the sins of this world. He was saying to us to eat His flesh by believing in this.

"My Flesh Is Food Indeed, and My Blood Is Drink Indeed" (John 6:55)

Our Lord was saying, "If you believe that I took upon your sins and was condemned for them by being baptized by John the Baptist and crucified to death, then your hearts will be relieved from the heavy burden of your sins. Whoever eats My flesh and drinks My blood has attained everlasting life." We believe in this Word wholly.

Since we have received everlasting life by believing in the gospel of the water and the Spirit, we pay even more attention to what our Lord has said to us. As our Lord said, *"Do not labor for the food which perishes, but for the food which endures to everlasting life" (John 6:27),* we believe that He said this to us. While we have received the remission of our sins by eating the flesh of Jesus and drinking His blood by faith, we still need to set our minds clearly on whether we would labor for the food that perishes or for the food that does not perish. We need to realize what it is to labor for the food that perishes, and what the food that does not perish is.

To labor for the food that perishes is to be carnally minded, only to think of the peace and comfort of our own flesh. What, then, is the food that does not perish? It is to be spiritually minded. As we serve this gospel, fulfill our role as its witnesses, preach it all over the world, and labor for this work, many people will indeed attain everlasting life. Making it possible for others to receive eternal life is what we must do. We need to discern clearly between laboring for the food that perishes and laboring for the food that does not perish, and we must set our minds on one of these two and work accordingly.

We Are Laboring to Preach the Gospel of the Water and the Spirit throughout the Whole World

Sometimes, even while serving the Lord, we wonder skeptically, "Is it really right to work like this?" And there are also times when we labor for the food that perishes, as there are times when we labor for the food that does not perish. Of course, we can go astray sometimes because of our weaknesses, but we should fundamentally set our minds on the right direction.

We need to set our minds clearly. It is to preach the gospel throughout the whole world that we are laboring like this. We are devoting ourselves to the literature ministry: We pray for this ministry, translate our books and publish them into many languages, and distribute them for free to whomever wants to read them. Most of our workers raise financial means for this ministry and support it with their own labor and sweat. None other than this is laboring for the food that does not perish. Do we really believe this when we are working? If we want to labor for the food that does not perish, then we need to set our minds on the work that does not perish. While it is possible for us to be mindful of both carnal affairs and spiritual affairs, we should set our minds on the work that does not perish, dedicate our hearts to it, and trust in it entirely. It is only then that we can become workers of righteousness, making it possible for others to receive everlasting life.

It is my sincerest hope that we would all serve the Lord and live for Him always. I admonish you to really set your minds on the work that does not perish, dedicate your hearts to it, and believe with all your hearts, not just with your thoughts, that it is the most precious work for you to labor for the bread of life. Although you are capable of doing both carnal and spiritual works, I want your hearts to realize that one is entirely wrong and the other is entirely right, and to dedicate your hearts and minds wholly to the right work and labor for it. While we can also work for the food that perishes, we must have the resounding and unshakable belief that it is only right for us to cherish the gospel and serve it, and we must become the people of faith offering ourselves to this work and dedicating all our strengths to it.

I have poured all my heart into preaching the gospel throughout the whole world. I am not saying that it's now enough, since we have been serving the gospel to this day; rather, what I am saying is that because this is the right thing for us to do, we should set our minds on the right work and have the firm belief that it is only proper for us to live like this for what is right. Regardless of how we might have lived so far, now we need to realize what is truly right and follow it. If we know what is right, but do not dedicate our lives to the food that does not perish, then our faith is all in vain. Do you know what it is to labor for the food that does not perish? Do you believe that it is right for us to live for this food? Have you set your minds on it and are you living entirely for this work? What is proper is not to just end with knowledge, but to set your minds on the right work, and to dedicate your lives wholly to this work.

Because we have the flesh, we sometimes fall into the work of the flesh. This is not proper. What the Bible says is right, we must believe wholly that it is indeed right at 100 percent. We shouldn't just think that one type of work is merely better than the other. What is wrong is entirely wrong, and what is right is entirely right. We have to set our minds unambiguously like this. Only if we place our hearts on what is right at 100 percent can we do the right work. And by doing this work, we can bear the fruit of everlasting life.

How are we then? Of course, our hearts may change from morning to evening, our thoughts may be as fickle as a reed and as unclear as fog, but we still have to make the decision of faith to place all our hearts on what is right at 100 percent. Only then can we do the work of everlasting life and bear the fruit of everlasting life. For our hearts to waver back and forth is only too human, but even so, to be unable to admit what is right at 100 percent is a shortcut to go astray. That is why we must labor entirely for what is right, realize that it is wrong for us to live for the food that perishes. And we also have to believe at 100 percent that working for the food that perishes is indeed wrong. If we evaluate these two works on a relative basis, we will not have clear faith in what is right, because the two get all mixed up. We really need to admit what is right as right at 100 percent, and what is wrong as wrong at 100 percent. Only then can we live entirely for the right work dedicating our hearts to it. Otherwise it is impossible.

What does Jesus say in today's Scripture passage? He tells us to labor for the food that does not perish. But are the Christian sinners all over the world really laboring for the food that does not perish? Aren't they following Jesus so that they would become rich, famous, and happy all from believing in Jesus? Jesus, in contrast, says that we must do the work of God. God's work is to labor for the food that does not perish. To enable others to receive everlasting life is to do what the Lord wants us to do. We have to believe that it is 100 percent right for us to work for the spreading of the gospel of the water and the Spirit. We really have to dedicate ourselves to this work and live for it.

My fellow believers, we need to make up our minds clearly. And when it comes to our work, we need to make it clear that what the Bible says is right is 100 percent right, and what the Bible says is wrong is 100 percent wrong. Yet even when this is made clear, since we are only humans living in this world, do we not often compromise on certain issues? There are many such cases. However, when it comes to our hearts' fundamental principle, we must never compromise.

We should be spiritually minded rather than carnally minded. And I believe that once someone believes that to be spiritually minded is 100%, he will be changed. That's because it is our human nature to dedicate our hearts to what we regard as 100% right. The Bible says that a virtuous wife does her husband good and not evil:

"She seeks wool and flax,
And willingly works with her hands.
She is like the merchant ships,
She brings her food from afar.
She also rises while it is yet night,
And provides food for her household,
And a portion for her maidservants.
She considers a field and buys it;
From her profits she plants a vineyard.
She girds herself with strength,
And strengthens her arms" (Proverbs 31:13-17).

I believe that we have to also work for the Lord like such a virtuous wife. We the believers in the gospel of the water and the Spirit are the ones who have received the Holy Spirit by eating the food of everlasting life, and the Bible says that those who have the Holy Spirit in their hearts do what is right. In other words, they labor for the food that does not perish. They yearn for the will of the Lord to be fulfilled, so that when the Groom comes they would be commended for having preached the gospel to others and served it. They toil and labor for this work, they set their minds to believe that it is only right for them to carry out this work devotedly, and they live their lives accordingly.

Rather than looking back and forth at both the world and the Lord's domain, and rather than wavering between the two, we must labor setting our minds on what is right at 100%. On certain issues, we sometimes make small compromises with the family, since we are all human beings, but because we never compromise on the fundamentals, we return and do what is right. We are the ones who do the work of God. Through us, as we carry out God's work, His heart is quenched, more and more people come to hear and believe in the gospel, and these people then receive everlasting life.

Of each and every person who eats the flesh of Jesus and drinks His blood by faith, there is no one who does not receive the remission of sin, and no one who does not attain everlasting life. And of all the people who labor for this food of life that does not perish, who preach the gospel believing 100% that it is right to serve this work, and who hear the Word and believe in it trusting that the gospel of the water and the Spirit is 100% right, there is no one who does not receive eternal life. That is why you and I must set our minds on spiritual work. And on the question of how right the spiritual work is, we need to score ourselves always. Is the spiritual work 100% right? Or is it only 70% right and 30% wrong? Or is it even 100% percent wrong?

We must set our minds unequivocally that it is 100% right for us to do spiritual work. Only when we have such a determination can we follow the Lord and become His precious workers who labor for the food that does not perish, and only then can those who receive the gospel from us attain the remission of their sins. Those in whom the Lord is pleased are blessed by Him in both body and soul, and bestowed with His grace and love. It is such people that we are to become.

You and I have probably come across a critical juncture in our lives facing the question of how we ought to live our remaining lives. What is far more important and what requires far more attention than any question that we have faced so far is this question of how we should live. Jesus said clearly, *"Do not labor for the food which perishes, but for the food which endures to everlasting life" (John 6:27)*. And the Lord is asking, "How right do you really think it is to labor for the food that does not perish, and how much do you admit and believe in this commandment?" If the Lord asks us this, then we should all answer by faith, saying, "Lord, it is 100% right to labor for the food that does not perish." Are you willing to answer like this?

We are preaching the gospel of the water and the Spirit, but it is not so easy to live for this work. When the Lord said with only His Word to let there be light, there was light; to let there be trees and plants, there were trees and plants; and to let there be birds flying in the air and fish multiplying in the sea, there were birds and fish. Everything was indeed fulfilled exactly according to His Word. Although we believe in the Lord's Word, we know very well just how slow and difficult it is to obey His Word completely. We are so fragile that we get tired easily at the slightest hardship. It is really hard for us to work by ourselves for the food that does not perish.

However, our Lord still uses such people like us as His workers, for He is powerful. He is amazing. When a machine begins to sputter, it can be easily fixed and made to work again, but human beings are not like this. It requires sophisticated techniques and tremendous faculties to use us, but despite this, the Lord is able to use us as His instruments. That's because

He made us.

When it comes to working for the gospel, we must have the belief that it is 100% right to do so. We may say so with our words, but what is important is to set our minds. We may say, "I'll think about it at home." But when we are at home, we don't really think about it. We have to make up our minds here and now. A foolish person may think about this work for a hundred years and yet still not make up his mind, but the wise can make the decision in five minutes.

My fellow believers, you must be passionate. I was told a story that was unbelievable: Someone was so passionate that when he was dating in his car, he did not even realize his car was floating down by increasing river flows. We can imagine how passionate he was while dating in his car. We must be passionate. Not only when we are dating, but also when we are working, we must be passionate about what we do and set our minds clearly and resolutely. If we are lukewarm, neither hot nor cold, then nothing can be achieved.

What happens when you pour cold water on hot coffee? It would turn lukewarm and lose its taste. Each of us has a distinctive personality. When we the born-again work for the gospel, we must work passionately submerged in that work, and throw ourselves to this work while believing that this work of serving the Lord is 100% right. "Though I have not been entrusted with a great mission, because I am living wholly for the gospel, its flowers are blossoming all over the world." The righteous need to have this kind of conviction and passion for the righteous work. God has made us such people. This age is indeed an age of uncertainty, but we need to have the unfaltering belief that what we are doing and what we believe in are definitely right.

Once you have received the remission of sin, you have to

start a new life oriented to the righteous work; you have to get out of your country, from your family and your father's house, to a new life that God shows you. You have to set up your mind clearly to work for the gospel for the rest of your life. What would happen if you drag your feet? You would soon be surrounded by all kinds of filthiness. This world does not leave you alone if you remain undecided. When you hear the Word of God, you must clearly approve it whatever it says is right; if it is right, then you must accept it; and if you reject the Word, then you must clearly provide the reason for rejecting it. If you drag your feet indeterminately, the Devil will come and devour you. If you still wonder, "Is this gospel right?" and if you still drag your feet even after ten long years of attending the Church wavering between this and that, the Devil will come and devour you.

We have been saved. We have been saved by eating the flesh of the Lord and drinking His blood. Have you eaten the flesh and drunk the blood given by the Lord? When did you do that? To believe that all your sins were passed onto Jesus when He was baptized is to eat the flesh of Jesus. You ate it by faith. How did we drink Jesus' red blood? We drank the blood of Jesus by believing that He shouldered our sins and died for us on the Cross. Has your thirst now been quenched? That is why Jesus said, *"My flesh is food indeed, and My blood is drink indeed" (John 6:55).* When we eat the flesh of Jesus by faith, our eyes are opened wide and our stomachs are filled. When we drink the blood of Jesus, our hearts are quenched.

My fellow believers, as we live on, sometimes we make mistakes; sometimes we are insufficient; and sometimes we even make irreparable blunders. However, when we think about how Jesus took upon our sins through His baptism and was condemned on the Cross in our place, our inside is all quenched. So I can't help but say, "Lord, You really died a good death. Thank You."

Would Jesus have been in pain on the Cross? Or would His heart have been satisfied? When He was crucified, He would have been in pain. While He was hung for six hours, He would have suffered immensely. But when He died, He felt relieved of the heavy burden of sin by the completion of His atoning ministry. To blot out all the sins of the world, Jesus came to this earth and accepted them all when He was baptized at the age of 30, and so how heavy must these sins have weighed Him down? Although He was in so much pain when He was crucified while shouldering more sins than the thick clouds in the sky, when He died, He was satisfied to have fulfilled all the works of salvation from sin. When the Lord said with His last breath, *"It is finished!" (John 19:30),* He was filled with joy. The Bible prophesied this, saying, *"He shall see the labor of His soul, and be satisfied" (Isaiah 53:11).* What happens when we finish some work? Our hearts feel greatly relieved. Like this, Jesus was filled with joy when He finished off all the sins of the world and said, "It is finished!"

Jesus was baptized and died on the Cross for our sins. It was because He was filled with joy at the last moment that He said, "It is finished!" and promised, "I will return again." He did not complete everything in pain alone. If He had completed His mission painfully up to His last breath, He would have said lastly, "This time I came like this, but you should save yourselves on your own the next time. You should reach it for yourselves." However, because the Lord forgot all about His pain, He said, "I will return to take you away exactly as I ascend." The Lord told us that He would take us and live together in the Millennial Kingdom and in the everlasting Kingdom of Heaven.

You and I must have this belief that it is 100% right to live preaching the gospel of the water and the Spirit. "I will continue to do this work, for it is entirely right at 100%." We must have such a belief in our hearts. Only when we have this kind of heart filled with faith at 100% can we live our remaining lives by faith. Only then can we be filled with conviction and overflow with joy until the day the Lord returns. Otherwise it's too hard to follow Him. Does it upset and exasperate you just to think about how much you have labored so far? Sure, it has been very hard, but we are still rejoiced, for it is right for us to have worked for the gospel by faith to this day. So, as we make a midterm assessment, we are confident that there won't be any problem in the future, either.

My fellow believers, this is not some kind of hypothesis, but it is our wholehearted faith. We need to set our minds once again, and we need to place our hearts on God's work again. We must really have the belief at 100% that what the Lord says is right is indeed right, and that it is only proper for us to do the work that does not perish. When we place our hearts on this work at 100%, we will renew our strength and mount up with wings like eagles (Isaiah 40:31), all that we do will be blessed by God through the Lord, and we will complete everything that remains in Him who give us power. If we dedicate our hearts to what is right at 100% percent, then there is no problem. But if we do not offer ourselves like this, then it's impossible for us to follow the Lord and to achieve the works He has entrusted to us.

Despite my actual insufficiencies, I have labored diligently so far. Though it has been hard, I believe that it's the right thing to do. And although I am still insufficient even now, because I believe that it is right for me to live for the salvation of souls, I have lived my life like this thus far. I have labored to this day because our righteous lives are the food that does not perish and is approved by the Lord, because I am convinced that people will receive everlasting life if they believe in this gospel of the water and the Spirit, and because this is what has actually been fulfilled. In the future, I will continue to work just as I have worked to this day, believing with my heart that it is 100% right.

We have published our books on the elementary principles of the gospel of the water and the Spirit from various angles. From now on, we will speak on how to live our everyday lives by faith. I believe that all that remains for us to do is to believe in the gospel of the water and the Spirit, to separate ourselves from those who are not born again, to believe wholeheartedly that it is right to labor for the food that does not perish, set our minds firmly, and give glory to God and bear the fruit of everlasting salvation. There isn't anything big that we can do for the Lord, but all that remains is to live our lives believing in what He says is right. There is nothing else but this. The lives of the righteous who have been born again of water and the Spirit are a continuation of the life that is lived for the Lord by offering the heart to Him day by day.

In case of any human work, we can finish it after attaining the expected goal. But this life of faith must be lived until the day the Lord returns. However, although this life may seem hard to live, it's not so hard if we live it by believing in what is right and offering our hearts 100% to the Lord, for He will empower us. On the contrary, it is quite easy, as it is written, *"Come to Me, all you who labor and are heavy laden, and I will give you rest. Take My yoke upon you and learn from Me, for I am gentle and lowly in heart, and you will find rest for your souls. For My yoke is easy and My burden is light"* *(Matthew 11:28-30).* The reason why it's not so hard to lead our lives of faith is because the Lord empowers us. If we believe that what the Lord said is right and set our hearts on it, then the Lord will give us new strength. Because He renews our strength, we can march forward by faith, and through this we come to thank the Lord, for we experience for our selves how He is helping us. I give my thanks to God.

I am eagerly waiting for our spiritual growth series to be published soon. I am sure that this series will work in many people's lives and yield a plentiful harvest from every nook and corner of the world. I know that we have to pray for this, and that to dedicate our hearts wholly to this work, believing that it is right to labor for the food that does not perish, is to bear the fruit of the Holy Spirit. We live by faith relentlessly not to show off our own glory or the pride of the Church, but to spread all over the world the food that does not perish. We continue to do the work of God, preaching the gospel of the water and the Spirit to let all the souls throughout the whole world be born again. We will do our best to preach the gospel day by day. So I believe that we need faith, and that it is right for us to offer our heart's faith in everyday life. I know that you also believe so.

My fellow believers, we must eat the flesh of Jesus and drink His blood by faith. If any Christian has not had the flesh of Jesus and His blood by faith, then he believes in Jesus erroneously. He is someone who is laboring for the food that perishes. Those who believe in Jesus only to be happy in this world, to be rich and famous, will depart from Jesus as soon as they prosper even slightly. There are so many Christians who eventually leave Jesus behind.

However, you and I cannot leave Jesus no matter what. Because we have received the true remission of our sins by believing in the gospel of the water and the Spirit with our whole hearts, we are 100% convinced that it is right for us to live like this. Happy are those who live their lives dedicating their hearts wholly to the right work and believe in it.

I hope and pray that you would not just know what is right in your heads, but put your hearts on it 100% and believe in it. ✉

We Must Eat the Bread From Heaven by the Faith In the Gospel of the Water And the Spirit

< John 6:28-58 >

"Then they said to Him, 'What shall we do, that we may work the works of God?' Jesus answered and said to them, 'This is the work of God, that you believe in Him whom He sent.' Therefore they said to Him, 'What sign will You perform then, that we may see it and believe You? What work will You do? Our fathers ate the manna in the desert; as it is written, 'He gave them bread from heaven to eat.'' Then Jesus said to them, 'Most assuredly, I say to you, Moses did not give you the bread from heaven, but My Father gives you the true bread from heaven. For the bread of God is He who comes down from heaven and gives life to the world.' Then they said to Him, 'Lord, give us this bread always.' And Jesus said to them, 'I am the bread of life. He who comes to Me shall never hunger, and he who believes in Me shall never thirst. But I said to you that you have seen Me and yet do not believe. All that the Father gives Me will come to Me, and the one who comes to Me I will by no means cast out. For I have come down from heaven, not to do My own will, but the will of Him who sent Me. This is the will of the Father who sent Me, that of all He has given

Me I should lose nothing, but should raise it up at the last day. And this is the will of Him who sent Me, that everyone who sees the Son and believes in Him may have everlasting life; and I will raise him up at the last day.' The Jews then complained about Him, because He said, 'I am the bread which came down from heaven.' And they said, 'Is not this Jesus, the son of Joseph, whose father and mother we know? How is it then that He says, 'I have come down from heaven'?' Jesus therefore answered and said to them, 'Do not murmur among yourselves. No one can come to Me unless the Father who sent Me draws him; and I will raise him up at the last day. It is written in the prophets, 'And they shall all be taught by God.' Therefore everyone who has heard and learned from the Father comes to Me. Not that anyone has seen the Father, except He who is from God; He has seen the Father. Most assuredly, I say to you, he who believes in Me has everlasting life. I am the bread of life. Your fathers ate the manna in the wilderness, and are dead. This is the bread which comes down from heaven, that one may eat of it and not die. I am the living bread which came down from heaven. If anyone eats of this bread, he will live forever; and the bread that I shall give is My flesh, which I shall give for the life of the world.' The Jews therefore quarreled among themselves, saying, 'How can this Man give us His flesh to eat?' Then Jesus said to them, 'Most assuredly, I say to you, unless you eat the flesh of the Son of Man and drink His blood, you have no life in you. Whoever eats My flesh and drinks My blood has eternal life, and I will raise him up at the last day. For My flesh is food indeed, and My blood is drink indeed. He who eats My flesh and drinks My blood abides in Me, and I in him. As the living Father sent Me, and I live because of the Father,

so he who feeds on Me will live because of Me. This is the bread which came down from heaven—not as your fathers ate the manna, and are dead. He who eats this bread will live forever.'"

The Souls That Were Lost before God

When our Lord was on this earth, the people of Israel were so poor that they did not have enough food to feed themselves, as they were exploited by the Roman Empire as a colony. Our Lord met the sick and healed them, and performed the miracle of five loaves of bread and two fish for the poor to feed them with the food of the flesh.

Seeing the people of Israel, our Lord had pity on them. He felt compassion for them because He saw them as lost sheep, a flock without a shepherd. When the people of Israel followed Jesus all the way to the wilderness, Jesus had compassion for them, for even as they needed to be fed, as they had the flesh, they had nothing to eat. So the Lord said to His disciples, *"You give them something to eat" (Luke 9:13)*. Philip then said to Jesus, *"Two hundred denarii worth of bread is not sufficient for them, that every one of them may have a little."* It was impossible for the disciples to feed all those people.

However, our Lord fed them full. He performed the miracle of five loaves of bread and two fish. As Jesus took two fish and five barley loaves, and blessed this food that was enough for only a single lunch, over 5,000 men were fed. If women and children are included, perhaps as many as 15,000 people were fed. Our Lord performed such a miracle.

When the people met Jesus, many of them were healed from their sicknesses, were fed with the bread of the flesh, saw amazing miracles, and heard the marvelous Word of the heavenly Truth. So a great multitude began to follow Jesus and tried to take Him by force to make Him the king of Israel. These people thought, "If You would just become our king, we wouldn't have to worry about food. You could just bless a bag of wheat once and it would be enough to feed the whole nation and still have leftovers to fill seven barns." So the smart ones tried to make Jesus their king, thinking that they would have nothing to worry about the nation's economy and food supply if only Jesus would be made king. However, Jesus refused firmly. "I will not become your carnal king." Jesus kept running away from them, and the people tried to take Him by force and make Him their king.

Then, Jesus went to Capernaum with His disciples crossing the Sea of Galilee by boat. The multitude of followers who were standing at the shore of the Sea of Galilee saw that Jesus had crossed to the other side, and so they followed Him there. As they tracked to the other side of the sea to find Jesus, they must have gotten hungry again. When the mealtime came around, they were thinking, "Wouldn't the Lord give us something to eat again?" At that time, our Lord said to them, *"Most assuredly, I say to you, you seek Me, not because you saw the signs, but because you ate of the loaves and were filled. Do not labor for the food which perishes, but for the food which endures to everlasting life, which the Son of Man will give you, because God the Father has set His seal on Him"* *(John 6:26-27).*

So the people asked Him, "What shall we do, that we may work the works of God?" Jesus then answered them and said, *"This is the work of God, that you believe in Him whom He sent" (John 6:29).* Jesus already knew what was in their hearts. He was telling them to believe in "the gospel of the water and the Spirit" given by Jesus Himself. They then asked Him, *"What sign will You perform then, that we may see it and believe You? What work will You do? Our fathers ate the manna in the desert; as it is written, 'He gave them bread from heaven to eat'" (John 6:30-31).*

Jesus wanted to feed them with the bread of life. However, since the people of Israel believed in God, they related this to the Old Testament's manna from heaven that God had given to their forefathers to eat while living in the wilderness. So they asked, "Can you then give bread like the manna to all of us, like Moses in the Old Testament?" Our Lord then answered, *"Most assuredly, I say to you, Moses did not give you the bread from heaven, but My Father gives you the true bread from heaven. For the bread of God is He who comes down from heaven and gives life to the world" (John 6:32-33).* The people said, "If You have the power, give us this bread. Feed it to us. Then we will believe." And Jesus replied, "It was not Moses who brought down the manna in the Old Testament, but it was God, and to give you life, I also give you My flesh. So eat My flesh and receive everlasting life."

Jesus said, "I am the bread of life," and told the people to eat this bread from Heaven, for it would give them life. What kind of bread is this? As Jesus said that His flesh was the bread of life, the people gathered there could not help but wonder about it. They could understand the bread of the flesh, but what was this bread of life that He spoke of all of a sudden? Here, we need to know the fundamental reason why Jesus spoke of the bread of life.

The people of Israel wanted the bread of the flesh from Jesus when they were following Him around. Jesus, on the other hand, wanted to give them the bread of life. These two desires did not correspond with each other. What Jesus wanted to give to them was not what the people of Israel were looking for. So referring to Himself, when Jesus said, "I am the bread of life," and "Eat My flesh," the people of Israel could not understand Him.

Jesus then explained to them in John 6:35-40: *"He who comes to Me shall never hunger, and he who believes in Me shall never thirst. But I said to you that you have seen Me and yet do not believe. All that the Father gives Me will come to Me, and the one who comes to Me I will by no means cast out. For I have come down from heaven, not to do My own will, but the will of Him who sent Me. This is the will of the Father who sent Me, that of all He has given Me I should lose nothing, but should raise it up at the last day. And this is the will of Him who sent Me, that everyone who sees the Son and believes in Him may have everlasting life; and I will raise him up at the last day."*

Jesus Is the Bread of Life

As Jesus described Himself as the bread of life, the Jews began to complain about Him, saying, "As we know, You are Joseph's son, and so how can You say that You are the bread from Heaven? The bread of life? Nonsense! We know all about your family. Your father Joseph and Your mother Mary are our neighbors, and we saw You growing up. Your father is our friend, and so how dare You say that You are the bread of life from Heaven? Our forefather ate the manna; will You give us this manna also? If so, then bring down the manna for us now."

Jesus then said to them, "No one can come to Me unless the Father draws him to Me; I will raise him on the last day." In other words, our Lord was talking about how God the Father had sent Him to the world to save its people. Yet the people were asking Him only for the food of the flesh. So, He said, "I am the bread of life and you will be saved and receive everlasting life if you believe in Me, but you do not believe in Me even as you see Me."

"How can we believe in You? We know that You are Joseph's son, and so how can we believe in You?" There had to be some meaningful dialogue between Jesus and the people of Israel, but we see that this was impossible, with both sides only advocating their own point.

Our Lord said that He was the bread of life. He said, "Even though your forefathers ate the manna in the wilderness, they all died, but what has come down to that wilderness was not given by Moses, but came from Heaven." He then said, *"The bread that I shall give is My flesh, which I shall give for the life of the world" (John 6:51)*. In other words, Jesus was saying, "I am the bread from Heaven, and if one eats this bread, he will live forever." The Lord said that His flesh was the bread of life for the world. And Jesus said that the people had to eat His flesh.

The Jews then began to argue amongst themselves in a great commotion, as they simply could not understand what Jesus was saying. So they said, "How can this Man give us His flesh to eat?" Jesus then said to them, *"Most assuredly, I say to you, unless you eat the flesh of the Son of Man and drink His blood, you have no life in you. Whoever eats My flesh and drinks My blood has eternal life, and I will raise him up at the last day. For My flesh is food indeed, and My blood is drink indeed. He who eats My flesh and drinks My blood abides in Me, and I in him. As the living Father sent Me, and I live because of the Father, so he who feeds on Me will live because of Me. This is the bread which came down from heaven—not as your fathers ate the manna, and are dead. He who eats this bread will live forever" (John 6:53-58).* However, the people of Israel still could not understand Him to the very end.

The Flesh of Jesus Is Food Indeed

We have been born again by eating the flesh of Jesus and drinking His blood. The born-again can realize that Jesus' flesh is food indeed and His blood is drink indeed. In fact, the born-again people are eating the flesh of Jesus everyday and drinking His blood everyday. This Jesus, who said that His flesh was food indeed, is still feeding the righteous to fullness with His flesh. The righteous are eating the flesh of Jesus by faith. This flesh of Jesus refers to the gospel of true salvation, that Jesus has washed away all our sins by receiving baptism on His body from John the Baptist and thereby taking upon Himself all the sins of the world.

The Blood of Jesus Is Drink Indeed

Jesus said that His blood is drink indeed. That Jesus bore all the condemnation of all our sins is the drink that quenches us. If we eat His flesh, we are filled, and if we drink His blood, we are quenched. As those who believe in the baptism and blood of Jesus feed on Him by faith, His flesh has truly become the bread of life from the Kingdom of Heaven, and His blood has become drink indeed. The flesh and blood of Jesus have become the true bread of life for the believers. You and I who believe in Jesus know and believe that the flesh of Jesus is the bread of life.

Here, we need to be very careful not to misunderstand. We shouldn't believe that Jesus' death on the Cross is His flesh, that this alone is the food of life. That Jesus died on the Cross is indeed drink to us, but it is not food. Are you filled when you believe in just the Cross of Jesus? No. When you believe only in Jesus' blood on the Cross, you may feel quenched as you are freed from the condemnation of your hearts' sins, but there is no fullness of the heart.

Jesus accepted all our sins through His baptism in the Jordan River, and He has washed away all our sins through the water of His baptism. This flesh of Jesus therefore continues to be food for you and me. Is this true for you also? Because the people of Israel at that time were carnal, they did not realize this fact while they were following Jesus, but when we the born-again read this passage, we understand what it means.

It is written, *"For My flesh is food indeed, and My blood is drink indeed. He who eats My flesh and drinks My blood abides in Me, and I in him" (John 6:55-56)*. Anyone who does not eat the flesh of the Son of Man and drink His blood has no life in him. But those who eat the flesh of the Lord and drink His blood have everlasting life. What about you, then? Have you had the flesh of Jesus and His blood? How did you have them? Did you rip out an arm from Jesus' body, cooked and gnawed at it? Did you draw the blood on a bowl when you ripped out Jesus' arm and drink it? Just how much flesh did Jesus have that all these people ate it?

My fellow believers, we know that Jesus did not say this passage in carnal terms. The Word of the Lord is spirit and life to us (John 6:63). Jesus has given us His flesh and blood. Anyone who does not eat His flesh and drink His blood has no life. No matter who, anyone who does not have Jesus' flesh and blood has no life. No matter how someone might be the wisest and greatest theologian, if he did not have the flesh and blood of Jesus by faith, then he is far removed from everlasting life.

Jesus took all the sins of mankind upon His body, and He bore all our condemnation by shedding His blood on the Cross. By giving His flesh and blood to all human beings, He has given life to those who believe that He has saved His believers. No one can be saved from sin unless he believes with the heart that Jesus is the Way, the Truth, and the Life. Nor can he receive everlasting life. Only those who believe in the Word of Truth, that the baptism of Jesus, which is His flesh, has washed away all the sins of mankind can receive true life from God through faith.

Have you received this life? Have you become of those who have eaten the flesh of Jesus and drunk His blood? It is by faith that we have become such people, having eaten the flesh of Jesus and drunk His blood. From what Jesus said, "My flesh is food indeed," we can realize clearly that this Word of God is indeed an amazing truth. When one gets tired and weary in spirit from living in this world, if he realizes that he lacks spiritual food and thinks about the baptism of Jesus, then this baptism will become the food of life that will fill him spiritually.

The food that Jesus has given to us with His flesh never perishes and lacks nothing, so that we may have it forever, day and night, today and tomorrow. That Jesus received baptism on His body means that He has washed away all the sins of mankind with the water, and this flesh of Jesus that bore all sins through His baptism has become fullness and true food for souls. Anyone who believes in Jesus' flesh gets his heart filled. This fullness is not of the flesh, but of the heart. His soul is filled and strengthened. It is strengthened so much that those who are not born again simply cannot understand or experience this Word of Truth.

During the Early Church period, Christians carried on with their lives of faith underground, hiding in the catacombs to escape from persecution. Seeing this, many Romans accused them of being cannibals who ate the flesh of Jesus and drank His blood literally. Not knowing the Word of God, the Romans mistakenly believed that Christians gathered together everyday to slaughter human beings and devour them, eating the flesh of their victims and drinking their blood. So they violently persecuted them. For those who are not born again, it is just impossible to comprehend that the flesh of Jesus constitutes food.

The Catholic Church has its own false doctrine regarding the flesh of Jesus. According to the Catholic doctrine of transubstantiation, when someone eats the wafer, he is eating the flesh of Jesus. Catholics believe that when a priest blesses the wafer during their Holy Communion, this wafer is literally transformed into the flesh of Jesus, and that this is how they eat the flesh of Jesus. So during Mass, by eating this wafer, they believe that they just ate the flesh of Jesus. This, however, is not eating the flesh of Jesus.

The flesh of Jesus is eaten only by faith. One eats the flesh of Jesus only when he believes in His baptism and His Cross. It is by believing in the gospel of the water and the Spirit that we can eat the flesh of Jesus and drink His blood. It is when we believe in this Word that it becomes food and life for us. Jesus is the Son of God who came down from the Kingdom of Heaven. Only when we believe this and thus receive Him into our hearts may Jesus become life in our hearts and God's everlasting life shall come to us. Let us then all receive this everlasting life by faith!

When Jesus came to this earth, He received baptism on His body, died on the Cross, and has thereby blotted out all the sins of mankind. To believe in the Word of God that took away the sins of the world is the very faith that enables us to eat the flesh of Jesus. You cannot eat the flesh of Jesus just by holding the ritual of Holy Communion and eating a piece of bread. To eat Jesus' flesh is to believe in your redemption from sin that was fulfilled by Jesus, that He came to this earth to deliver you from sin, was baptized by John the Baptist and accepted all the sins of mankind, and has thereby washed away all your sins. This faith is the faith that enables you to eat the flesh of Jesus. It is by believing in the gospel of the water and the Spirit with our hearts that we eat the flesh of Jesus. When we believed with our hearts that all the sins of mankind were passed onto Jesus when He was baptized, and that He was vicariously condemned in mankind's place when He died on the Cross, Jesus became the food of life for us, our Savior from sin, and thereby made it possible for us to receive everlasting life through faith.

The Bible says, *"For with the heart one believes unto righteousness, and with the mouth confession is made unto salvation" (Romans 10:10)*. How, then, can we eat the flesh of Jesus and drink His blood? It is by believing in the gospel of the water and the Spirit that we can eat the flesh of Jesus and drink His blood. It is by nothing else but only by faith that we can have them.

Jesus said, *"For My flesh is food indeed, and My blood is drink indeed. He who eats My flesh and drinks My blood abides in Me, and I in him" (John 6:55-56)*. The Lord Jesus said that there is life in His flesh. Our Lord has offered His own flesh to sinners. He has fed His flesh to all those who believe in Him and filled them. This flesh refers to none other than the baptism that Jesus received. And Jesus has given us the drink of life too. In other words, Jesus was condemned for us by being crucified. In doing so, He has quenched our hearts, for He has made us never to be condemned for our sins.

It is because our Lord has given to the whole of mankind His flesh (His baptism), the spiritual food of life, that we have been filled from eating this flesh called the baptism of Jesus. Even at this very moment, there still are many souls on this planet who are starving to death in a spiritual famine, even as they are eating the food of the flesh, for they are unable to eat the food of life called the baptism of Jesus.

By accident, I came to listen to a certain pastor's sermon on TV a few days ago. The gist of his sermon was that we had to attain everlasting life and receive the remission of sin by believing in Jesus. However, after raising this critical issue to his congregation, this pastor did not give any answers as to *how* one should believe in Jesus. He was using John 6:28-40 in his sermon, but he had no idea how to interpret this passage. While he preached for half an hour, he was able to raise only questions and provide no answers. That's because he himself did not know the answer. A real sermon is to explain and answer how one can receive the remission of sin, how he can lead his life of faith properly, and how he can live an upright life. Yet the pastors who are not born again do not know what the food of Jesus' flesh is like. That's why this pastor just kept throwing questions at the congregation while preaching for half an hour, asking, "How should we live? What should we believe?" Such a sermon is likely to make Christian sinners even more sinful binding them with the legalistic faith.

When a preacher gives a sermon, he must provide answers to what he is preaching, for only then can the listeners eat the spiritual food and be filled. If he preaches without even knowing the answer himself, how could his sermon be called a sermon? Isn't it so, my fellow believers? Far too many people are starving now.

There are two kinds of food available to us: one is of the flesh, and the other is spiritual. As you and I know quite well, the food of the flesh is the edible produce we can get from the earth. But the spiritual food can be had only when we eat the flesh of Jesus. What the earth yields cannot constitute spiritual food. The spiritual food from Heaven is the flesh of Jesus. Only when we eat the flesh of Jesus do we eat this spiritual food, and only when we have the flesh and blood of Jesus do we receive everlasting life.

However, there are far too many Christians who do not even realize why Jesus came to this earth. By being baptized, Jesus became the Savior who has remitted away people's sins, and by offering His own flesh to us, He has given us everlasting life. The very fact that He has saved us from sin by receiving baptism on His body and shedding His blood constitutes our spiritual food. Despite this, many people do not believe in the baptism that Jesus received when He came to this earth. On the contrary, they only know that Jesus was condemned to death on the Cross and rose from the dead again. Even to this day they are still suffering, not realizing that Jesus, by being baptized when He came to this earth, has washed away all the sins of the sinners who believe in Him. How could this have happened?

People are hungry. Do you realize just how hungry they are spiritually? What about yourselves? Have you had the flesh of Jesus, the food of life, through your faith in His baptism? You must eat this flesh of Jesus. I am so thankful for the flesh that Jesus has given to us; it is food indeed. Had Jesus not been baptized, then no matter how sincerely we might believe in

Jesus, we could not have received the remission of our sins, nor could our souls and hearts have been at peace.

Reading today's Scripture passage, I realized how the flesh of Jesus (His baptism) is food indeed. And it saddened me deeply that the people of Israel could not recognize Jesus as who He really was. When Jesus said that His flesh was the food of life, I wish they would have just believed in Him and said, "Oh! So You are indeed the Messiah, the Savior, and the Lamb of sacrifice that came to this earth, was baptized, and would be condemned on the Cross." Their conversation with Jesus would not have been a dialogue of the deaf then. If they knew that Jesus was the Savior and believed so, then today's Scripture passage wouldn't have needed to be so long.

What happened when the Jews in today's passage failed to understand the flesh of Jesus, that the baptism of Jesus saved them from all their sins? When Jesus told the people to believe in Him, they said, "How can we believe in You?" to which Jesus said, "I am the bread of life from Heaven." Jesus said, "He who eats My flesh (Jesus' baptism) by faith eats the food of everlasting life, and he who drinks My blood drinks true drink." But the Jews retorted, "Are You then telling us to eat You literally?"

It was not just the Jews that were engaged in a dialogue of the deaf like this. Far too many Christians today who believe in Jesus without being born again are all engaged in such a dialogue of the deaf. They read today's Scripture passage, but they do not understand what it means. So not knowing the meaning of this Word of God, they only insist that we should live virtuously and piously. But what a flawed teaching is this? They speak of faith in Jesus only in terms of ethics and morals, saying, "You ought to live this way and that way." That's why Jesus cannot become their food even as they believe in Him, and why those who are not born again of water and the Spirit cannot feed souls with spiritual food.

Once I ate the flesh of Jesus by believing in the baptism of the Lord, my heart has always been full. Once I believed in the baptism of Jesus and His blood on the Cross, Jesus' baptism became the food of life in my heart, and His precious blood became true drink. When I read about the baptism of Jesus from the Word, this baptism became the food of the true remission of sin, and whenever I looked at the Cross, I thanked God for the fact that there truly is no longer any condemnation for me. When I believed in His salvation, that all the believers' sins were washed away through His baptism, and that their hearts are quenched by the bread of Jesus, the flesh (Jesus' baptism) and blood of Jesus became the true food of life for me. I am so thankful for this.

If One Believes in Only the Blood of Jesus, What Are the Consequences of This Faith?

Before I encountered the gospel of the water and the Spirit, I, too, had the faith that prevented me from eating the flesh of Jesus. I was drinking only the blood of Jesus at that time. During this time, for ten years I professed to believe in Jesus, but I only believed in His blood. So I had no food and was starving at that time. I was so bereft of spiritual food that I lived my life of faith based on my own emotions.

In those days, when I did not have true peace in my heart, singing hymns plainly was no fun. It was not exciting to sing solemnly. I was so starved and thirsty that I sang fanatically like a revivalist. Then without realizing myself I got immersed in my own emotions, and while I sang hymns like a fanatic, I felt a burning desire to serve the Lord. However, this lasted only a short while, and as soon as I stopped singing, I felt empty and was hungry again. Even while I worshipped, I wasn't filled at all, only feeling empty all the time. If we believe only in Jesus' blood, He cannot become food for our souls. So when I came to church to be fed, far from being fed I became even hungrier, and looking for satisfaction, I ended up going from one prayer retreat to another, from this revival meeting to that meeting. The result of believing only in the blood of Jesus was slightly quenching at best, if not continuously empty. That's because there was neither true faith nor the true water of life in my heart.

However, now that I ate the flesh of Jesus (the Word of Truth that Jesus has washed away all my sins by being baptized), the emptiness in my heart has disappeared. Now, true life overflows in my heart. Now, I can share the water of life with everyone else.

Jesus Has Washed Away Our Sins with His Flesh

From the moment I realized that all my sins were passed onto Jesus when He was baptized, my heart's thirst was quenched. From the moment I realized that Jesus was condemned on the Cross in my place, and from the moment I believed that Jesus accepted not only my sins, but all the sins of the entire mankind when He was baptized, I became full. That's because I truly received life at that time.

It is written, *"The LORD is my shepherd; I shall not want. He makes me to lie down in green pastures; He leads me beside the still waters" (Psalm 23:1-2).* My fellow believers, as we have eaten the grass to our hearts' content and drank the water at the riverside, we are filled and quenched, and being satisfied, we lie on green pastures and say, "I am so full. I am so full that I have nothing more to wish for!" My fellow believers, we have become such a contented people who are always smiling, happy beyond all description and lacking nothing.

My soul became full once I met our Lord in His Word. Whenever I feel slightly hungry, I always think about our Lord. I read the Word and meditate on it. I always remember that my sins were passed onto the Lord when He was baptized. He took upon Himself all of my sins. So my heart is always full. "Thank You, Lord, thank You so much. I am wholeheartedly grateful to You. I am so thankful that You have made me sinless. Lord, words cannot express just how grateful I am." I think about how truly insufficient I am on my own, and how our Lord bore all my sins; and believing in this with the heart, I eat the flesh and drink the blood everyday, and thereby rest with joy and peace in my heart.

We are living by feeding on the food of life for our souls. Not only I, but you have also attained salvation by believing in the flesh of the baptism of Jesus. By offering His own flesh and blood, Jesus has fed us with the food of life, bringing us back to life from sin. We believe in this. We believe that with His baptism and blood, Jesus has saved us all, who had been at the verge of dying of starvation. Is this not the case? By believing in the baptism of Jesus and His blood, we have eaten of His flesh and drunk His blood. If one does not eat and drink them by faith, he will surely die, but if he does eat and drink by faith, then he will surely attain everlasting life.

We must continue to eat the baptism of Jesus, that is, His flesh. Eating it once leads you to everlasting life, eating it twice leads you to fullness, and eating it thrice a day leads you to become people of faith. By having the flesh and blood of Jesus everyday, we gain new strength and are filled everyday. Do you believe this? We must indeed eat the food of life everyday.

My fellow believers, Jesus said, *"For My flesh is food indeed, and My blood is drink indeed. He who eats My flesh and drinks My blood abides in Me, and I in him. As the living Father sent Me, and I live because of the Father, so he who feeds on Me will live because of Me. This is the bread which came down from heaven--not as your fathers ate the manna, and are dead. He who eats this bread will live forever"* *(John 6:55-58)*. Do you believe this? My fellow believers, those who have Jesus' flesh and blood will live forever. The flesh of Jesus does not just fill us for only a short while. Jesus' flesh enables you to be washed from your sins and to receive eternal life, and it has become the food of everlasting life.

It is such an amazing miracle and a thankful blessing that we have come to eat the flesh of Jesus. What have we done to deserve this, to have both the flesh and blood of Jesus, when so many people only drank the blood? Today's sermon has addressed this point, highlighting how fortunate it was for us to be saved by a laser-thin margin. I have spoken about how we have made it through by a single difference and attained everlasting life, and how some others are bound to hell because of this slight difference.

What love and what grace is it that the Lord has saved us and met us, when there are so many people in this world who are smarter and more esteemed than us? I am so thankful for this, beyond any words. The flesh of Jesus is indeed the grace of God. It is the God-given food of Heaven. All that I did was just accepting by faith the gift that the Lord gave me all on His own. For all of us, too, there is nothing else to do but to just believe in the flesh and blood of Jesus, in His baptism and blood.

What we have received is everlasting life; we have come
to have faith in the flesh of baptism and the blood of the Cross
that Jesus has given us. This, we confess to our God, is not
because of our own goodness, nor because of the virtues of our
deeds, nor because we are particularly more talented than the
rest in any way.

We believe that it is because God had mercy for us and
loved us that He gave us the gift of salvation and everlasting
life, all on His own. God the Father led us to be saved, as it is
written, *"No one can come to Me unless the Father who sent
Me draws him."* God the Father has drawn us to the way of
eternal life, to the Church that has the proper teaching on the
flesh and blood of Jesus, and He has made us eat the flesh of
Jesus and receive everlasting life. When destruction comes to
this earth, Heaven will come to us. We now have nothing to
worry.

The Bible says, *"It is appointed for men to die once, but
after this the judgment" (Hebrews 9:27).* That God has made
us live forever means that He has made us not to end as
ephemeral beings, when our lives in this world were like the
morning mist to disappear in no time. So that we would enjoy
everlasting life and live forever, Jesus has made us God's
people by feeding us with His flesh and blood. All those who
believe in the flesh and blood of Jesus, who eat this flesh and
drink this blood, will live forever. My fellow believers, we can
eat and drink Jesus' flesh and blood at any time by faith. In
God's Church, we can always eat the spiritual food and drink.

That our Lord gave us His flesh and blood was to give us
everlasting life and eternal food. The flesh of Jesus was the
baptism of Jesus who washed away all our sins, and the blood
of Jesus was the punishment of the sins that He had borne

through His baptism. By believing in the flesh and blood of Jesus, the Son of God from Heaven, we have received the remission of our sins and attained everlasting life. ⊠

Jesus Christ, Who Became The Bread of Life to Us

< John 6:41-51 >

"The Jews then complained about Him, because He said, 'I am the bread which came down from heaven.' And they said, 'Is not this Jesus, the son of Joseph, whose father and mother we know? How is it then that He says, 'I have come down from heaven'?' Jesus therefore answered and said to them, 'Do not murmur among yourselves. No one can come to Me unless the Father who sent Me draws him; and I will raise him up at the last day. It is written in the prophets, 'And they shall all be taught by God.' Therefore everyone who has heard and learned from the Father comes to Me. Not that anyone has seen the Father, except He who is from God; He has seen the Father. Most assuredly, I say to you, he who believes in Me has everlasting life. I am the bread of life. Your fathers ate the manna in the wilderness, and are dead. This is the bread which comes down from heaven, that one may eat of it and not die. I am the living bread which came down from heaven. If anyone eats of this bread, he will live forever; and the bread that I shall give is My flesh, which I shall give for the life of the world.'"

In the Gospel of John chapter 6, the Lord says, *"I am the bread of life."* People felt full having eaten food for the flesh from Jesus. On the following day, they went seeking Jesus again, but Jesus told them not to labor for the food that perishes but for the food that endures to everlasting life. And so, people asked, *"What shall we do, that we may work the works of God?" (John 6:28)* Jesus answered, *"This is the work of God, that you believe in Him whom He sent" (John 6:29)*.

Then, people said, "If so, do you mean that You are the One sent by God and that You came down from Heaven? If so, do You have any evidence that You came down from Heaven? Please, show us the evidence. As it is written, Moses fed the people of Israel by having manna come down from heaven, but can You perform such a miracle?"

The Lord replied, "Your ancestors could not live eternally by eating such bread. But, because I am the bread that came down from Heaven, if you eat this bread, you will never die. I am the bread of life for the world." Then, He said, "Whoever eats this bread will have everlasting life, and on the last day, I will raise him up." The Lord said that He came in order to have everyone acquire life by He Himself becoming the bread of life for all the people of this earth.

In today's Scripture passage, the Lord said that the Jews murmured among themselves regarding Jesus, just as He said that He is the bread which came down from Heaven (John 6:41). Jesus said that He was the bread that came down from Heaven. That is why the Jews complained and murmured among themselves. They were saying, "As far as we know, aren't You the son of Joseph? We know your parents, yet how could You say that You came down from Heaven? Say things that make sense."

The Lord was the bread that came down from Heaven, just as He said, referring to Himself, "I am the bread which came down from Heaven." By eating this bread with faith, people are able to receive the remission of sin and acquire everlasting life with which we can never die. The Lord said that He came to this earth in order to have us receive salvation from sins, be delivered from death, acquire new life, and gain eternal life by giving all of us His own body. This is why Jesus said that He was the bread which came down from Heaven.

The Lord referring to Himself as the bread of life means that He has saved all humankind from sin by coming down to this earth in human flesh when we, the sinners, were about to die by getting drowned in sin. In order to save humankind from sin, the Lord took over the sins by receiving the baptism from John the Baptist with His body, was crucified, shed His blood unto death, and was resurrected from the dead on the third day. By receiving the judgment for our sins in this manner, the Lord has blotted out all our sins and permitted us to receive true salvation by believing in Him as the Savior. The Lord referred to Himself as the bread of life because He is spiritually the bread of life, which allows our spirits to live an everlasting life. These words refer to Him coming down to this earth and taking on all our sin with His body, as well as Him having died vicariously on the Cross and saving us by being resurrected from the dead. In short, they refer to the works that the Lord did by coming to this earth, that is, the completion of the gospel of the water and the Spirit.

Jesus Is the Bread from Heaven

Just as people sustain life by eating food for their flesh, those who truly believe in the ministries carried out by Jesus are entitled to receive eternal life. This is why Jesus said, *"I am the bread of life. He who comes to Me shall never hunger, and he who believes in Me shall never thirst" (John 6:35).* But, people took these words from a carnal perspective, instead of understanding them from a spiritual perspective. The Lord said, *"Do not murmur among yourselves. No one can come to Me unless the Father who sent Me draws him; and I will raise him up at the last day" (John 6:43-44).* Dear fellow believers, it is said that no one can come before Jesus unless the Father draws that person.

Then, who are the ones that the Father draws to Jesus? They are the ones who want to be cleansed of sins in their hearts and to receive salvation of the spirit, which would never perish, instead of things of the flesh that would rot away. God draws these people to His Son, Jesus, and has them know and believe in the fact that Jesus has become our savior by taking on our sins by receiving the baptism from John the Baptist, dying through crucifixion, and being resurrected from the dead, that is, the fact that Jesus has become the bread of life for all mankind. For us to believe in this Truth in our heart is to eat the bread of life and to acquire the salvation of everlasting life.

God the Father knows people's hearts well. It is said, *"For man looks at the outward appearance, but the Lord looks at the heart" (1 Samuel 16:7).* This is why God the Father draws those who want to acquire everlasting life by receiving the remission of their sins to His Son, Jesus, and has them eat the bread of life by faith. And thus, He allows them to gain salvation. In contrast, this means that God does not draw those who seek only the things that perish.

Thus, when we believe in Jesus, we must truly pursue the things of the spirit by heart. In doing so, we will be able to receive the remission of sin and acquire everlasting life by having attained such goals. As we believe in Jesus, we mustn't seek the things of being well off on earth, such as becoming rich, being famous, getting healed from sickness, and gaining power. It is the case that such people come to God in order to realize their greed, and it is the case that they believe in Him according to their lusts. That is why such people do not get to receive salvation. Truly, if we were to believe in Jesus as the Savior, we must believe in Jesus with the desire to receive the remission of sin in our own hearts. We must believe in Jesus with purposes such as receiving the remission of sin, becoming children of God, and living eternally in the Kingdom of Heaven prepared by God. Only when we go before God with such purposes, does God the Father help us, draw us, and as we listen to the Word of God, allow us to properly understand, believe, and follow it. Otherwise, it is said that we cannot come before the Father.

Dear fellow believers, we are in the middle of this revival meeting. We wrote the title of the meeting, *"Be converted, that your sins may be blotted out" (Acts 3:19),* on placards and placed them in several places. And we circulated leaflets, and so on. But, not that many people come to this evangelical meeting. Why aren't they coming? It is because their interest lies in something preposterous.

On a mountain, Jesus performed the miracle of five loaves of bread and two fish. With five barley loaves and two small fish at hand, Jesus blessed them, saying, "Let there be a blessing of God," and it is written that there were twelve baskets left over even after five thousand people had eaten. But, the thing was that these people, after having eaten this bread to one's content, sought after the bread for the flesh only, instead of recognizing the Lord who has performed such a miracle and trying to receive the remission of sin and to gain everlasting life by believing in the Word spoken by the Lord. Hence, just as Jesus started to speak about the spiritual Truth to those asking for bread, they all left, saying, "The words are difficult."

Only When We Believe in the Gospel of the Water and the Spirit, We Come to Eat the Flesh of Jesus and Drink His Blood

It's the same in this day and age. Instead of seeking for the things of the flesh, people should really come in order to have their spirits receive the remission of sin, become children of God, gain everlasting life before God, and receive the blessing of living for all eternity. But because their objectives are of the flesh, they are not coming to the church of God. Thus, it is the case that today's Christians believe in Jesus unavailingly.

Because we received the remission of sin by believing in Jesus who has come by the water and the Spirit, it is the case that we became children of God and those who have acquired everlasting life, and it is also the case that we will be resurrected on the last day. The fact is that we were able to receive such blessings because God the Father, having seen the center of our hearts, guided us before Jesus and had us recognize and believe in Jesus who is the bread of life. We have received the remission of sin by believing in the fact that our Lord has saved us by taking on our sins once and for all by His baptism, dying vicariously by being nailed to the Cross, and being resurrected from the dead. Also, God has taken us in as His children and has given us everlasting life, and by also believing in these, we were able to acquire the everlasting life, become participants of the resurrection of Jesus, and gain such blessings.

Last week, I visited the resting place of the late deacon Myungchan Kim who had died a few years ago. Fortunately, rain had come the day before, and the grasses were fresh. The words carved on his gravestone, "A righteous man, Deacon

Myungchan Kim, rests here waiting for the Lord's second coming," touched my heart once again. But one thing that's peculiar is that we can see many new graves near by with a similar epitaph. Only, they could not use the title "A righteous man or woman," as in "A righteous man, so and so." Why? It is because they weren't able to receive the remission of sin in their hearts, even though they may have led a life of faith as a deacon, an elder, a pastor, or a missionary throughout their entire life.

We the born-again saints, that is, the righteous, have clear hope. The fact is that God has prepared much more blessings for those who came before God yearning for things of the spirit, those who believe in the things given by God as is, and those who believe in divine and heavenly blessings that are eternal, instead of the things that will perish. And, we who believe in such things have received such blessings. Whatever the case, the focus of our hearts must seek the things of the spirit before God in order to receive salvation before God. If it is the case that we were to have no interest in the things of the spirit and in our hearts being cleansed of sins, but instead have interest in the things of the flesh, such as getting healed of physical infirmities and becoming rich, it would only be of no use for us to believe in Jesus. It is because God the Father does not let those who pursue the things of the flesh know the secret of Heaven, and does not lead them.

For what do we listen to the Word of God and believe in Jesus? You and I do believe in Jesus in order to receive complete cleansing of sins in our hearts, become children of God, acquire everlasting life, and be resurrected just as Jesus. In short, we believe in Jesus so that we may live in His Kingdom forever as kings along with Him, the King of kings. We believe in Jesus neither to be well off only on this earth nor to be well off in only the flesh. Rather, we believe in Him foremost for our spirits to be well off. Because we believe in Jesus with such purpose, it is the case that our Lord said, *"And this is the will of Him who sent Me, that everyone who sees the Son and believes in Him may have everlasting life; and I will raise him up at the last day" (John 6:40).*

In the Gospel of John chapter 6 verse 45, it is said, *"It is written in the prophets, 'And they shall all be taught by God.' Therefore everyone who has heard and learned from the Father comes to Me."* Who is the One that has shown this world the Father? It is the only begotten Son, Jesus. If so, whom did they, who are taught by Jesus, learn from eventually? The fact is that they have learned from God the Father.

Dear fellow believers, proper faith is something handed down from above. It means that there is a conduit for spiritual learning. From whom did you learn the Truth of salvation? Did you not learn the Word of the gospel of the water and the Spirit from the born-again servants of God, or brothers and sisters before you? You have learned from the predecessors of faith in the church of God. If so, it is the case that you have learned from God the Father. The reason is that they had heard and learned from Jesus, through these written Word. This Word itself is exactly what God the Father had said, and henceforth, if it is the case that servants of God should convey this Word to you after having heard and learned it from above, then you must realize that what you have learned from the servants of God is the same as having heard and learned from God the Father. The principles are the same. That is why Jesus said, *"It is written in the prophets, 'And they shall all be taught by God.'"*

Jesus is our Savior, but He is also the true Prophet. Thus,

He teaches us all things. The passage, *"It is written in the prophets, 'And they shall all be taught by God,'"* means that all the Scriptures of the Bible, which are spoken by the Lord, are the Word of the Prophet as well as the Word of the Truth. Jesus is really the First and the Last (Revelation 1:17); He is the truly the One who is in complete charge of the beginning and the end of human history. And, He is the One who teaches us the ultimate purpose of life precisely. He is the Creator who has made us, the Savior who has saved us from sins, and the Lord of the everlasting life who has given us the eternal life. Also, He is the resurrection for He is the Way, the Truth, and the Life. He, who has saved us from death, given us new life, has provided for our eternity, and had us receive blessings forever, is everything for us. This is what He was saying.

In the Gospel of John chapter 6 verse 46, it is said, *"Not that anyone has seen the Father, except He who is from God; He has seen the Father."* Who saw the Father? Only Jesus saw Him. That is why our Lord said the following in the Gospel of John chapter 6 verses 47 and 48. *"Most assuredly, I say to you, he who believes in Me has everlasting life. I am the bread of life."* It means that a person who eats Jesus, the bread of life, by faith into his or her heart has an undying life.

The Lord said, *"Your fathers ate the manna in the wilderness, and are dead. This is the bread which comes down from heaven, that one may eat of it and not die,"* (John 6:49-50). It means that Jesus is the bread which comes down from Heaven. It tells us that this bread is something that one may eat of it and not die. Jesus is the bread of life, which has given you and me true life. Jesus is the bread that gives the remission of sin and everlasting life. Dear fellow believers, do you believe in Jesus wholeheartedly? Do you truly believe in your heart that Jesus has saved you and me by taking on your sins as well as mine by receiving His baptism, dying vicariously on the Cross shedding His blood, and being resurrected from the dead? You and I who believe in this are the ones who have gained the everlasting life.

Everlasting Life Means That We Live Forever

The Lord has promised that, at the last day, He will raise those who have everlasting life. When the people of Israel were in the desert, Moses prayed to God, and God sent down the manna. And, these people ate that manna and maintained their carnal lives. But, they all died eventually. Some died of old age, some because of sickness, and some died in the midst of a war. Whatever the reason, they all died. But, what about the bread, which comes down from Heaven? People who have eaten it believing with their hearts never die. People who believe in the righteous works done by Jesus with their hearts do not die. People who believe in the fact that Jesus has saved us from sins, that He has given us everlasting life, and that He will raise us in the end will not die for all eternity. It was possible for the Apostles of the Early Church to be courageous in martyrdom because they believed in everlasting life. I hope for you to know the fact that there is everlasting life inside you and me.

The Lord said, *"I am the living bread which came down from heaven. If anyone eats of this bread, he will live forever; and the bread that I shall give is My flesh, which I shall give for the life of the world" (John 6:51).* Could we receive the cleansing of all the sins in our hearts by doing some virtuous deed and sanctifying ourselves? Never. We are able to receive the remission of sin, become children of God, and acquire the everlasting life only by believing in and accepting wholeheartedly the fact that Jesus, the One sent down by God the Father, came down to this earth and cleansed our sins by the gospel of the water and the Spirit. The Truth is that one can neither receive the remission of sin nor acquire everlasting life without going through the One set forth by God, His Son Jesus. This is why one must believe in the One sent down by God the Father, Jesus, who is the bread which came down from Heaven.

Thus, We Eat Bread and Drink Wine Whenever We Hold Holy Communion

The Lord told us to remember the bread and the wine. He said, *"For My flesh is food indeed, and My blood is drink indeed" (John 6:55)*. The Lord said, *"I am the bread of life,"* because He has taken on our sins by coming to this earth in human flesh. It is because He has cleansed our sins by taking on our sins with His flesh and vicariously received the judgment. The Lord is the bread of life. Only when we know and believe in Him with our hearts, we get saved from sins and acquire everlasting life. So then, we are truly born again anew and able to lead a worthwhile life.

In the Gospel of John chapter 6 verse 51, Jesus said, *"I am the living bread which came down from heaven. If anyone eats of this bread, he will live forever; and the bread that I shall give is My flesh, which I shall give for the life of the world."* The Lord refers to Himself as the living bread, but what is that bread? It is His flesh. It means that the flesh of Jesus is the bread of life. In the flesh of Jesus, there is the prefect faith. Jesus has saved us perfectly from all our sins by taking on our sins on His flesh through His baptism, going to the Cross with those sins, getting nailed, shedding blood, and receiving the judgment for our sins on our behalf. The fact that Jesus is the bread of life to us tells us the Truth that Jesus has taken on all our sins by receiving the baptism on His own flesh. Having faith in the salvific works done by Jesus is eating Jesus' flesh and drinking His blood. This is precisely the way to gain salvation. This is precisely the way to acquire everlasting life.

Is there anyone more blessed than a person born in this world who has received the remission of sin and everlasting life from God? As we live in this world, we can die from a fire, a traffic accident, or from some undeserved events. It is such a great blessing that we have acquired everlasting life while living in a fate of not knowing when we will die.

We sometimes get tired and irritated while we are heavily burdened by work, whether it is the work of God or the work of the world. As for those of you who believe in Jesus, if your hearts are weary and not joyous, you must think once more about the work that the Lord has done for you. We were those who had no choice but to go to hell. Yet, the Lord, by becoming the propitiation for us, has saved us perfectly. If we truly believe in our hearts the love of Jesus, we cannot but be thankful. We have received the remission of sin and became children of God. He has given us eternal life, and when our flesh dies, He will raise us at the last day. And, we will be given true rest.

Jesus is the living bread from Heaven. Jesus came to this earth to give you and me His flesh as the living bread. The Lord told you and me to eat this bread, and said that we will live eternally if we eat this bread. It is the case that we eat the bread of life by believing with our hearts and gain everlasting life.

In order for us to eat this bread of life, we must know

about the flesh and blood of Jesus. Also, we must realize our own sinful nature, and furthermore, we must realize that, before God, we are those headed for hell if we were to be judged according to the Law of God. "After being born on this earth, I wasn't able to accomplish anything, but I must at least receive the remission of sin. I want to receive the remission of sin, become a child of God and then go to Heaven." There has to be this fervent thirst in our spirits. By having faith with a sincere heart in the fact that 'Jesus has blotted out your sins as well as mine by the gospel of the water and the Spirit,' we are able to acquire everlasting life, be thankful, and truly share this bread also by faith.

We do not lead a life of faith with the things of the flesh. Whether or not a certain work is going well, life of faith would be carried out well only if we were to lead a life of faith by believing in the salvific ministries of the Lord and having faith in God. We are able to receive salvation, gain everlasting life, and receive all the blessings by believing in our hearts the things that He has given us.

Dear fellow believers, do you believe in the fact that Jesus gave this world His flesh of life? Do you believe in the Truth that He has saved us by coming down to this earth in human flesh, receiving the baptism from John the Baptist, dying crucified, and being resurrected from the dead in order to save you and me? We must be thankful before God. We must believe in our hearts the things that He has done for us. Those who believe have received the remission of sin and have gained the everlasting life. I am truly thankful for that.

People who believe in "transubstantiation" believe that when the celebrant of that rite blesses the wafer of Holy Communion, it actually turns into the body of Jesus. Thus, they think that they are eating the bread of life, the flesh of Jesus, by eating this wafer. For this reason, they mystify Holy Communion, and think that the act of receiving and eating the wafer itself is receiving a tremendous grace. But, that is clearly wrong.

Jesus said that His flesh was to give life to this world. He has saved us from sins and given us everlasting life by being born on this earth in human flesh, taking on our sins upon His flesh by receiving the baptism, dying vicariously on the Cross, and resurrecting from the dead. And, having faith in this Truth with our hearts is precisely to eat the bread of Jesus. One can receive the remission of sin and the everlasting life by eating the bread given by Jesus.

Jesus, who has said that I am the living bread from Heaven, is referring to the baptism He had received on His flesh. The Lord came down to this earth and gave Himself to us in order to have us acquire everlasting life and to remit us of our sins by having us eat Him with faith. It is the case that Jesus gave Himself to us by receiving the baptism, shedding His blood, and resurrecting from the dead. We have gained salvation and everlasting life by believing with our hearts the remission of sin and the new life God has given us.

Did you become children of God by faith? If you have now received the remission of sin, you must no longer be bound by the things of the flesh and be dragged around by them. What reason is there for the righteous to be tied down by fleshly works and to continue to get stressed? We the righteous must think of everything from a spiritual perspective. If we have food and clothing, we will be content with that (1 Timothy 6:8); we must live spiritually, doing the most worthwhile work on this earth. It is more than enough to have something to eat and a warm place to lie down with a roof and a wall to block out rain despite being made of vinyl. Yet, must we live lavishly? No, we don't. All these things disappear completely after a short while. These things will disappear when you and I die, and some of them will disappear even before we die.

We must often revert back to our spiritual hearts by thinking about God-given salvation and by having faith in it. We would still be lacking even if we were to place all our hearts in spiritual things. I hope for you to guard your spiritual heart by having faith in the Lord, not being bound by fleshly concerns and not being frustrated by things that do not go according to your wish. True faith manifests itself when we are faced with some hardship. True faith never changes.

We believe in the fact that Jesus came to this earth for us, received the baptism, died vicariously on the Cross, and was resurrected from the dead. That is why we received the remission of sin, gained the everlasting life, and became children of God. Also, that is why we are doing the work of God.

Dear fellow believers, I am joyful. Because the Lord has given you and me the everlasting life, you and I are both joyful. We are not joyful because there is something other than this. What else in this world should give us joy? We are thankful just to have a place of worship, where, inside this building, we can find shelter from rain, offer worship services, and share the gospel with each other.

Of course, there are times when we get irritated because things are not working out according to our own desires. But, it is a good thing to think about the work that God has done for us, and it is also good to think about the life in eternal Kingdom of Heaven where we would be together with the Lord forever. Life is like living as a student boarder, staying on this earth just for a while and then going back. Therefore, we must long for the home place where we will be residing for all eternity.

But, there also are many difficulties while living on this earth. Our hearts get tied up in situations and circumstances again and again, and they fall into the visible world. We get arrogant, lose our drive, and become laidback. It is possible for us to lose faith and just float along downward following the demands of the flesh. But, this is neither the proper life of faith, nor the way of living by faith. When you are faced with such spiritual hardships, think about the work that the Lord has done for you. Then, even if there is no fruit on the fig tree and even if there is no herd in the stable, you would be able to thank God just for the work of saving you from eternal hell.

NASA's Goddard Space Flight Center predicted that this year would be the hottest year in history. On this earth, there will be numerous disasters such as great earthquakes, large floods, typhoons, and tidal waves. If so, shouldn't every nation anticipate and prepare for these natural disasters? We shouldn't prepare only physically, but also in our hearts. That is why people who haven't yet received the remission of sin must eat the bread that came down from Heaven. Those who still have sins in their hearts must believe in the gospel of the water and the Spirit with their hearts before anything else, and receive the remission of sin.

People who haven't received the remission of sin are miserable. It is because if there is a sin in one's heart, he or she will be going to eternal hell. If there's a sin, one would have nothing to do with God, but only after having received the remission of sin does one get to live all the while receiving the blessings of God from that moment on. Dear fellow believers, it is the case that we have received the remission of sin, gained the everlasting life and become children of God by believing with our hearts the work God has done for us. We must be thankful that we are doing the worthwhile work by having become workers of God. And, we must go on living all the while being always thankful for that fact.

We have eaten the bread which came down from Heaven, received the remission of sin, and acquired the everlasting life. So now, for what must we go on living in this world? From now on, we must go on living by serving the gospel of the righteousness. Do you know it is no small blessing for us to go on living while serving God and having become the ones without sin, that is, the righteous? It's an immense blessing. Where is a blessing that is greater than this?

We the righteous must spread the gospel to many others, and should we not be able to do so, our hearts become ill at ease. After having received the remission of sin by wholeheartedly believing in the bread which came down from Heaven, if we are not doing God's work, then we should be doing the works of this world. When we are doing the works of this world, do you think there won't be difficulties such as these? Do you know how many miserable people there are in this world? While on this earth, we should be content with having food and clothing (1 Timothy 6:8). Being able to eat three meals a day and to serve God should be more than enough. Yet, is serving the Lord something miserable? It is something blissful.

Jesus is truly the bread from Heaven. God gave you and me the bread of life. Dear fellow believers, do you believe in this fact with your heart? Did you eat that bread with your heart? That bread is something that you eat by having faith in your heart.

Is preaching the sermon the only way for us to serve the gospel of God? Providing support for the spreading of the gospel by earning material things is also a way of serving the gospel. If preaching the sermon three or four times a week is everything that a person does just because he is a pastor, then he is not a true servant of the gospel of the Lord. We are thankful everyday because we are eating the God-given food of life and because we are doing the precious works that God has entrusted us. Dear fellow believers, are you weary? If so, remind yourself of the flesh and blood of Jesus who has given us hope.

Jesus told us, *"But seek first the kingdom of God and His righteousness, and all these things shall be added to you"* *(Matthew 6:33).* We must truly realize what we must believe, how to live by faith, and what we must do before God. First, we should gain salvation by knowing and having faith in the flesh and blood of Jesus, and then we should go on living spreading this Truth.

I give thanks before God. ⊠

How Can We Eat
The Flesh of Jesus?

< John 6:41-59 >

"The Jews then complained about Him, because He said, 'I am the bread which came down from heaven.' And they said, 'Is not this Jesus, the son of Joseph, whose father and mother we know? How is it then that He says, 'I have come down from heaven'?' Jesus therefore answered and said to them, 'Do not murmur among yourselves. No one can come to Me unless the Father who sent Me draws him; and I will raise him up at the last day. It is written in the prophets, 'And they shall all be taught by God.' Therefore everyone who has heard and learned from the Father comes to Me. Not that anyone has seen the Father, except He who is from God; He has seen the Father. Most assuredly, I say to you, he who believes in Me has everlasting life. I am the bread of life. Your fathers ate the manna in the wilderness, and are dead. This is the bread which comes down from heaven, that one may eat of it and not die. I am the living bread which came down from heaven. If anyone eats of this bread, he will live forever; and the bread that I shall give is My flesh, which I shall give for the life of the world.' The Jews therefore quarreled among themselves, saying, 'How can this Man give us His flesh to eat?' Then Jesus said to them, 'Most assuredly, I say to you, unless you eat the flesh of the Son of Man and drink His blood, you have no life in you. Whoever eats My flesh and drinks My blood has eternal life, and I will raise

him up at the last day. For My flesh is food indeed, and My blood is drink indeed. He who eats My flesh and drinks My blood abides in Me, and I in him. As the living Father sent Me, and I live because of the Father, so he who feeds on Me will live because of Me. This is the bread which came down from heaven—not as your fathers ate the manna, and are dead. He who eats this bread will live forever.' These things He said in the synagogue as He taught in Capernaum."

What it is that we should do to really love our neighbors and help them? Would it be really beneficial to them if we help them financially? My advice to you, my brothers and sisters of faith, is not to give free handouts to your unfortunate neighbors. This actually does not help them at all. Assisting them to stand up on their own feet is the real help. Of course, we can't just ignore when someone extends his hands to us asking for our help, and so we should help that person in anyway possible, but before we do so, we need to first consider carefully whether or not our assistance would really be of any use to him. And ultimately, we have to preach the gospel of the water and the Spirit to him and free him from all his sins. That is the real help and love.

John chapter six speaks about the bread of life. Jesus said, *"I am the living bread which came down from heaven. If anyone eats of this bread, he will live forever" (John 6:51).* Why did Jesus say to the Jews that He was the bread that came down from Heaven? And why were the Jews drawn to this Word?

When Jesus came to this earth, Israel was a tributary state to Rome. So it was a constant struggle for the Israelites to just survive and meet their basic needs for food, clothing, and shelter. Because many Jews were starving to death, when the Lord spoke about bread, it was probably inevitable that this would draw their attention. They thought that it was in their interest to gather around Jesus, since they thought that He would fill them with bread.

In John chapter six, Jesus at first said that He was the bread that came down from Heaven. And then He said, "I am the bread of life." In verse 51, Jesus also said, *"I am the living bread which came down from heaven. If anyone eats of this bread, he will live forever; and the bread that I shall give is My flesh, which I shall give for the life of the world."* Like this, Jesus explained gradually how He gave us everlasting life.

Taking one step further, in John 6:53-57, Jesus said, *"Most assuredly, I say to you, unless you eat the flesh of the Son of Man and drink His blood, you have no life in you. Whoever eats My flesh and drinks My blood has eternal life, and I will raise him up at the last day. For My flesh is food indeed, and My blood is drink indeed. He who eats My flesh and drinks My blood abides in Me, and I in him. As the living Father sent Me, and I live because of the Father, so he who feeds on Me will live because of Me."* In other words, Jesus explained in progressive detail how He saved us, and how He thus gave us everlasting life.

Why did Jesus say that He is the bread of life that came down from Heaven, and that anyone who eats Him will receive eternal life? Jesus said that His flesh is food and His blood is drink. Why did He say this?

Just as our Lord said, we must eat the flesh of Jesus and drink His blood. The people who heard Jesus might have thought that He was saying something heinous, thinking, "Does He regard us as cannibals?" But there was nothing dreadful about what He said. We must actually eat the flesh of Jesus by faith. And we must also drink His blood by faith. Only then can we live in both body and spirit. Unless we do so, we cannot live.

Let's turn to John 6:53-54: *"Most assuredly, I say to you, unless you eat the flesh of the Son of Man and drink His blood, you have no life in you. Whoever eats My flesh and drinks My blood has eternal life, and I will raise him up at the last day."*

We must eat the flesh of Jesus and drink His blood without fail. The Lord made it clear that unless we eat His flesh and drink His blood, we have no life. Since Jesus said that we must infallibly eat His flesh and drink His blood in order to attain life, we must indeed eat His flesh and drink His blood without fail.

Why Must We Eat the Flesh of Jesus?

That we must eat the flesh of Jesus means that we must believe that Jesus took upon our sins on His body by receiving baptism when He came to this earth. In other words, only when we believe that our sins were passed onto the body of Jesus can we attain everlasting life. If we don't believe that our sins were passed onto the body of Jesus through His baptism, even as we profess to believe in Jesus, then we will starve to reach spiritual death. Just as our bodies would die of malnutrition unless we eat everyday, our souls will also face spiritual death unless we eat His flesh as frequently as possible.

To eat the flesh of Jesus is to believe that He bore all our sins on His body. Only if we believe that our sins were passed onto Jesus can our souls be filled and attain prosperity. If you don't believe that your sins were passed onto the body of Jesus, then even if you believe in Him, you will still starve spiritually and waste away.

Is it because of our own merits that we have been saved? No, of course not. It's because God loved us that He has saved us with His power. It is entirely by the grace of the Lord that we have been saved from all our sins. If we were saved because of our own goodness, then we wouldn't have to eat the flesh of Jesus. However, we humans have absolutely no real virtue. There is nothing good whatsoever to mankind. Therefore, it is impossible for us to reach our salvation unless the Lord Himself saves us. Had God not written this Word of salvation in the Bible, none of us then could be saved.

My fellow believers, take a look at yourself and see how you were remitted from your sins. Do we have any virtue at all? It's because the Lord has saved us that we reached our salvation and became God's people; if our salvation had required our own perfect acts even slightly, then we could not have been saved. We humans are utterly evil. You yourself are an exceedingly evil person. If you think that's not the case, then it's only because your circumstances have not yet fully exposed your wickedness. The reality of mankind is such that when the circumstances are ripe to expose its wickedness, a parent would even devour his own child.

Do you think it's impossible for a mother to cannibalize her own son? As described in 2 Kings chapter six, when Ben-Hadad king of Syria gathered all his army and besieged Samaria, a great famine followed and the people inside the city were all starving to death. Among the starving people in Samaria, two women talked to each other and reached an agreement. "We will all die if we don't do something. An idea struck me; today, we will eat your son, and tomorrow we will eat mine. What do you think of this plan?" "Okay. That sounds good."

So they ate one woman's son, and the next day, it was the other woman's turn to give up her son. But this woman hid her son and refused to give him up. So the woman who had first given up her son sought justice from the king. "Your majesty, that woman suggested that we should eat our children, and so yesterday we ate my son, and today we are supposed to eat her son, but she is refusing to give him up." When the king heard these words, he tore his clothes in agony.

My fellow believers, this event written in the Bible is a true story. God recorded this so that we would admit the fact that mankind is more than capable of committing such atrocities when faced with extreme conditions. This shows just how evil mankind is. There are parents who kill their own children if they give them too much trouble, and there are also children who kill their parents to take over their wealth. Yet to save such people like us, our Lord came to this earth incarnated in the flesh of man, His creature, and bore all our sins on His body.

You must believe that all your sins were passed onto the Lord Jesus when He was baptized. Not to believe in this fact is for you to starve to death. Just as you would die unless you eat food, if you don't believe that all your sins were passed onto the body of Jesus, then you will starve to death spiritually. That is why Jesus is saying that we have to eat His flesh. It is written, *"The bread that I shall give is My flesh, which I shall give for the life of the world" (John 6:51).* The only way for our God to enable us to live forever was to shoulder our sins on His body. So by believing in this, we must eat the flesh of Jesus. When Jesus said, *"My flesh is food indeed, and My blood is drink indeed,"* He meant, "Eat My flesh and drink My blood, or otherwise you will die. Whoever eats My flesh and drinks My blood will receive everlasting life." Have you eaten the flesh of

Jesus?

The Lord has given us His flesh. However, when He said to the Jews, "Eat My flesh, for it is your food," they only derided Him, saying, "What? Aren't You Joseph's son? How can a man be bread?" The Jews just could not understand what Jesus was saying when He told them, "Eat My flesh and drink My blood."

Even now, many people still do not know what Jesus meant when He said that one should eat His flesh, and so they believe in a fabricated hypothesis called "Transubstantiation," which claims that the bread and wine prepared for Holy Communion actually turn into the flesh and blood of Jesus through the blessings of the presiding priest. Such people believe like this and eat the wafer with all piety, saying that Jesus told them to eat His flesh.

However, this is not what Jesus meant. When Jesus told us to eat His flesh, He meant that we should believe in the following: By shouldering all our sins and their curses on His body in our place, Jesus has truly enabled us to avoid condemnation and destruction. Even after being saved, we cannot help but continue to sin, for we are still weak in our flesh. However, to ensure that our souls would never die for such sins, Jesus took all our sins upon His body by being baptized. This is what Jesus told us to believe when He said that we must eat His flesh. In other words, Jesus has saved us perfectly by shouldering all our sins on His body.

Are Today's Christians Then Truly Eating the Flesh of Jesus?

Among today's Christians, few really know and believe in

the gospel of the water and the Spirit. That's why Jesus told us to eat His flesh and drink His blood. By drinking only the blood of Jesus, we cannot live. Only when we eat the flesh of Jesus does it turn into our food, thus enabling us to live forever. This Word of God is the Truth. Every Word of God is the Truth. We must all infallibly believe in this Word about the flesh and blood of Jesus with our hearts.

We commit sin constantly. As we are weak and insufficient, we think evil and we commit wrongdoings. Nevertheless, Jesus shouldered all the sins that we commit while living on this earth, and that is why we can live. He has shouldered all the sins of both those who have received the remission of their sins and those who have not. Had Jesus not borne our sins on His body, then we who have received the remission of our sins would not be able to live either. If that were the case, our hearts would lose the strength of faith today, even though we may have believed yesterday. In other words, since we are still committing sin every day out of our weaknesses, we may suffocate to death under the weight of sin because of our wickedness if the Lord had not taken away all our sins when He was baptized.

That is why the Lord said to us, "My flesh is food indeed." Whenever we are weak, we believe that our Lord has saved the entire human race from sin by taking away all the sins of the world, and this is how the Lord becomes our food.

We must always believe with our hearts that the Lord is our Savior. In other words, even though we are weak, we must nevertheless believe resolutely based on the Word that the Lord is our Savior. When we have this kind of faith, we can live without shame even though we are living in a corrupt world, for we have the righteousness of God and eternal life in our hearts. Because the Lord has given us His flesh, by taking it as our food, we carry on with our lives boldly today and tomorrow.

We Will Die If We Do Not Eat the Flesh of Jesus and Instead Only Drink His Blood Everyday

Everyone has to have both food and drink for energy and metabolism. You have to have them both; if you have only one, then you will surely die. The same goes for your spiritual life. You and I eat the flesh of Jesus and drink His blood everyday. We must have them today, tomorrow, and for the rest of our lives. Whenever we fall into weaknesses, we believe, "The Lord took away my sins. He bore all my sins," and this is how we feed on the bread of life. Whenever we are insufficient, we must remember that Jesus took away all our sins by being baptized at the Jordan River, and once again eat this bread. That is how we live without hunger, but always filled. The flesh of Jesus constitutes our food. Yet despite this, most Christians are starving to death, all because they do not eat the flesh of Jesus.

When we eat Jesus' flesh, we are filled and strengthened. Jesus described His body as bread. Jesus was born in Bethlehem, and the word Bethlehem means "a house of bread." Jesus said that He is the bread for our food that came down from Heaven. That is how He has enabled everyone to live by eating His flesh. We are living on the true bread of life.

Verses 49-50 in today's Scripture passage say, *"Your fathers ate the manna in the wilderness, and are dead. This is the bread which comes down from heaven, that one may eat of it and not die."* The people of the Old Testament died even though they had eaten the manna. The manna, which was like white coriander seed and tasted like wafers made with honey (Exodus 16:31), was the pure food that God brought down. This manna refers to the Word of God, Jesus Himself. In other words, the Israelites still died even after believing in God's Word. However, now, if you eat the flesh of Jesus and drink His blood, then you will receive eternal life. This passage means that when we believe in the Word of God, we must both eat the flesh of Jesus and drink His blood by faith.

The life of the flesh is in the blood (Leviticus 17:11). This means that by offering His life for us and bearing our condemnation in our place, the Lord has given us life, for His blood is His life. In other words, even though we had to die for our sins, we were saved precisely because Jesus gave us His life.

The Lord said, *"He who eats My flesh and drinks My blood abides in Me, and I in him" (John 6:56).* Many people say that they can be saved just by drinking the blood of Jesus without eating His flesh, but that is completely wrong. You are not saved simply by believing only in the Jesus who died on the Cross. You can live only if you eat the flesh of Jesus. Even today, I live by eating the flesh of Jesus. I will eat His flesh tomorrow also. Of course, this does not mean that I eat the flesh of Jesus like a cannibal, but it means that I believe that Jesus took all my sins and blemishes upon His body by being baptized. To believe is to eat. I have to eat His flesh everyday as long as I live on this earth. There is no one who can live without eating the flesh of Jesus.

However, almost all Christian believers are only having drinks. Why don't they eat the flesh of Jesus, when the Bible clearly states that they should eat it also? By being baptized by John the Baptist, the representative of mankind, Jesus accepted the sins of the world once and for all, and by being crucified on behalf of the entire human race, He bore its condemnation. It is by believing in this that we have attained our salvation and received everlasting food. Everyone is saved only by believing that Jesus took upon all his sins through His baptism, and that He was condemned in his place. This is the very Truth that Jesus spoke in John chapter six.

In verse 57 of today's Scripture passage, Jesus said, *"He who feeds on Me will live because of Me,"* and in verse 58, He said, *"He who eats this bread will live forever."* Those who have accepted Jesus by faith have eaten this bread. Those who believe in what Jesus has done for them will live forever. On the day of our Lord's return, He will raise all such believers from their graves and have them live forever.

Our Lord has become the true bread for us. The reason why I preach the gospel of the water and the Spirit is because it is our everlasting food. Because the Lord has blotted out all our sins with the gospel of the water and the Spirit, we have reached our salvation simply by believing in this Truth. It's only because the Lord has saved us that we've received our salvation. Had He not really saved us through the gospel of the water and the Spirit, there would then be no way for us to be saved. Had the Lord not taken upon Himself all our sins, then we could not have been saved. Therefore, only the fact that Jesus has saved us through the gospel of the water and the Spirit is the true bread that makes us live forever.

Is there any virtue or merit to us? No, there is none. We were completely insufficient creatures, nothing more than piles of sin, who could receive the remission of our sins only if the Lord came to this earth incarnated in the flesh and take away all our sins to save us. It is only because Jesus has saved us through the gospel of the water and the Spirit that we have received our salvation. Our salvation is completely devoid of our own efforts or merits, not even 0.001 percent. It is attained 100 percent by the grace of the Lord.

We have received our salvation because of the Lord. I praise the Lord. Even though we were inevitably bound to be condemned, our Lord has still saved us. Were it not for the Lord, we would all be cast into hell. We would all lose life. Had the Lord Himself not given us His flesh and blood, how could we live otherwise? It's only because the Lord has saved us that we've reached our salvation. He has become our bread of life. Because we have eaten the bread given by the Lord, we live for Him today and tomorrow, for eternity.

Because the Lord has given us His flesh and blood, we have received everlasting food, and because the Lord has become everlasting food, we will live with Him forever. I give all my thanks to our Lord. ✉

Believe in Jesus Who Came from Heaven as Your Savior in Your Heart

< John 6:41-51 >

"The Jews then complained about Him, because He said, 'I am the bread which came down from heaven.' And they said, 'Is not this Jesus, the son of Joseph, whose father and mother we know? How is it then that He says, 'I have come down from heaven'?' Jesus therefore answered and said to them, 'Do not murmur among yourselves. No one can come to Me unless the Father who sent Me draws him; and I will raise him up at the last day. It is written in the prophets, 'And they shall all be taught by God.' Therefore everyone who has heard and learned from the Father comes to Me. Not that anyone has seen the Father, except He who is from God; He has seen the Father. Most assuredly, I say to you, he who believes in Me has everlasting life. I am the bread of life. Your fathers ate the manna in the wilderness, and are dead. This is the bread which comes down from heaven, that one may eat of it and not die. I am the living bread which came down from heaven. If anyone eats of this bread, he will live forever; and the bread that I shall give is My flesh, which I shall give for the life of the world.'"

The Lord Is the Bread of Life

In today's Scripture passage, our Lord said that He came down from Heaven. It was to give us eternal life that the Lord came down from Heaven. He came from Heaven to become our bread, to feed us this bread of life, and to thereby save the souls dying from sin. Our Lord Jesus is not of the earth. He emphasizes the fact that He came down from Heaven in obedience to the will of the Father. The reason for this is because He is not of the earth, but He is the Son of God the Father in Heaven.

Therefore, we must recognize that Jesus, the only begotten Son sent by God the Father, is our Savior and Lord, and we must believe so. Indeed, we should never think of Him merely as one of the four great sages or just a founder of a religion. Our Lord said that He is the bread that came from Heaven. It can't be emphasized enough just how important it is that He came down to this earth from Heaven according to the will of the Father to save us sinners from all our sins.

There are two types of faith among today's Christians: Some believers mistakenly believe in the man-made doctrine of prayers of repentance, while the people of the right faith believe in the gospel of the water and the Spirit proclaiming that Jesus came down from Heaven and saved us from the sins of the world. Every Christian adheres to either one of these two types of faith. The former believers have made up their own doctrine of salvation and believe in it as they like, but they can never blot out their sins from their hearts no matter how ardently they might believe in Jesus, and therefore they will be cast into hell in the end. We should never follow their way.

Our Lord said clearly, *"I am the living bread which came down from heaven" (John 6:51).* The Son of Man is the bread that came down from Heaven. Even though our Lord was born on this earth through the body of a woman, He is the Savior who came down from Heaven. He is God Himself who, in order to become our true Savior, came to this earth incarnated in the flesh of man. That is the gist of today's Scripture passage.

All of us must believe in this passage. The Lord does not want us to believe in Jesus just as a matter of religion. Why did Jesus say to these Jews that He was the bread that came down from Heaven? Why did He repeatedly underscore the fact that He had come down from Heaven, that He was now speaking according to the Father's instruction, and that He had come only because He was sent by the Father? It was to make it clear to you and me that Jesus is the God of salvation who came down from Heaven, and to make us believe in this. That is an absolutely indispensable Truth that cannot be emphasized enough.

Jesus, in whom we believe, is not just a slightly better man than us, who are all equally human, but He is the Creator God Himself who is incomparably more exalted than us. He is the One who created the universe and everything in it, and He is the One who came to this earth as our Savior. In other words, when we had fallen into sin deceived by Satan's temptation and were suffering, when we were sentenced to hell for eternity and placed under the curse, the Lord came down to this earth forsaking His throne of glory in Heaven and saved us from the sins of the world. Jesus is the One who truly came down from Heaven, and He is our Savior. We are saved from our sins when we believe in what Jesus from Heaven did for us on this earth. It is absolutely indispensable to have this kind of faith.

Our Lord said in John 6:43-44, *"Do not murmur among yourselves. No one can come to Me unless the Father who sent*

Me draws him; and I will raise him up at the last day." As a matter of fact, we find grace only if God the Father leads us to Jesus. Unless God leads us to be saved by knowing and believing in the gospel of the water and the Spirit, no one can believe in Jesus as the Savior. Jesus, who made the universe and everything in it, also reigns over our salvation, our life and death, and our fortune and misfortune. As well, Jesus is the Triune God together with God the Father, who is His Father and our Father, and the Holy Spirit. It is this Triune God who has led us to meet Jesus, believe in Him, reach our salvation, and put on the glory of Heaven.

This world is indeed full of countless Christians. Yet even though there are many Christians professing to believe in Jesus, what is the state of today's Christianity? Those who believe in Jesus properly within the Word of Truth are extremely few. To blot out our sins, Jesus came down from Heaven by being born through the body of the Virgin Mary; at the age of 30, He was baptized to shoulder all the sins of mankind; He then carried the sins of the world to the Cross and was crucified to death; in three days, He rose from the dead again; and now, He is sitting at the right hand of the throne of God the Father. Few Christians believe in Jesus with such understanding. In fact, even though every Christian should have this kind of faith, there are far many more Christians who lack it than those who have it.

What kind of faith exalts God? It is the kind of faith that does not seek to establish one's own righteousness, but instead believes entirely in what God has done for us to save us, thanks Him, and gives all glory to Him. This is the kind of faith that God wants from all of us.

Every Christian must believe infallibly and unambiguously that Jesus came down from Heaven. We must believe in Jesus who has become our Savior by coming from Heaven, exalt Him, and give our thanks to Him. We must believe that He took upon our sins by being baptized; we must believe that He carried them to the Cross to bear the terrifying punishment of crucifixion; we must believe that He gave us new life by rising from the dead again; and we must believe that He has given us the Millennial Kingdom and the everlasting Kingdom of God that will come soon. To believe in all these things clearly and based on the Word is the right faith. God wants us to have faith in what He has done for us. We must believe in His righteousness and exalt it. God is pleased to accept precisely such people who know, praise, and exalt His righteousness, love, and salvation. I admonish all of you to become this kind of people who believe in the glory of Heaven that God has prepared for us and thank Him for it.

To explain the purpose of creating us mankind, the Bible says, *"Blessed be the God and Father of our Lord Jesus Christ, who has blessed us with every spiritual blessing in the heavenly places in Christ, just as He chose us in Him before the foundation of the world, that we should be holy and without blame before Him in love, having predestined us to adoption as sons by Jesus Christ to Himself, according to the good pleasure of His will, to the praise of the glory of His grace, by which He made us accepted in the Beloved"* (Ephesians 1:3-6). God made the universe and everything in it, created mankind, and placed you and me on this planet earth, as well as everyone else, all in order to reveal just how exalted He is, how merciful He is, how full of love He is, how He has given such perfect salvation, and how many blessings He has given to us mankind—to thereby make us praise the glory of His grace with our faith.

I thank God for enabling us to praise Him. His love truly

knows no bound, His power is truly amazing, and His mercy is truly fathomless. He is indeed marvelous. Our Lord is saying that it was because He wanted to receive such praise, thanks, and prayers from us that He made us born on this planet earth, and then born of the gospel of the water and the Spirit one more time.

We Must Have Faith in the Gospel of the Water and the Spirit

We must now become the kind of people who praise and exalt the righteousness of God. We must believe that Jesus, God Himself, came down to this earth from Heaven in order to save us from our sins; that He was born through the body of a virgin incarnated in the flesh; that He took upon all our sins at the age of 30; that He was condemned for all the sins of the world on the Cross; and that He has made us God's everlasting children. You and I must grasp the status of Jesus, our Savior who came down from Heaven, exalt Him accordingly, thank Him for saving us with our wholehearted faith, and receive the blessing of salvation by this pure faith. The Lord is pleased by our faith and wants to receive our praise and glory. You and I both need this kind of faith.

Jesus emphasized repeatedly to the Jews that He had come from the Father. He did this so that they would reach an understanding of His divinity. However, the Jews rejected Him to the end. God wants everyone to believe that Jesus is God Himself and the Savior who came down from Heaven to save mankind from its sins. In other words, Jesus does not want us to know Him merely as one of the great men in human history. Therefore, it cannot be allowed that anyone should consider

Jesus just as one of the four famous, great sages of world history. God told us to believe in Jesus who came down from Heaven. Jesus is the Savior who came from Heaven to save you and me from our sins. The Lord wanted us to know what He had done for us, and to thank and praise Him from the depth of our grateful hearts. That's because He had made us mankind in order to be glorified through us.

If you want to have the right faith, you must believe in the gospel of the water and the Spirit wholeheartedly. You must not regard Christianity only as one of the many religions of the world, nor believe in it as such. You should never believe in Jesus as if you were choosing just one religion from many. God will be disappointed and enraged if you believe like this. We have to recognize Jesus as God. Jesus created the universe and everything in it. He made not only the mountains, the seas, and the rivers, but He also made the galaxies in the universe, and everything invisible as well. My fellow believers, is this how you believe?

Yet despite this, too many Christians today think that Jesus who came down from Heaven was born of the earth. Having misunderstood Him like this, they believe in Him mistakenly. Just how gravely wrong is this? My fellow believers, if the Jesus in whom you and I believe were merely a highly influential and respectable man on this earth, then He could not have become our Savior. That's because the status of the One who can save all of mankind on this earth bound in sin and destruction must be not of someone born of the earth, but it must be that of God Himself. Only when God Himself comes can our salvation be perfected. My fellow believers, do you believe like this? You must grasp this and believe so.

God is really frustrated. He is not frustrated at you, who are righteous, but at the Christians of this world who still have not been born again. That is because even though God loved the world so much that He sent His only begotten Son, and even though Jesus, God Himself, forsook His throne of glory in Heaven and came to this earth to save us sinners from our sins, people still do not recognize this Jesus who came from Heaven and only think of Him as someone born of the earth. This is the same sin that the Jews in today's Scripture passage committed by refusing to believe in Jesus, saying, *"Is not this Jesus, the son of Joseph, whose father and mother we know? How is it then that He says, 'I have come down from heaven'?" (John 6:42)*

My fellow believers, not to believe is sin (John 16:9). When someone says that he believes in Jesus but not as God Himself, his faith is fundamentally of his own making, and therefore he may be pious when it suits his heart, but if something goes wrong, he is bound to display his true color by renouncing his life of faith. This kind of capricious faith, one that embraces Jesus only if needed and forsakes Him when no longer needed, is not true faith.

It is precisely because Jesus, who came down from Heaven, is God Himself that He is our Savior, our Shepherd, our Judge, and our everything. That is why we should never believe in Jesus in whatever way we want. He is the Creator who made us, and our Savior. How could we believe in the Creator just arbitrarily, when our everlasting life and all heavenly blessings depend on Him?

In the ancient Roman Empire, its emperors were regarded as gods. In ancient China, the Zhou dynasty called its king "the son of the heavens," which is another way of calling him the son of God. In modern-time Japan also, its king was called the "heavenly emperor," deifying him to the status of a divine son, and this deification united the country and led to the rise of

Japanese militarism that eventually launched the Pacific War. Do you infer from this that Jesus ranks somewhere among such emperors? No, Jesus is the very God who created the universe and everything in it, irrespective of whether you and I believe so or not.

When some angels in the realm of His creation rebelled against Him, Jesus drove them out and created mankind in the image of God. And as God loved the world so much, He made you and me be born on this earth to make us His children, and sent Jesus His only begotten Son. God the Father, the Son, and the Holy Spirit had planned to make us God's own children by saving us, and fulfilled it all. The One who came from Heaven according to this will is called Jesus. Coming from Heaven, He has saved us through the water, the blood, and the Spirit (1 John 5:6-8). This Truth is written in the Bible so clearly that no one can refuse to believe in it.

Whom Does God the Father Lead to Jesus?

Those who hunger and thirst for righteousness, who mourn over their sins, who are poor in spirit, and who cannot find satisfaction from the things of the earth—these are the people whom God leads to Jesus. Such people's hearts are naïve and honest like a child before God, even though they may have no possession or knowledge. In other words, if there are people who, even though they do not know Jesus that well, suffer because of their hearts' sins, and therefore are desperately looking for the Savior, then the Father leads such people to Jesus. That is why the Lord said, *"No one can come to Me unless the Father who sent Me draws him."* If you have now met Jesus by believing in the gospel of the water and the

Spirit, it is because the Father has led you that you have come to know this Jesus and believe in Him.

However, there are way too many Christians on this earth who exalt their own righteousness rather than the righteousness of God, even as they profess to believe in Jesus. They keep raising themselves up high, claiming, "As I prayed earnestly to God, I saw a vision in my dream, and I was saved. I was empowered when I fasted and prayed." In the end, they are claiming that they met the Lord all because of their own merits, thanks to their own piety and godliness.

That is not what true faith is like. True faith exalts God and praises Him. God Himself came down from Heaven, and to become our Savior for us, He was baptized, crucified to death, and resurrected from death. To believe that Jesus has become our true Savior through the gospel of the water and the Spirit, to thank Him with this faith, and to revere and believe in what God has done for us—none other than this is the right faith.

We just sang praise a short while ago. When we praise, Jesus saturates our hearts and our thoughts. Through our praise, the salvation of Jesus and His love and absolute power completely imbue our souls, as sponge is soaked with water. In other words, what He has done for us fills our hearts while we sing praise. Why? Because it's an undeniable fact that He has saved us perfectly, and we recognize this completely with our hearts. That is why while we praise, our hearts are filled with thankfulness and reverence for God.

To praise is to commend. Commending God for loving us, saving us from sin, and blessing us is to praise Him. This is how we actually believe, and we want everyone else to also have the same faith. However, for those who think that they met Jesus through their own righteousness, whom should they praise? Such people should praise themselves. They should sing, "♪I've met the Savior through my piety; ♪I've been saved thanks to my self." To be more precise, such people should not even praise the Lord at all, since there is hardly anything that the Lord has done for them, and if anything was achieved at all, it's all because of their own merits.

Jesus said in John 6:45, *"It is written in the prophets, 'And they shall all be taught by God.' Therefore everyone who has heard and learned from the Father comes to Me."* God the Father wants everyone to hear and learn His Word, and to come out to Him by believing in His Word. God wants the pure souls who, suffering from the sins of their hearts, are looking for the Savior to meet the righteous who have been saved through the gospel of the water and the Spirit, come to know the real God through them, find Jesus in the Word, and reach their salvation. That is why the Bible says that God *"desires all men to be saved and to come to the knowledge of the truth" (1 Timothy 2:4).* What about you then? Have you also learned about Jesus and reached your salvation through those who have truly met Him, those who have truly been saved?

From whom you learn is critically important. In the Old Testament, the one whom God abhorred and hated the most was Jeroboam. After the passing of Solomon, king of Israel, his son Rehoboam succeeded the throne. At that time, Jeroboam and the people asked Rehoboam to lighten the heavy burden that his father Solomon had placed on the people. Jeroboam was originally an officer in King Solomon's court favored by the king. However, as King Solomon came to worship pagan gods, God had prophesied that He would tear the people of Israel into two and make Jeroboam king of ten tribes, and because of this prophesy, Jeroboam had fled to Egypt to escape from Solomon's persecution.

With the death of Solomon, Jeroboam was now back in

Israel, pleading the new king to lighten up the yoke imposed on the people. However, King Rehoboam ignored this request of Jeroboam and the people, and he also ignored the advice of the elders from his father's court. Instead, he listened to his devious friends' advice, and deciding to oppress the people even more, he said to them, *"My father made your yoke heavy, but I will add to your yoke; my father chastised you with whips, but I will chastise you with scourges" (1 Kings 12:14).* As a result, the people turned against the house of David, and ten of the twelve tribes of Israel, excluding the tribes of Judah and Benjamin, crowned Jeroboam as their king and founded another kingdom. Israel was now divided into north and south, like today's Korea.

Jeroboam became king completely unintended. After assuming the throne, Jeroboam thought about his situation, and he reckoned that since he had become king even though he was not of the royal family, it was undeniably an act of high treason. So fearing potential backlash in the future, he came up with a cunning scheme. What was most important for the people of Israel was the sacrificial system enshrined in the Tabernacle and its priests. Jeroboam thought that every year, on the tenth day of the seventh month, the people would go up to the Temple of Jehovah in Jerusalem to offer sacrifices, and since Jerusalem was under Rehoboam's control, the people might turn their hearts back to Rehoboam the king of Judah and rise up against him. So, he made two golden calves, placing one in Bethel and the other in Dan, and made the people worship them there. Not only this, but Jeroboam also changed the date of the Day of Atonement that was set for the tenth day of the seventh month to the fifteenth day of the eighth month, and he even appointed ordinary people to priesthood, when the priesthood of the Tabernacle was open to only Levites. It is from then on that lawlessness came to prevail in Israel, and the people's faith was ruined.

Jeroboam ignored the Word of God and changed the statutes established by Him all on his own. God abhors the most this sin of corrupting the Truth deviously by changing it ever so slightly. In other words, God hated Jeroboam's sin the most. That's why He put Jeroboam to death. As Jeroboam's son followed in his father's sinful ways even after he succeeded him, God put him to death as well. In fact, most of the succeeding kings of Israel walked in the way of Jeroboam, and as a result, they bore the same wrath of God that was brought upon the house of Jeroboam.

It is so important from whom you learn, and under whom you lead your life of faith. Jesus said, *"Everyone who has heard and learned from the Father comes to Me" (John 6:45).* The Lord wants you to believe and learn from those who have heard and learned the Bible according to how God the Father has taught, and for you to also teach others as you have learned. That is why our Lord, having completed everything on this earth, said the following upon His ascension: *"Go therefore and make disciples of all the nations, baptizing them in the name of the Father and of the Son and of the Holy Spirit, teaching them to observe all things that I have commanded you" (Matthew 28:19-20).* This means that only the born-again disciples of Jesus can truly bear yet more disciples. The Apostle Paul therefore also said to Timothy, *"But you must continue in the things which you have learned and been assured of, knowing from whom you have learned them" (2 Timothy 3:14).*

God our Father wants every soul to understand and believe in Jesus properly. In other words, God wants the believers who have learned from the Father to teach the lost properly, and for the lost to also believe properly. God demands such faith from us. You and I are very fortunate. We believe in Jesus who came down from Heaven, and we believe that He has become our Savior by being baptized, dying on the Cross, and rising from the dead again. As we have been saved by this faith, and as we are now preaching this Truth of salvation, God is truly pleased with us.

We are spreading the gospel all over the world. God is helping us in many ways to proclaim His gospel throughout the whole world. By allowing the 2002 FIFA World Cup to be hosted by Korea, God made my country known across the world. As the Korean team reached the semi-final against all odds, my country made a lasting impression in the minds of people all over the world. We are preaching the gospel of the water and the Spirit throughout the whole wide world, and God has strengthened and fostered an ideal environment for us, so that no one may ignore us. I believe that God has done these things because He is pleased by us believing in and preaching the gospel of the water and the Spirit, and to make it possible for us to spread this gospel of Truth further and wider across the entire world. I am so thankful for this.

More recently, we have printed stickers and name cards of our mission in several languages to introduce our website all over the world. Our coworkers in each country are now sharing these name cards and stickers with their people. Through this, the weary souls who are looking for the Truth will visit our website and find the way of life. Although many people have already visited our website, their number will increase exponentially in the days to come.

Before closing, let me share with you just one more verse here from John 6:46. *"Not that anyone has seen the Father, except He who is from God; He has seen the Father."* Jesus said here that only He who is from God has seen the Father. There is no one who has ever seen God physically. Only Jesus has seen the Father. However, He also said, *"He who has seen Me has seen the Father" (John 14:9)*. We the born-again therefore have seen Jesus, and therefore we have also seen the Father. Indeed, among all Christians, only those who believe in the gospel of the water and the Spirit have seen the Father, and only they are able to share His love and salvation.

Today, there are so many people professing to believe in Jesus. Yet many of today's Christians front their own righteousness, and still others take pride in their own denominations. Furthermore, they make no mention of the gospel of the Truth, that Jesus has come by the gospel of the water and the Spirit and saved us humans from all our sins. Many pastors preach the Word of God just a little only as a dressing, and their sermons mostly invoke the congregation to offer more church donations. They raise someone who is slavishly faithful to his own church and pastor through his own piety and righteousness, and make him testify his zealousness so that the congregation would serve the church like him. This kind of faith is a false faith. The correct faith is to believe in what God has done for us, not to front one's own devotion or righteousness. There also are some Christians who blindly claim to have no sin even as they have no clear foundation of the Word, but such people's faith is an arbitrary faith that deceives themselves (1 John 1:8).

What kind of faith should you and I have then? He who came down from Heaven has saved us through the gospel of the water and the Spirit. He fulfilled all His promises of salvation to perfection, exactly as He had prophesied. We the born-again believe in every Word of promise and in the next world of glory to come that God has promised to us. That's why we live our lives with thanksgiving and glorifying God. It is when we have faith in the God-spoken Word, not our own arbitrary faith, that God is pleased. Even though we are too insufficient and weak before God, by believing in this God of utter perfection and unsurpassed majesty, in what He has done for us and will do in the future, and by commending Him, we can still put on all His grace. That is how we can offer our praise to commend Him. God has given this kind of grace to you and me. And He wants us to spread this grace all over the world.

Even though you and I are insufficient, God Himself came down from Heaven, and He has clothed us in His heavenly grace and glory. That is how we have come to live our lives filled with blessings and gratefulness, all by believing in Him. And that is how we have also come to attain everlasting life. My fellow believers, do you believe that God has given you eternal life? Eternal life means that you will never die but live forever in happiness.

God had promised in the Old Testament that He would save us from all our sins, and when the time came, our Lord came to this earth and saved us perfectly through the gospel of the water and the Spirit according to His promise. Likewise, God will also fulfill His promise to give us paradise on earth. So we wait in hope. Sooner or later, you and I will reign over this planet earth for a thousand years. After we reign the Millennial Kingdom for a thousand years, the Lord will then resurrect the dead—that is, those who did not believe in the gospel of the water and the Spirit—into immortal bodies for the last judgment, cast them out into hell, and forever seal the lid. And the righteous who are born again of water and the Spirit will enjoy eternal life with God forever in His everlasting Kingdom.

Because we believe that the Lord has given us such blessings, we have hope. Because of this faith of ours, we are filled with happiness day after day. Born again through the gospel of the water and the Spirit, you and I are now preaching this true gospel whenever and wherever. Even though we are insufficient, we thank God with our faith, and we gladly carry out this work with satisfaction. If we only look at our circumstances, there are many things that frustrate us; however, when we ruminate on all the blessings that the Lord who came down from Heaven has given us, we are able to live with forever grateful hearts. I give all my thanks and glory to God for giving us such blessings. ✉

Jesus Has Given Us
The True Everlasting Life!

< John 6:47-51 >

"Most assuredly, I say to you, he who believes in Me has everlasting life. I am the bread of life. Your fathers ate the manna in the wilderness, and are dead. This is the bread which comes down from heaven, that one may eat of it and not die. I am the living bread which came down from heaven. If anyone eats of this bread, he will live forever; and the bread that I shall give is My flesh, which I shall give for the life of the world."

Have you been in peace? Time flies by so fast, but with the passing time, the world has really undergone many changes. The people who are translating our books into English haven't been keeping the deadline, so we are suffering many setbacks in the works of the literature ministry. I have the wish for them to be committed to the work just as if it were their own work. That is why we must pray for the co-workers of the gospel and our workers to be healthy and faithful. Also, we must pray to God to safeguard international and domestic political situations, as well as the socio-economic environment of our country. When we are faced with difficulties, we must pray, and when we do gain strength, we must work diligently.

In today's Scripture passage, the Lord said, *"Most assuredly, I say to you, he who believes in Me has everlasting life" (John 6:47)*. God wants to give us everlasting life. And,

God the Father has given everlasting life to those who believe in the true salvation His Son, Jesus, has accomplished. By believing in the God-given everlasting life, we have gained that everlasting life.

For us, everlasting life is something truly great. Qin Shi Huang (259 BC - 210 BC), the First Emperor of China, wanted to live forever, not wanting to die, so he sent his subjects all over to bring him the elixir of life. What this means is that he had tried everything he could possibly do to avoid death. Nevertheless, he died in the end. As he died, he made a wish to be buried along with his subjects, wives, concubines, and material riches. Thus, many people were buried along with him. According to the most recent excavations, he had built a 4 stories deep underground city in preparation for his death, and that royal tomb is said to be almost 2km² in size. He had many soldiers shaped out of clay, and had them to be on guard. From his underground city, 7,000 of these 6 feet tall 'clay figures' were discovered, but the surprising part was that all these numerous clay soldier figures had facial expressions and clothes different from one another. Can you imagine how earnestly he had wished to be king even after death for all eternity, so much so that he did such things? However, he died merely at the age of 51.

Do you think only the First Emperor of China yearned for everlasting life? All human beings want to live forever. Do you know just how many people have tried to gain everlasting life? Everyone dreams of everlasting life, but it is something impossible. Human beings by themselves can never live eternally. Therefore, it's no exaggeration to say that the ultimate quest for all humankind is how to acquire everlasting life.

However, God gave everlasting life to those who believe

in the Lord. We are those who have acquired the everlasting life by faith. It means that, by faith, we have acquired the life in which we will never die. No matter how much we want to live forever, it is something impossible, but for God loved us so much and wanted to live with us forever, He has given us everlasting life through the propitiation of His Son. How wonderful is this blessing? I am so thankful that we have gained such everlasting life. God granted us everlasting life, and we have become its recipients. Truly, it is the case we have come to possess everlasting life. Of course, our flesh dies once, but later on, even our flesh will live again. And, the fact is that we will live together with God as His children, never having to die. The fact is that we have received this everlasting life before God. It is such a marvelous grace, as well as a great blessing.

How Can We Become Beings That Do Not Die?

Then, by doing what could we become beings that do not die? We acquire the everlasting life neither by sanctifying ourselves nor by obtaining certain abilities. We have come to receive and enjoy it because of God the Father. What a marvelous love and blessing is this? What is marvelous is the fact that God has the wish to live together with us forever. Through His Son, Jesus, God has blotted out all our sins. Not only has He given us the remission of sin, but also, He has granted us eternal life. This is truly a marvelous blessing. For God has given us this unilaterally, despite the fact that we are not worthy, it is such a marvelous and great grace.

We are beings that do not die. We are those who have the everlasting life. If we were to think about ourselves, we are not worthy enough to have everlasting life. There are times when we wish in our hearts to return to being a pile of dirt as soon as possible for living seems tedious and when we hope that there is no afterlife. Nevertheless, it isn't the case that there is no afterlife, no judgment, no resurrection, as we hope. Also, it isn't the case that there is no prize of the Millennial Kingdom. God said, *"And as it is appointed for men to die once, but after this the judgment" (Hebrews 9:27),* and the fact remains that everything will happen according to God's decision.

He wanted to give us the everlasting life. So, He sent down Jesus and gave everlasting life to those who have received the remission of sin by believing in Jesus as the Savior. Thus, we who believe have gained the everlasting life. It means that God has made us into beings of everlasting life. And therefore, we have become somewhat different beings. We became self-conscious of the value of our existence. Sometimes, we could consider ourselves to be a weak and worthless being. However, the fact is that you and I are no longer a worthless and weak being, but rather, a being that has acquired the everlasting life. It is tremendously important for us to live in recognition of this fact.

From time to time, I also underestimate myself. Prior to being born again, there was a time when I had lamented, saying, "Why did God make me be born and go on living in such hardship? All that I have is this body of mine." Although it was when I was young, I used to sit on top of a grave and fall into nihilism, saying, "If I die, I will be buried like this. In any case, this will be my final destination, so what meaning is there for me to go on living?" And so, I tried very hard to find out the reason for my being on this earth. Still, I wasn't able to find a meaning in my life, but then, I started to believe in Christianity, trying to live virtuously. But, as I entered into this religion, called Christianity, I came to realize that living virtuously wasn't easy and saw my sins getting revealed more and more.

And then, I came to be enlightened of the gospel of the water and the Spirit by the grace of God. When I first perceived the gospel of the water and the Spirit, I was so elated by the fact that there was no sin inside my heart. The Holy Spirit within me was so moved that I could not stay still, and so I started preaching this gospel of the water and the Spirit, hoping that everyone else would be without sin, just as my heart is without sin. As I preached this genuine gospel, one thing became more certain and that is the fact that people in this day and age do not know the gospel Truth of the water and the Spirit. That is why I have been dedicating myself to the spreading this gospel all over the world thus far.

To give us everlasting life, God the Father had us be born into this world, and, on the other hand, sent His Son to receive the baptism, die on the Cross, and be resurrected from the dead. Also, by recording the Word of the Truth, He had us become aware of the fact that we are beings that live eternally. It means that God has turned you and me into beings that never die. The fact is that God has turned us into His children who will live along with Him, enjoying everlasting joy with divine authority. We must know that God had made plans to give us everlasting life. That is why God forgave our sins and took those of us who believe in Him as His children. I give thanks to God, who has allowed us to live for all eternity.

We must properly realize what kind of a being we have become. Neither overestimating too much nor underestimating too much, all we have to do is to properly know and believe in accordance with what the Word that God has told us. You and I who believe in the gospel of the water and the Spirit have come to possess the everlasting life.

The Lord said, *"I am the bread of life" (John 6:48)*. By sending His only begotten Son down to this earth, God the Father had us receive the remission of sin. We have come to acquire the everlasting life by believing in Jesus' baptism and His blood of the Cross, which were carried out by Jesus with His flesh. Because God had the desire to turn us into beings that live forever, He has clothed us with such enormous grace.

It is said that those who believe in the Son have the everlasting life. Jesus came down to this earth from Heaven in human flesh and took on our sins with His body. And then, by bearing our sins and receiving the punishment for them and by being resurrected from the dead, He saved us. It means that Jesus had given Himself as the bread of life for us in order to save us when our spirits were in want, unable to avoid death and curse due to our sins. The fact is that it was made so for us to gain eternal life if we were to eat the flesh and blood of Jesus, who is the bread of life. By believing in the works carried out by Jesus, we have eaten the flesh and blood of Jesus, and thus, we have gained the true life. This is why Jesus said, *"I am the bread of life" (John 6:48)*. We are able to gain eternal life by having eaten the flesh and blood of Jesus by faith.

For us to gain new life and to maintain that true life is possible only by believing in our hearts that Jesus has become the bread of life. One does not live forever by eating some elixir of life. Not considering Jesus, let us say that one gets to live forever by eating the elixir of life, but wouldn't this be very unfair since the rich and the powerful would consume all of it first?

God the Father had us humankind acquire new life by giving His Son, Jesus. The fact is that He has given us the bread of life through Jesus. The true road to gaining new life and living forever is having faith in the works done by Jesus who has become our Savior. The pathway to everlasting life is the faith of believing in Jesus' works in which He received the baptism, died on the Cross, and was resurrected. If we were to have faith in Him in our hearts and to believe in His baptism, His death on the Cross, and His resurrection, we would be eating the bread of life and acquiring life without death. It is said, *"There is no other name under heaven given among men by which we must be saved" (Acts 4:12).* It was made so that one would only be able to receive salvation from death by believing in Jesus. Only when one eats the Son of God who is the bread of life does that person receive the everlasting life. The Lord allowed anyone who eats this bread to live an eternal life.

We must remember that Jesus came to this earth so as to become the bread of life. And, we must have faith in it. Jesus, who had received the baptism on His flesh as the bread of life, taken on all our sins, received the punishment on the Cross on our behalf, and suffered death instead of us, granted everlasting life to those who believe in Him as the true Savior. You must know God's intention to give us everlasting life, and believe in Jesus, who has become the bread of life, as your true Savior. By having faith, you must eat the bread of life, and be in the blessings of gaining everlasting life. It is because if you believe, you will gain everlasting life, but if you do not, you will receive everlasting damnation.

The true bread that gives humankind the everlasting life is Jesus. Except for Jesus, we mustn't have faith in anyone else, and we mustn't rely on anyone else. We must remember and believe that there is only the Holy Trinity, that is, God the Father, Jesus and the Holy Spirit, who can solve the problems of sins of people, as well as their problem of life and death.

Jesus became our true bread of life. He became our true bread of life so that we will be without sins and thus, we may live along with God for all eternity as the children of God without sins in our hearts. Do you believe in Jesus who had become our true bread by receiving the baptism, dying on the Cross, and being resurrected? I believe so, also. Thus, the fact is that you and I have acquired the everlasting life. Therefore, we are not afraid of death. And so, we neither overestimate nor underestimate ourselves. The only thing is that we must give all the glory back to God by becoming aware of the everlasting life that God has granted us and believing in it. We must become conscious of that. We have gained a life of eternal living through having faith in Jesus who has become the bread of life.

It is customary in Korea to give greetings by sharing steamed rice cakes with those near by, whenever one moves to a new neighborhood or opens up a new store. One shares steamed rice cakes in order to establish a good relationship, along with the intention of making a request for much guidance. We who are born-again are those who share the bread of life. We are currently doing the work of spreading throughout the world the way to an everlasting life. The current work of spreading the gospel of the water and the Spirit is the work of sharing the bread of life. Inside your hearts and mine, there is the bread of life. For we are those with the bread of everlasting life, we are sharing that bread through the gospel of the water and the Spirit. The fact is that spreading the gospel of the water and the Spirit is doing the work of sharing the bread of life with people.

Therefore, we are those who have the key to remit the sins of people (Matthew 16:19). You and I have acquired eternal life by eating by faith the bread of life that Jesus has given us, and now, we have become delivering messengers of the bread of life. When people listen and believe in this gospel of the water and the Spirit, they gain everlasting life. They have gained the most precious gift. Isn't gaining the everlasting life such a marvelous blessing? This gospel we are spreading is something great, and therefore, the mission of spreading this gospel is a work that's so very precious.

The Lord said, *"Your fathers ate the manna in the wilderness, and are dead. This is the bread which comes down from heaven, that one may eat of it and not die. I am the living bread which came down from heaven. If anyone eats of this bread, he will live forever; and the bread that I shall give is My flesh, which I shall give for the life of the world"* (John 6:49-51). For the people of Israel, the event in which their ancestors had eaten the manna was something that had happened such a long time ago. And so, they thought of it as just a tale, and considered it be just some religiously mysterious experience that their long ago ancestors had gone through. But, in the Gospel of John chapter 6 verse 50, our Lord says, *"This is the bread which comes down from heaven, that one may eat of it and not die."* God truly wanted to send down from heaven the bread of life by which we would live, and He actually did send it down. He wanted to feed us the bread of life by giving us His flesh, and He had us become those who live eternally by feeding us the flesh of Jesus, which we ate by faith.

In earnest, Jesus now tells us to eat His flesh. It meant that He would give us life by granting us His flesh. What does it refer to? He was referring to the gospel of the water and the Spirit, in which you and I believe. By being born on this earth in human flesh, Jesus wanted to blot our sins. And so, in order to give us the blessing of everlasting life, He took on all the sins of all humankind by receiving the baptism from John the Baptist, carried His flesh to the Cross, got crucified, and resurrected from the midst of death. Then, He gave those who believe in Jesus, who has become the living bread that came down from Heaven, the remission of sin, the power to become children of God, and the blessing of everlasting life.

Jesus was born on this earth through the body of the Virgin Mary. And He had accomplished our salvation with the righteous work that He had done throughout His 33 years of life; He has saved us by His receiving the baptism from John the Baptist, going to the Cross bearing the sins of the world, getting crucified, shedding blood, dying, being resurrected from the dead, and rising up to Heaven. Truly, our Lord gave us His flesh in order to give us the everlasting life.

It isn't the case that Jesus came to this earth and said, "Believe in Me unconditionally. I am the Son of God. Just believe in Me blindly." The fact is that He took on all the sins of humankind by receiving the baptism from John the Baptist onto His flesh so as to actually become the bread of life. By having done so, it is the case that He had cleansed our sins completely, and had ended the punishment set out for us by going to the Cross bearing our sins and receiving the judgment on our behalf. Then, by being resurrected from the dead, He had given everlasting life to those who believe in Him, the bread of life which came down from Heaven. This is how Jesus has given us the eternal remission of sins.

Thus, we must know and believe in the righteousness of Jesus, and that it is within the gospel of the water and the Spirit. Jesus identified Himself as the bread of life which came down from Heaven, and it is the case that we are able to acquire everlasting life by eating this living bread by faith. We must eat the bread of life of salvation by knowing God's intention to give us the remission of sins and the eternal life and by having faith in the work of Jesus having blotted out our sins perfectly through the baptism He had received, the blood of the Cross, and His death and resurrection. Only by doing so, do we get to receive true salvation and the everlasting life.

I am sure that it is never enough, no matter how much I preach the gospel of the water and the Spirit repeatedly. Fundamentally speaking, something important must be emphasized for all eternity. In order to give us the bread of life, God sent His only begotten Son to this earth, had Him take on the sins of the world by having His flesh receive the baptism, had Him go to the Cross and die by being crucified, resurrected Him, and had Him sit next to the throne of God, even now. And thus, when we eat the bread of life by having faith in that Jesus, we are able to acquire the everlasting life.

Yet, can we believe selectively in some of the things and not in others among the works that the Lord has done? To give us life, Jesus came to this earth, received the baptism, and saved us by dying on the Cross. Yet, can we slight some of the works that Jesus had done but consider others to be important? All the works that He had done were for us. They are all essential. To give us everlasting life, the Lord remitted our sins and took us in as God's children. I believe the Lord gave us the gospel of the water and the Spirit in order to give us eternal blessings. Do you believe as I do?

The Lord said, *"The bread that I shall give is My flesh, which I shall give for the life of the world" (John 6:51).* What does the flesh of the Lord mean? What was the reason behind Him being born on this earth in human flesh? Wasn't it to save us by receiving the baptism from John the Baptist, dying nailed to the Cross bearing the sins of the world, and being resurrected? Did He just come and got hung on the Cross? "I am the Son of God. Did I not raise the dead? I am going to die on the Cross for you. Thus, believe in Me." Is that it? That's not the case. The fact is that people are dying because of sins, and so in order to become children of God and to acquire the everlasting life, we must eat the flesh of Jesus by faith. The baptism Jesus had received after being born on this earth, the work of Him getting nailed to the Cross, the work of Him being resurrected from the dead—we must eat all those works by faith. We must engrave in our hearts that we were able to gain everlasting life because He had given us His flesh. We must believe that.

He came to this world so as to blot out our sins and to destroy the work of the devil. Who is the devil? He is someone who makes people servants of sin by having them commit sins and in the end, temps people with the purpose of having them fall into destruction with him. But, the Lord came to have humankind be freed from being servants of the devil by blotting out all the sins of humankind and destroying the work that the devil does. We must know and have faith in the will of God. Also, we must accept the works that God has done and believe in them as they are.

It isn't the case that we get saved by believing in doctrines that came out from human thoughts, such as the doctrine of salvation, the doctrine of sanctification, the doctrine of repentance, and so on. Rather, we must believe in the gospel Truth of the water and the Spirit, by which God has saved us from sins by sending His only begotten Son to this earth. Only by having faith in all the works that He has done according to such plan, do we get saved. The fact is that we get to acquire the everlasting life by listening, knowing, and believing in that gospel Word of salvation. By giving us His flesh, the Lord gave life to those of us who believe in the Truth. Were you able to acquire life by believing in the gospel of the water and the Spirit? Did you gain the everlasting life? If so, you will never die.

In the last hour, when tribulations should come, my flesh will die instantly. I have an impatient character, so when the subordinates of the antichrist try to put me into a boiling caldron to kill me, I will probably have stopped breathing even before getting thrown into the caldron. But, later when the Lord comes, He will have me live again. At that moment, even our fleshes will be made to live. Our spirits have already acquired resurrection and everlasting life. They have become spirits that were moved from death to new life, and now, we are waiting for our weak flesh to resurrect so that we will be in a body that never dies. The Lord said that He would even make our flesh to live again. Just as He had resurrected, He said that our flesh would resurrect, also. We must become those who will live enjoying the everlasting life.

In truth, if we were to think ourselves about the fleshly aspects, we are really nothing of worth. It is because we are beings that always commit sins and are selfish. Yet, I actually did gain the everlasting life. This was possible not because of me but because of God. Just as Abraham was accounted for righteousness by having faith in the Word of God, we have gained the everlasting life also through having faith in the Word that tells us God has given us everlasting life. Thus, we mustn't think of ourselves with contempt. Truly, we must honor ourselves just as God thinks of us as honorable, and we must go on living with a faith and heart like that of Abraham. How could I express the blessing of everlasting life into words?

I am so thankful to God for giving us the everlasting life. And I think of you as the honorable. Also, I don't think you are more lacking than I. You are not bound by the world. Rather, you are God's workers, His disciples, His children, and those who will enjoy the everlasting life with Him. I do believe so. Thus, we must respect each other. We cannot but ignore those who do not believe this gospel despite being aware of it because God ignores them also. But as for those of us who believe, we must respect each other because we are the honorable. As for those who do not believe, we hope that they will believe, and as for those who believe, we consider them to be honorable. We must remind ourselves of the fact that God has made us into beings that live forever, and think about the everlasting life we will be enjoying for all eternity. Also, we must treat each other honorably.

When the time comes for our flesh to change, we probably won't recognize each other. For a flesh that has been resurrected, there is no gender distinction (Matthew 22:30). If the memory of life on earth would come back then, perhaps that itself would be hell. It is because we might grind our teeth, saying, "That jerk did such and such to me," and say curse words. For those who are headed for hell, such hatred and the desire to imprecate may remain, but for those who will be living eternally in Heaven, there is no such heart.

We are all so fortunate to have gained everlasting life in this last days. The fact that we have acquired the everlasting life by believing in the gospel of the water and the Spirit is a blessing worthy for us to dance with joy all throughout our lives. It doesn't matter how we are living on this earth. It doesn't matter even if we lose everything. It is because we have acquired the everlasting life in Heaven and because we have become those who have received the blessing of being able to live the rest of our life together with the gospel. God gave us the everlasting life through Jesus. And thus, nothing damaging can ever happen even if we aren't able to do the things that we want while on this earth and there would be nothing to resent in our hearts.

When I first preached the gospel of the water and the Spirit after having received the remission of sin, it felt so good. However, though I felt good, there was a time when I had thought, "If I live like this, isn't my life going to suffer losses? Shouldn't I also live for something for me?" But as I got to know the Lord and served Him more and more, I discovered that He was serving me rather than me serving Him. Like so, the Lord stood by me and guided, and thus, I was able to follow and serve the Lord without having lost the everlasting life, even now.

The Lord gave me the everlasting life, so what could I possibly lack? There is a feeling of satisfaction in my heart. As it is said, *"Blessed are the poor in spirit, For theirs is the kingdom of heaven. Blessed are those who hunger and thirst for righteousness, For they shall be filled" (Matthew 5:3, 6),* I am truly filled in my heart. It is because my spirit is filled with the Holy Spirit. For the Word of God has become the food of life, my spirit is truly filled. I am so very thankful for that.

I am very well aware that it's not easy for you to lead a social life, and also a life at work places. Even so, all such hardships can be offset because there is the blessing of God where He has blotted out all our sins, taken us in as His children, given us everlasting life, and bestowed us with eternal riches and glory. It is written, *"For I consider that the sufferings of this present time are not worthy to be compared with the glory which shall be revealed in us" (Romans 8:18).* Therefore, such hardships can be overcome, and although we may be lacking, we are thankful for entrusting us with God's work. Also, even if it were not the case, we are still thankful. We are thankful for saving us and giving us the everlasting life.

We are thankful for entrusting us the work of spreading this gospel of the water and the Spirit. We are thankful for allowing us to live together with God. For we have received such great grace from the Lord, there would no exhausting of this grace even if we were to share it over and over.

For God is supplying us this grace for all eternity, we get to praise God, give back the glory before God, and thank God, always. By the strength He has given us and by the grace He has shown us, we are thankful before Him, and thus, we are able to do His work with zeal.

For all these grace, we are thankful. Most of all, we are thankful for giving all of us the everlasting life. ✉

How to Participate in Holy Communion With the Right Faith

< John 6:52-59 >

"The Jews therefore quarreled among themselves, saying, 'How can this Man give us His flesh to eat?' Then Jesus said to them, 'Most assuredly, I say to you, unless you eat the flesh of the Son of Man and drink His blood, you have no life in you. Whoever eats My flesh and drinks My blood has eternal life, and I will raise him up at the last day. For My flesh is food indeed, and My blood is drink indeed. He who eats My flesh and drinks My blood abides in Me, and I in him. As the living Father sent Me, and I live because of the Father, so he who feeds on Me will live because of Me. This is the bread which came down from heaven—not as your fathers ate the manna, and are dead. He who eats this bread will live forever.' These things He said in the synagogue as He taught in Capernaum."

Describing Himself as the bread of life, our Lord said, *"The bread that I shall give is My flesh, which I shall give for the life of the world" (John 6:51).* He then went on to say, *"Most assuredly, I say to you, unless you eat the flesh of the Son of Man and drink His blood, you have no life in you. Whoever eats My flesh and drinks My blood has eternal life, and I will raise him up at the last day. For My flesh is food indeed, and My blood is drink indeed. He who eats My flesh and drinks My blood abides in Me, and I in him" (John 6:53-56).* Hearing this, even Jesus' own disciples said, "This is a hard saying; who can understand it?"

We eat the flesh of Jesus and drink His blood by believing in the gospel of the water and the Spirit. It is when we eat the flesh of the Lord that our hearts are made sinless. In other words, whoever eats the flesh of the Lord is made completely sinless, with all the countless sins in his heart blotted out. If we believe in the Word that Jesus took upon all the sins of the world once for all through His baptism at the Jordan River, then our sins are absolutely blotted out. We become sinless people when we eat the flesh of Jesus by believing that all the sins of the world were passed onto Him when He was baptized on His body.

No matter how a feast is prepared before us with all kinds of delicacies, unless we eat them, we would not be filled. Likewise, those who do not eat the flesh that Jesus has given them cannot receive the remission of their sins, and therefore their sins remain all intact. We are made sinless only if we eat the flesh of Jesus by believing that the Lord took upon our sins by receiving baptism on His body and has thereby made us sinless. That is why we must eat the flesh of the Lord time after time. And we must also drink His blood spiritually as often as possible. The bread of life that the Lord has given us is the flesh of Jesus and His blood.

Whoever eats the flesh of Jesus and drinks His blood by faith is a blessed man. I am so thankful that the Lord has given us His flesh. Feeding on the Lord's flesh everyday, we are able to say to God, "I have no sin." What a tremendously bold faith is this? What would have happened to us had Jesus not given us His flesh? Where would we find and attain the Truth that makes us sinless? Could we become sinless through our own good deeds? Could we become sinless by giving up all our possessions? Could we become sinless by living virtuously? Or could we become sinless by being sanctified? No, were it not for the flesh of Jesus, we could never have become sinless. It is by eating the flesh of Jesus and drinking His blood that we have become sinless before both God and mankind.

We Have No Sin, for We Have Eaten the Flesh of the Lord and Drunk His Blood

Jesus offered His body to us, and we have become sinless by eating the Lord's flesh. By believing in what the Lord has done for us with our hearts, we have now become sinless in our hearts. In John 6:63, the Lord said, *"It is the Spirit who gives life; the flesh profits nothing."* In other words, it's inconceivable to actually eat the flesh of Jesus and drink His blood physically, and so we shouldn't think of it in carnal terms. The Lord has blotted out all our sins with His flesh and blood. By eating this flesh of the Lord, we have become completely sinless. How amazing it is! We have become sinless by eating the Lord's flesh! The flesh of the Lord has so much power that whoever eats the flesh of Jesus is made sinless. We eat this flesh of the Lord by believing that Jesus took upon the sins of the world by being baptized at the Jordan River, that He bore the condemnation of our sins by being crucified and shedding His precious blood on the Cross while shouldering the sins of the world, and that He has thereby given us true life.

Whenever we are weak and feel as if we still have sin, we

must eat the flesh of Jesus and drink His blood by faith. That is what we should do as spiritual people before God. Even among the disciples of Jesus, there were some who did not believe that He was the Son of God, and there were also others who did not believe that He had taken upon all the sins of the world. Likewise, among today's Christians also, many do not believe that Jesus accepted the sins of the world by being baptized by John the Baptist, even though this is the clear Truth.

The Lord Said That We Will Live Forever If We Eat His Flesh and Drink His Blood

Because God the Father had planned our salvation in Jesus to deliver us through His flesh and blood, and because the Lord completed this plan perfectly, God has now made it possible to receive everlasting life for everyone who believes in the Lord's work exactly as He has done it. By offering His own body and blood for us, the Lord has given us the everlasting remission of our sins, and He has also made us God's children. Now, God abides with us until the end of this world as the Father, the Son, and the Holy Spirit.

However, almost all Christians partake in Holy Communion only as a religious ritual, without understanding what the bread and wine shared in Communion really mean. The bread and wine shared in Holy Communion should not be taken thinking only of the blood of the Cross. Rather, the bread of Holy Communion must be had with the clear understanding and belief that Jesus took upon the sins of this world through His baptism by John the Baptist, and the wine must be had with an equally clear understanding and belief that Jesus was crucified to death because He had already shouldered the sins of the world. Therefore, to participate in Holy Communion properly, one must know and believe in the gospel of the water and the Spirit.

If we believe in the flesh and blood of Jesus, then we will receive the remission of our sins and live with everlasting life. So, if anyone tries to blot out his sins by himself without believing in the flesh of Jesus and His blood, then he is nothing more than a fool. Therefore, if you still have sin in your heart, you must infallibly understand the reason why Jesus told us humans to eat His flesh and drink His blood, and uniting yourself with Him by faith, you must receive the remission of your sins. By believing in the baptism of Jesus, we have been washed from our sins in Christ, and by believing in His blood on the Cross, we have escaped from the condemnation of our sins completely. Given this, if you are still trying to blot out your sins all on your own by offering prayers of repentance, then your faith is very flawed and arrogant. After all, who among you could ever blot out one's own sins? There is no one in this world who can do this. If you try to do this, you will be disappointed greatly. Now that God dwells in our hearts, we should live by trusting in the flesh and blood of Jesus. You can carry out God's work by believing in the gospel of the water and the Spirit.

Our Lord came to this earth incarnated in the flesh to save us from all the sins of the world, and to take upon all the sins of mankind once and for all, He was baptized by John the Baptist on His body. As well, to bear the condemnation of our sins, He was crucified and shed His precious blood unto His death, and He then actually rose from His physical death. That is how Jesus has brought the true remission of sin and eternal life to all of us who have eaten His flesh and drank His blood by faith. Those who have such faith and such understanding praise the

Lord with faith. By giving His flesh and blood, Jesus has enabled every believer to receive the everlasting remission of sin and eternal life.

There are two sacraments that the Lord has established in the Church—that is, for His disciples: One is the sacrament of baptism, and the other is Holy Communion. The sacrament of baptism is partaken as a sign of faith by those who have been born again by believing in the gospel of the water and the Spirit, to confirm and confess their faith. Just before ascending to Heaven, the Lord said to His disciples, *"Go therefore and make disciples of all the nations, baptizing them in the name of the Father and of the Son and of the Holy Spirit, teaching them to observe all things that I have commanded you; and lo, I am with you always, even to the end of the age" (Matthew 28:19-20).* The Lord commanded us to preach the gospel of the water and the Spirit to people and lead them to receive the remission of their sins; to make disciples of the redeemed and baptize them for their faith in the baptism of Jesus; and to teach those who have thus become disciples everything that the Lord has taught and commanded us.

Secondly, the Lord commanded us to perform Holy Communion in remembrance of how He has given us His flesh and blood. The bread and cup that we receive at Holy Communion symbolize the body and life that our Lord gave us to blot out our sins. Both these two sacraments instruct us to believe that since our Lord was baptized and shed His blood to death on the Cross when He came to this earth, He has indeed blotted out all our sins. That Jesus gave His flesh to us means that He took all our sins upon His body once and for all through His baptism. All of us must therefore realize that Jesus accepted the sins of the world through His baptism, carried them to the Cross, died in our place, and has thereby blotted out all our sins; and we must forever engrave this Truth in our hearts by faith.

Do you now believe that Jesus has given us His body? To blot out all our sins, the Lord willingly offered His own body to us. That Jesus came to this earth in the image of mankind was to take upon all the sins of us humans through the baptism He received from John the Baptist. Those who believe that Jesus gave up His innocent and unblemished body for our sins and bore them through His baptism are now able to receive the perfect remission of their sins. Since Jesus Himself willingly offered His body in order to accept our sins and be condemned for them to blot them out completely, we have now become sinless by believing in Him. You must understand this properly when you take the bread and cup of Holy Communion. Just as our physical lives are sustained only if we eat the bread of the flesh, it is by believing that Jesus shouldered our sins on His body by being baptized that we can eat His flesh and attain everlasting life.

Today's Christianity preaches only the cup of Jesus—that is, His blood; in reality, however, the Lord has actually given us and fed us both His flesh and blood. We must reach the proper understanding of the reason why Jesus gave us His flesh. That our Lord gave us His flesh means that He shouldered our sins by being baptized by John the Baptist. Therefore, whenever we receive the bread and cup of Holy Communion that constitute the flesh and blood of Jesus, we must remember that we have been saved from sin by believing in His flesh and blood, and we must thank Him for this. When we partake in Holy Communion to eat the flesh of Jesus and drink His blood, we must participate by placing our faith in the gospel of the water and the Spirit.

We Give All Our Thanks to God

Who are we that the Lord would care so much for us? Human beings deserve to just live in their miserable state only to return to a handful of dust, and be cast into the eternal fire of hell for their sins and pay the everlasting wages of sin. Yet despite this, God the Father loved us so much that He sent His own Son to this earth as our Savior. Since Jesus came to this earth according to the will of the Father, was baptized by John the Baptist, shed His blood to death, and has thereby removed all our sins and condemnations and made us God's children, all of us who believe in this Truth are infinitely indebted to the Lord for loving us so much. We are so thankful beyond all words that we have been saved from our sins through God's love.

Whenever I think about the souls that have received the remission of their sins by believing in the gospel of the water and the Spirit, I'm overwhelmed by gratefulness. Whenever I hear from our brothers and sisters overseas bringing the good tidings that they were born again from reading our books, my heart is rejoiced and happy beyond all description, as if I, myself, had received the remission of sin. Just as those who have received the remission of their sins first are rejoiced in their hearts for those who receive the remission of their sins after them, God is also happy to see the born-again souls who believe in the gospel of the water and the Spirit. As it is because of God's love that we have been saved from our sins, we thank Him for His love and salvation.

Have you been saved from all your sins by believing in the gospel of the water and the Spirit, fulfilled by the love of God and His salvation? Of the flesh and blood of Jesus, we should never overlook either one of them. If we were to leave out even just one of either the baptism of Jesus or His blood on the Cross, then we would render God's love and His grace of salvation in vain, and therefore we must cherish this Truth in our hearts in faith. We cannot but praise God for His love and salvation.

We give all our thanks to God the Father, for He has saved us perfectly and made us His children through the flesh and blood of His Son Jesus, despite the fact that we cannot help but commit sin. The Lord has given us the wisdom to understand the spiritual things of Heaven. I give thanks to God for bestowing such salvation and love on us. I am so grateful to the Lord and love Him so much for blotting out all our sins. Every time I pray to God the Father, there is hardly anything else to say but to thank Him.

Were it not for the flesh of Jesus and His blood, how could we have been saved? Remembering us and out of His love for us, God has saved us from all our sins through the gospel of the water and the Spirit, and that is precisely why we have reached our salvation by faith. Because we are always insufficient, we cannot help but live as sinners and continue to commit sin with our thoughts, hearts, or acts. Yet despite this, we have still attained our salvation, for Jesus has saved us from all our sins by being baptized by John the Baptist and shedding His blood on the Cross.

Now that we have eaten the flesh of Jesus and drunk His blood by faith, we are qualified to enter Heaven. If there is anyone whom you really love, then you should preach to that person the gospel of the water and the Spirit for his sake. That is how the gospel is spread. I believe that in not too distant future, people all over the world will come to accept this precious and beautiful gospel of the water and the Spirit.

Is there anyone among you who still has not been born

again? If you are such a person, you must cast aside your carnal thoughts and have the flesh and blood of Jesus by faith. Other than the God-given Truth, what else could you rely on in this world? I believe that it is the most peaceful and happiest life for us to know the power and wisdom of God and to rely on these by listening to and believing in the gospel Word of the water and the Spirit inside God's Church. It is such a tremendous blessing that we are able to listen to this gospel of the water and the Spirit with our ears and hearts while we are living on this earth. How wonderful is it then, now that we are able to say that we are indeed sinless, for we have heard the gospel of the water and the Spirit and believed in it? I am so happy that I am now able to have the flesh and blood of Jesus written in the Word of God by listening to the gospel of the water and the Spirit in His Church.

The gospel Word of the water and the Spirit is the most spiritual Word that came down from Heaven. This gospel is the Word of Truth, the way of life, and the forever-unchanging Truth that people had heretofore never heard. My fellow believers, even though your bodies may have suffered a bit while living in this world, what a thankful life are you now living in your sinless state, having been made sinless by hearing the Word and believing in it? You and I have received the most precious gift in the world called the gospel of the water and the Spirit. Now, I ask you all not to treat too lightly this precious gift that you've received from God. I admonish you not to make a mockery out of God with your lack of understanding and faithlessness, neither knowing nor believing in the flesh and blood of Jesus. God the Father has made us His children by giving us His Son's life, more precious than even His own life. As the Holy Spirit now dwells in your heart, who have joined God's sinless people by believing in the gospel of the water and the Spirit, I am sure that you will never be able to bring yourself to mock this gospel. So I ask you to cherish the gospel of the water and the Spirit and keep it forever.

We are thankful that we can now spread to everyone throughout the world the correct understanding of the flesh and blood of Jesus within the gospel of the water and the Spirit. Our hearts are overflowing with joy that we are able to preach to each of our nations, as well as to everyone all over the world, the gospel of the water and the Spirit that holds the secret of the flesh and blood of Jesus. Given the fact that our God has loved the entire human race like this, it would be an act of utter ungratefulness if we were to ignore this love that has come by the flesh and blood of Jesus. So, as we cannot just let this Truth be known and kept by us alone, we want to spread throughout the whole world the secret of the flesh and blood of Jesus that manifests God's love. I ask you all to also pool your hearts together and pray for this ministry.

From now on, everyone in this world will eat the flesh of Jesus and drink His blood by faith. It is my sincere hope and prayer that the love of God and His blessings, which come by believing in the flesh and blood of Jesus spiritually, would also be bestowed on you in abundance. ⊠

Jesus, Who Has Given Us The Bread of Life

< John 6:54-63 >

"'Whoever eats My flesh and drinks My blood has eternal life, and I will raise him up at the last day. For My flesh is food indeed, and My blood is drink indeed. He who eats My flesh and drinks My blood abides in Me, and I in him. As the living Father sent Me, and I live because of the Father, so he who feeds on Me will live because of Me. This is the bread which came down from heaven—not as your fathers ate the manna, and are dead. He who eats this bread will live forever.' These things He said in the synagogue as He taught in Capernaum. Therefore many of His disciples, when they heard this, said, 'This is a hard saying; who can understand it?' When Jesus knew in Himself that His disciples complained about this, He said to them, 'Does this offend you? What then if you should see the Son of Man ascend where He was before? It is the Spirit who gives life; the flesh profits nothing. The words that I speak to you are spirit, and they are life.'"

The Lord Has Blotted Out All the Sins of Yours and Mine

By coming to this earth, our Lord took on all the sins of my soul, blotted out all of them, and received the judgment for them. In doing so, He had us become people without sin. To become a spirit without sin, a person who has no sin, is truly an extraordinary event. Except for those who have received salvation, there isn't a person that does not have sin.

You have a flesh, but you also have a spirit. Because Jesus, who is God, has blotted out all the sins of our spirits, we have become the righteous without any sin by our spirits having received salvation. What could be a greater blessing than to have become a person without sin? We must realize that the blessing that has come to us by having become those without sin is something very great. The greatest blessing is the fact that we have become the sinless. It is because there are so many advantages once we become a person without sin. First of all, we have come to be able to live in this world without any hesitation. The fact that we can go on living honorably in this world without the fear of the judgment is a blessing that only a person, whose sins have disappeared by the water and the Spirit, can have. Before our Lord, truly, we give thanks and give back the glory.

Dear fellow believers, the thought that we are the only ones enjoying this blessing of sinlessness made me feel sorry for those who are outside of this blessing. Even God did not want this precious gospel to be known only among us. Thus, I have a wish that by spreading this gospel, we could have people be without sin like us. Because this work is also the command of our Lord (Matthew 28:19-20), we are gladly spreading this gospel all over the world. Our Lord requested us to spread to all people, how great and perfect God's love truly is. He told us to let all the nations know how much God loves us and how the Lord blotted out all our sins and gave us everlasting life.

Because Our Lord Has Blotted out All Our Sins by the Gospel of the Water and the Spirit, We Have No Sin in Our Hearts

Dear fellow believers, as human beings, how could people say that they are without sin? The Lord said, *"But I say to you that whoever looks at a woman to lust for her has already committed adultery with her in his heart" (Matthew 5:28).* As people commit sins with their eyes whenever they open their eyes, how could they become a person without sin? What I am asking is how could a creation become a person without sin like God? Do you know that you are without sin because the Lord had blotted out all your sins? Dear fellow believers, it is something that is possible only by the grace of God. Actually, we were able to receive salvation from sin because God took pity on us and saved us.

What I am saying is that since the fact that we are living honorably by having become those without sin is completely by the grace of God, how could we be the only ones to possess and enjoy this precious Truth? In this world, there are so many people in hardship due to sin. Because of sin, they moan, feel ashamed, commit suicide, and have sicknesses in their hearts and bodies. And, there are so many people who are dying because nothing seems to go right, because they have become spiritually blinded, and because they have become physically confused. Yet, how can those who have received the remission of sin before God turn away from the will of God and be ignorant, all the while possessing and enjoying this precious Truth all to themselves? This is what I am trying say.

God loves not only us, but also all the people. And, He has saved every single person from sin. The only difference is that there are those who have received the grace before God by knowing and believing in that Truth and then, there are those who haven't received the grace because they do not believe in that Truth for they have no knowledge of it, and the truth of the matter is that God loves everyone.

When a great multitude started to follow the Lord, He took pity on them, and fully fed more than five thousand people by blessing the five loaves of barley bread and two fish that a lad had taken out. People, after having eaten this food, tried to make Jesus their king. But, perceiving their intentions, the Lord departed the place. The disciples went over to the other side of the Sea of Tiberias by a boat, but it seems as though Jesus hadn't gone with them. Thus, when the disciples in the boat met a great wind and were afraid, not knowing what to do, it is written in the Bible that Jesus came walking on the sea and had calmed it.

On the following day, those who tasted the blessing called "the miracle of five loaves of bread and two fish" found out that Jesus wasn't there, and started to look for the Lord. Jesus was someone who had healed the sick, resurrected the dead, and fed over five thousand souls with just a single food basket. Because it was very difficult for them to go on living, for their country was under the colonial rule of Rome, these people had started to think that if they were to make Jesus, who had fed them fully, their king and serve Him, they will be free from destitution and also drive out the Roman Empire. That is why people had started to look for Jesus. But, the motive behind it was not in gaining the blessing of everlasting life by receiving the remission of sin but rather, in eating bread for the flesh to their content.

Like so, even today, there are many Christians who believe in Jesus in order to receive bread for the flesh. Why do they believe in Jesus? They believe in Him to receive blessings for the flesh. The Lord tells us to enjoy God's blessing of everlasting life by being born again and also to lead the life of a disciple who passes on that blessing. Yet, the faith of the multitudes was seeking Jesus only to satisfy the desires of the flesh. That is why our Lord said, *"You seek Me, not because you saw the signs, but because you ate of the loaves and were filled" (John 6:26),* to the great multitude who came expecting more bread after having seen Jesus performing wonders. The Lord knew that they came to Him seeking bread for the flesh. What He is telling us is that when a person seeks the Lord, he or she shouldn't seek Him to get bread to eat, but instead, he or she should confirm and believe the signs that tell us that Jesus is the Savior who has blotted out all our sins. It means that when Jesus performed the miracle of five loaves of bread and two fish, people should have recognized that He is the Son of God, as well as God who had created the heavens and the earth, and the One who has come to give people life.

Jesus wanted those people to know that He is the Son of God and the Savior who was going to blot out the sins of all human kind. However, they perceived Him at best as just some person who had given them some bread for the flesh. Because they perceived Jesus merely as the one who feeds them bread for the flesh, He felt awkward as He told them, "How come you do not labor for the food that does not perish, but instead, follow Me seeking food that perishes? Didn't you follow me now in order to eat some more bread? Did you chase after me to this faraway place just to eat some more bread, as if you were going to a house in celebration? Jesus felt very regrettable: "If you seek everlasting life from Me, I shall give you the everlasting life, and if you seek remission of sin in your heart, I shall give you the remission of sin once and for all and turn you into children of God. And, if you seek blessings of Heaven, I can give you all the blessings of Heaven. Yet, how come you only seek the things of the earth?"

Let us take a look at scripture passages from the Gospel of John chapter 6 verse 28 through 40. *"Then they said to Him, 'What shall we do, that we may work the works of God?' Jesus answered and said to them, 'This is the work of God, that you believe in Him whom He sent.' Therefore they said to Him, 'What sign will You perform then, that we may see it and believe You? What work will You do? Our fathers ate the manna in the desert; as it is written, 'He gave them bread from heaven to eat.'' Then Jesus said to them, 'Most assuredly, I say to you, Moses did not give you the bread from heaven, but My Father gives you the true bread from heaven. For the bread of God is He who comes down from heaven and gives life to the world.' Then they said to Him, 'Lord, give us this bread always.' And Jesus said to them, 'I am the bread of life. He who comes to Me shall never hunger, and he who believes in Me shall never thirst. But I said to you that you have seen Me and yet do not believe. All that the Father gives Me will come to Me, and the one who comes to Me I will by no means cast out. For I have come down from heaven, not to do My own will, but the will of Him who sent Me. This is the will of the Father who sent Me, that of all He has given Me I should lose nothing, but should raise it up at the last day. And this is the will of Him who sent Me, that everyone who sees the Son and believes in Him may have everlasting life; and I will raise him up at the last day.'"*

Dear fellow believers, why did our Lord come to this earth and perform miracles and wonders? The Lord did so in order to teach us that He is the Son of God and the Savior of all human beings. If Jesus came to this earth and healed the sicknesses of people only, it is the case that the healed and would live for just a few years or a few decades and go to hell after dying with sins still in their hearts. Then, there would be no benefit for Jesus to have come to this earth. Our Lord performed miracles and showed signs to people so that the Lord Himself is the Savior, and that He is the One with the power to blot out all so many sins of us humans once and for all.

Various miracles performed by Jesus were the foreshadowing of the remission of sin. The Lord performing the miracle of five loaves of bread and two fish was to teach us what sort of faith would have us gain the everlasting life: "I give you My flesh, and I give you My blood. In doing so, I give you all My life. You receive the remission of sin and gain the everlasting life by eating My flesh and blood." The Lord performed the miracle of five loaves of bread and two fish in order to teach us the Truth that Jesus Himself is the bread that comes down from Heaven and that if people should eat the bread that comes down from Heaven, they will gain everlasting life. Dear fellow believers, many false prophets today are performing numerous wonders and miracles, but they are all deceptions. Our Lord performed the miracles in order to blot out all our sins by coming down to this earth and to teach us that He is the Son of God and our Savior, the Redeemer.

As Jesus said He is the bread, what did all the people pay attention to? They were interested in the bread itself. They thought that they would not go hungry if they could only eat the manna from heaven, just like in the times of Moses. That is why they said, "Our fathers ate manna in the desert, just as it is written He had us eat the bread from Heaven." In reply, our Lord said, "Manna did not come from Moses, but rather, it came from My Father." In the Old Testament, God gave people of Israel manna when they were wandering in the desert for 40 years, and they were able to survive without having to cultivate food. Similarly, in the New Testament times, God gave His own life to us and had us live for all eternity. He was saying that by taking the example of God giving manna when the people of Israel were living in the desert long ago, God the Father, by sending Jesus, has now had people receive remission of sin by eating and drinking Jesus' flesh and blood and thereby gaining everlasting life.

People Have Great Interest in Food That Perishes

The multitude was greatly interested in the issue, "What can I do to eat and be full today?" However, our Lord was interested in having people receive remission of sin and having them live eternally by giving up Himself for them to eat and drink. Jesus gave up His flesh and blood so that we may live on this earth in eternal abundance and also to have us enter the Kingdom of Heaven, for one will never get hungry and thirsty for all eternity by eating them just once. Our Lord came to this earth not for the satisfaction of our flesh but for our spirits to be liberated from sins and to live in peace for all eternity.

Why do you believe in Jesus? Do you perhaps believe in Jesus in order to have your flesh be well off? You mustn't work for the food that perishes. Instead, you must do the work of the food that does not perish. If one is healthy inside, the outside will become healthy, also. Dear fellow believers, if we believe the Lord in our hearts and know the genuine gospel in greater detail, and if the gospel penetrates our hearts deeper, then our infirmities of the flesh will be healed, also. However, if there are sins in our hearts, our hearts will become sick and our spirits will also become sick. And thus, our bodies will eventually shut down. We must realize this fact. That is why it is said in the Bible, *"The spirit of a man will sustain him in sickness, But who can bear a broken spirit?" (Proverbs 18:14)*

Our Lord came to this earth to blot out the sins of our spirit. This is a fact that you must know. It isn't the case that the Lord came down to this earth wearing the flesh to have us eat and live well and to make us rich. Dear fellow believers, do you understand this? The great multitude sought Jesus when He was living in the land of Judea because they wanted to eat the bread for the flesh. However, we should not be like these people. Our Lord blotted out all the sins of human kind by giving up Himself in the whole to people all over the world. Jesus did so in order to have all the people gain everlasting life by believing in Him

Dearly beloved fellow saints, our spirits must become well off first of all. If our spirits become well off first, everything else of ours will then become well off. All the blessings will come to us. A person, who unites with God's Church in faith after having received the remission of sin, dwells in the Word, and lives with the clear conviction that his or her spirit has no sin, will have a body that is healthy, also. A path opens up to everything that the person does. It is because the Lord gives that person all the blessings that just cannot be expressed into words. Although nothing may be visible to the eye now, the person will be able to taste the blessings and the helpings of the Lord, which He provides at times.

However, if the spirit were to turn bad, dear fellow believers, all would come to an end. If the spirit were to go bad, everything would become dark, and even with both eyes open, one would not be able to find the way around. Even in a bright daylight, one would be fumbling about and wandering around asking, "Where is the road?" If the spirit were to go wrong, one would start to wonder, "Alas, what should I do? What must I do? What must I do to find a way to live? What work should I do? What business must I start? How do I solve family problems?" But, one would find no answer to all these questions. That is why the spirit must be well off first of all. If we were to receive in our hearts the remission of sin, which makes sins go away completely because of our Lord, a path will open up. Therefore, our spirits must be well off first. The spirit must be well off for everything else to go well.

There was a time when my body was in very bad shape. By the way, because of my illness, I started to believe in the Lord in my early twenties. And almost twenty years have passed since I had really met the Lord through the genuine gospel of the water and the Spirit. However, my body wasn't in any better shape. Did things get better right away just because I met the Lord and my spirit became well off? That isn't so. The fact is that my body became really better without my being aware as I was meditating everyday on how our Lord had blotted out my sins, reaffirming it with the Word everyday, listening to the Word everyday, sharing fellowship with the other saints in the Word, and spreading the fact that He had blotted out all our sins with the Word. As my heart got better, my body got better, eyes of the flesh became clearer, and our Lord blessed me with everything I did.

At first, after having received salvation, there were more losses from the perspective of flesh, but as time passed, our Lord started to bless me unnoticeably, and more than anything else, I started having a stronger faith. The Lord gave me the faith that He, who has saved me and blotted out all the sins of my soul, will take responsibility for my everything and bless me. After I came to possess that faith, although there have been many occasions when I had made Him feel regretful, the Lord has never disappointed me, not once. Truly, there were many times when I had made God feel regretful to my lacking, and there also were many times, really, when I had made other people feel regretful. But, the Lord had not made me feel regretful, not once.

Why did our Lord come to this earth? The Lord didn't come to do His bidding. The reason the Lord came down from Heaven was to carry out the will of God the Father, as it is said, *"For I have come down from heaven, not to do My own will, but the will of Him who sent Me. This is the will of the Father who sent Me, that of all He has given Me I should lose nothing, but should raise it up at the last day" (John 6:38-39).*

Do you want to receive the remission of sin? Do you want to become a child of God, without any sin inside your spirit? If you truly want it, you will no doubt receive the remission of sin. Who are all those in the passage, "all He has given Me"? They are none other than those who come out seeking the Lord with the desire to receive the remission of sin. Take a look at Zacchaeus (Luke 19:2-5). Although he might have committed many shameful sins and thus his heart might be filled with sins, but he went forth before the Lord because he wanted to be without sin before God and go to the Kingdom of God.

Dear fellow believers, if such a person goes before God, He will give such person His love. The fact is that, for the people who truly long for the Kingdom of God, God the Father decided to blot our all our sins by sending His only begotten Son, Jesus, down to this earth. And Jesus, following the will of God, came down to this earth actually, received the baptism at the Jordan River, and perfected our salvation by dying on the Cross shedding His blood.

"She Will Bring Forth a Son, and You Shall Call His Name JESUS"

In the Gospel of Matthew chapter 1 verses 21-23, it is written, *"And she will bring forth a Son, and you shall call His name JESUS, for He will save His people from their sins. So all this was done that it might be fulfilled which was spoken by the Lord through the prophet, saying: 'Behold, the virgin shall be with child, and bear a Son, and they shall call His name Immanuel,' which is translated, 'God with us.'"*

The Virgin Mary conceived the baby Jesus. The fact is that she had conceived Him by the Holy Spirit. The Holy Spirit is God. In order for God to save us humans, He had to be born in human flesh. Because people could be saved only if Jesus were to take on all the sins of human flesh with His own flesh, our Lord had to come to this earth by the body of the Virgin Mary. And through an angel, God gave a name for the Baby who was to be born: *"And she will bring forth a Son, and you shall call His name JESUS, for He will save His people from their sins"* *(Matthew 1:21)*.

It is said that Jesus was conceived by the Holy Spirit. The Holy Spirit is God. What it means is that in order for God to come as the Redeemer of human kind, He had to be born as baby Jesus, having borrowed Mary's body. It is said, *"Behold, the virgin shall be with child, and bear a Son, and they shall call His name Immanuel"* *(Matthew 1:23),* and as it were, 'Immanuel' means that God is with us, (Isaiah 7:14), and it tells us that God has come to this earth in human flesh.

Now, we must find out why God came to this earth in human flesh. It was because there had to be a body to take on all the sins of people in order for Him to take over the sins of the world. It is just like the way of offering a sacrifice in the

Old Testament where there had to be a sacrificial animal without blemish to blot out the sins incurred by humans by passing them over to it. And that is why Jesus, in order to become sacrificial offering for all of us, human beings, came to this earth in human flesh.

In the Book of Leviticus in the Old Testament, if people wanted to receive the remission of sin, they received it by offering a lamb without blemish. If a person with sins brought forth a lamb, a goat, or a cow without blemish and laid his or her hand on it, all the sins got passed onto that sacrificial offering. And, that sacrificial offering without blemish died on behalf of the person who had passed on the sins. Just as it was said, *"For the life of the flesh is in the blood, ... for it is the blood that makes atonement for the soul" (Leviticus 17:11),* people passed on their sins to an animal made of flesh and bled it to death. It is the case that people of the Old Testament received the remission of all their sins in this manner.

Our God, in order to save us in a way similar to this, came down to this earth Himself in human flesh. And so, we will find out how He has saved us by looking at the Scripture passages in the Gospel of Matthew chapter 3. These are the written Word on how Jesus has given us the flesh.

"Then Jesus came from Galilee to John at the Jordan to be baptized by him. And John tried to prevent Him, saying, 'I need to be baptized by You, and are You coming to me?' But Jesus answered and said to him, 'Permit it to be so now, for thus it is fitting for us to fulfill all righteousness.' Then he allowed Him. When He had been baptized, Jesus came up immediately from the water; and behold, the heavens were opened to Him, and He saw the Spirit of God descending like a dove and alighting upon Him. And suddenly a voice came from heaven, saying, 'This is My beloved Son, in whom I am well

pleased'" (Matthew 3:13-17).

There are three Persons of the Godhead—the Father, the Son, and the Holy Spirit. Three may differ in terms of status, but they are all actually God. Jesus is God. The Holy Spirit is also God. God the Father is God, too. All three Persons of the Godhead had the same intention, and from among them, Jesus, who is the Son of God the Father, came to this earth in human flesh. By being born on this earth through Mary, Jesus received the baptism from John the Baptist who was the representative of all humankind. That is why God the Father bore witness to His Son, saying, *"This is My beloved Son, in whom I am well pleased" (Matthew 3:17),* after Jesus had received the baptism. Who bore witness to what? The fact is that God the Father bore witness that the baptized Jesus is His Son. By this baptism, all the sins of the world were passed onto Jesus. That is why, on the following day of the baptism, John the Baptist said, pointing out Jesus, *"Behold! The Lamb of God who takes away the sin of the world!" (John 1:29)*

Our God sent down the bread of everlasting life from Heaven. That bread was none other than His Son, Jesus. He had sent down Jesus, the Creator of all things, the King of all kings, the Lord of all hosts, the Son of God who is also God Himself, to this earth. Jesus, who was sent down to this earth in human flesh, took on all the sins of humankind by receiving the baptism. God had the sins of the world be passed on to His Son, and had all humankind receive the remission of sin by faith, for Jesus had taken on all the sins of humankind with His flesh.

Some people say, "Jesus received the baptism at the Jordan River to show a good example of humility. That is not so. He didn't ornate the first work of His public life with the baptism in order to show His humble character. There wasn't a single work that was wasteful among the works that He had done after having come to this earth. Why did the Lord, who has come to save you and me, start off the work of our salvation by going to John the Baptist, bending down His head before him, and receiving the baptism? Why do all Four Gospels start to record the ministry of the Lord by starting off with the baptism of Jesus, and why do all the disciples mention, on countless occasions, the baptism that Jesus had received? Why does the Apostle Paul proclaim, *"For as many of you as were baptized into Christ have put on Christ" (Galatians 3:27)*?

Our Lord came down to this earth to save us, and as He turned thirty, He took on all the sins of humankind unto His flesh. His flesh had been without sin. Why? It was because Jesus wasn't born of reproductive relationship between a man and a woman. In order to wear human flesh purely as God, He had merely borrowed Mary's body. And, in order to take on the sins of all human beings unto His flesh, which was void of sin then, He had received the baptism at the Jordan River. This is what is meant by "Jesus has given His flesh for us."

Why Did Jesus Have to Receive the Baptism from John the Baptist?

John the Baptist was a messenger of God sent by God. In the Old Testament era, the High Priest Aaron, as the representative of all Israelites, performed the laying of both hands on the sacrifice on the 10th day of the 7th month, which would blot out the sins of the people of Israel all at once (Leviticus 16:20-22, 29). The High Priest passed on a year's worth of sins of the people of Israel to the flesh of that sacrificial offering once and for all by laying both his hands on it as the representative in accordance with the sacrificial system established by God. As such, there was the need to send a representative of humankind onto this earth in order for God to blot out all the sins of humankind by having them passed onto Jesus. That is why, 6 month prior to the birth of Jesus, He had John the Baptist be born through Zacharias, a descendant of the High Priest Aaron (Luke 1:5-25).

God is a God of the Covenant. Just as He had promised through the sacrificial system and His Word of prophecies, God came to this earth actually and offered His sinless flesh for all humankind. To do so, through whom did He take on our sins? It was through John the Baptist. Jesus had received the baptism from John the Baptist, the messenger of God and the representative of all humankind. The Lord personally witnessed that John the Baptist was the representative of all people, saying, *"For this is he of whom it is written: 'Behold, I send My messenger before Your face, who will prepare Your way before You.' Assuredly, I say to you, among those born of women there has not risen one greater than John the Baptist; but he who is least in the kingdom of heaven is greater than he" (Matthew 11:10-11).*

He said that he who is least in the Kingdom of Heaven is greater than he because John the Baptist was the representative of earth. A representative of earth, no matter how great, is still less than the least in the Kingdom of Heaven. But, the fact is that John the Baptist is the greatest on earth. The greatest born of a woman refers to the representative of all human beings. Also, the Lord, making reference to the Book of Malachi chapter 3 verse 1, said, *"Behold, I send My messenger before Your face, Who will prepare Your way before You" (Malachi 3:1).* It means that God, in order to blot out people's sins, sent a representative of people 6 months before His coming to this earth. Who was he? He was none other than John the Baptist.

"'Behold, I send My messenger,
And he will prepare the way before Me.
And the Lord, whom you seek,
Will suddenly come to His temple,
Even the Messenger of the covenant,
In whom you delight.
Behold, He is coming,'
Says the LORD of hosts" (Malachi 3:1).

Whom does the messenger of God mentioned here refer to? Jesus says personally that he is John the Baptist. Jesus bore witness that Elijah who was to come is none other than John the Baptist (Malachi 4:5).

Near the end of the Old Testament era, the nation of Israel was destroyed and there wasn't any hope for they had departed from God. Then, God, through the prophet Malachi, promised to send a representative of all people as His messenger High Priest. He promised to send down a representative of all people prior to the Lord and take on all the sins of humankind by receiving the baptism. In order to save us, the fact is that He had already set up a perfect program.

"And from the days of John the Baptist until now the kingdom of heaven suffers violence, and the violent take it by force" (Matthew 11:12). From the days of John the Baptist until now, the Kingdom of Heaven suffers violence from the invaders, the men of faith. In chapter 3 of the Gospel of Matthew, why did Jesus have to receive the baptism? In the Gospel of John chapter 6, Jesus says, "Whoever eats My flesh and drinks My blood has eternal life. As you do so, you can abide in Me just like I abide in the Father. But, should you not eat My flesh and not drink My blood, you and I have nothing to do with each other." Between Jesus' flesh and His blood, if a

person were to ignore either one of them, the person would neither be able to abide in Jesus nor be able to gain everlasting life.

"Oh, I like the blood of Jesus, but not the flesh." Is there anyone who speaks such words? In order to blot out our sins, our Lord came to this earth in human flesh, took on all our sins by receiving the baptism with His body, and thus, has made us be without sin in our hearts. If it is the case that He has planned to save us, we must believe it so. If we were to ignore either the flesh or the blood of Jesus, it would be like ignoring God's plan for salvation.

Our God received the baptism in order to save us. And that is why Jesus commanded John the Baptist, "Permit it to be so now." "Are you the High Priest of the earth? Are you the representative of humankind? Do not say anything, but lay your hands on my head as I tell you to do. Only if you do so does all the sins of the world come over to me. It is only right for us to make all people be without sin by doing so. It is only fitting to fulfill all righteousness."

Dear fellow believers, is this fitting or is it not? It is fitting. Is it the case that Jesus had saved us just by saying, "Hey, I am dying for you. Believe in me," as were dying on the Cross without having taken on the sins, even though they lie within us? If he had done so, the fact would be that sins would still be within us, so the sins of the heart would never go away. The reason is the same as to why there are sins still inside the hearts of those who do not believe in the baptism of Jesus.

You cannot ignore Jesus' baptism. Dear fellow believers, if our spirits were to receive the remission of sin, we cannot but have faith in the fact that our Lord had received the baptism at the Jordan River and that He had taken on all my sins at that moment. Without having faith in the baptism of Jesus, which is our true food, how can we say that our spirits are without sin? Our God is the just God. Because we commit sins all throughout our lives with our flesh, we are those who must die due to our sins. Yet, the Lord came to this earth in human flesh just like ours in order to blot out all our sins, and saved us from sins by taking on all the sins of all people through the baptism that He had received and then sacrificing His flesh on the Cross.

Jesus received the baptism at the Jordan River. What does the word 'baptism' mean? First of all, the word 'baptism' means "to cleanse." Dear fellow believers, how do our hearts get cleansed? As our hearts are full of sin, how do they get cleansed? The sins in our hearts get cleansed because the sins were passed onto Jesus. Our sins were passed onto Jesus because He had received the passing on of sins through the representative of all people, and because our sins were passed on, it is the case that sins of our hearts disappeared completely through cleansing. When we look into the sacrificial system in the Old Testament, don't sins get passed on, just as a sinner lays his or her hands on a lamb? Then, is there a sin inside this person? No, there isn't. For there is no sin, it is the case that sins have been cleansed away. This is redemption. Redemption refers to there being no more sins through the payment of price for sins.

On the day of the great redemption, the High Priest Aaron lays his hands on the sacrificial offering on behalf of the people of Israel. Because the sins of the people of Israel get passed on to the sacrificial offering completely by doing so, it is case that the sins of these people get cleansed. Thus, it is the case that one receives the remission of sin by having faith in that fact. Just like this, the fact is that Jesus, in order to cleanse our sins, took on all the sins of all of us humankind by receiving the baptism Himself from John the Baptist who is the representative of all humankind. It is the case that sins get cleansed by believing in our hearts this fact.

Secondly, in the word 'baptism,' there is the meaning, "to bury." In other words, it implies death. Dear fellow believers, why did Jesus die? Jesus died at the Cross because He had taken on our sins at the Jordan River. Jesus was someone who had no sin. Not even once did He commit a sin. No matter how hard we look at the Gospels, there isn't a single passage that says Jesus did something by mistake. Jesus did not have any imperfection, spiritually or before the Law. The passages state that He is the Son of God, spotless, flawless, and without blemish. This is why the Bible states, *"For He made Him who knew no sin to be sin for us, that we might become the righteousness of God in Him" (2 Corinthians 5:21).*

Why did Jesus come to this earth and received the baptism? In order to take on the sins of us human beings, He had received the baptism. Jesus, by giving us His immaculate flesh, completely took all our sins onto His flesh. Because He had to receive the judgment in order for Him to save human beings from sin, it is the case that He had received the baptism of taking over worldly sins by giving us His flesh. Jesus took on all our sins completely. Our Lord gave us His flesh. He had us eat His flesh. Just as He said, *"Permit it to be so now, for thus it is fitting for us to fulfill all righteousness" (Matthew 3:15),* the sins of all people went away and all righteousness was fulfilled the moment when Jesus received the baptism. It tells us that the work of all the sins of this world going away and the righteousness getting fulfilled in its place was accomplished through the baptism of Jesus.

Just as the sacrificial offerings in the Old Testament took over sins, it is the case that Jesus had taken over all the sins of the world by receiving the baptism. Just as the sin of the people of Israel went away the moment when the scapegoat died after having taken over the sins of all the people of Israel and then having gone to the wilderness crying "maah, maah," Jesus came to this earth as the Lamb of God, and in order to blot out all the sins of humankind, He finished off the judgment for all sins by taking on the sins through the baptism and then dying on the Cross. The fact is that Jesus took on all the sins by receiving the baptism.

Thirdly, in the word 'baptism,' there is the meaning "to pass onto." From a sinner's point of view, only when his or her sin is passed into the sacrificial offering, does he or she become without sins and receive redemption. Jesus was a sacrificial offering for redemption. In order to save you and me from sin and to save all humankind from sin, Jesus Himself became the sin offering that has taken on all sins. If it were the case that the Lord did not take on all our sins, then how would it be possible for our sins to go away? "I do not want to. I have no sin. Yet, why must I taken on sins? Please, don't say that, Father. I have no sin. I did not make mistakes. There is no sin in My heart. I am Holy. With the only difference being that I am Your Son, am I not equal to You? Yet, why must I become a sinner by taking on the sins of all those vulgar beings? I do not want to do so." If Jesus had done so, it would have been the end for us. If Jesus hadn't received the baptism, there would have been no hope whatsoever for us humankind. It is because all of us humankind would have had no choice but to go to hell.

When Jesus was receiving the baptism, God said, *"And suddenly a voice came from heaven, saying, 'This is My beloved Son, in whom I am well pleased'" (Matthew 3:17)*. It means that although He was without sin, in order to uphold the will of God to save humankind, Jesus put forth His head toward John the Baptist and voluntarily took the sins upon His body, which was without a single sin. That is why God said, *"In whom I am well pleased" (Matthew 3:17)*. God was pleased by the fact that Jesus had died vicariously by becoming the sacrificial offering for a short while and bearing the sins of the world, and God had Him live again, though He was dead.

Our Lord died after having lived on this earth for 33 years. For 30 years, He had lived His private life, and as for the following 3 years, He had lived His public life. The 3 years span from the moment when He had received the baptism until His death on the Cross. Jesus died after having lived His public life for 3 years. In order to blot out all our sins, Jesus received the baptism, and gave us His own flesh. Today's Scripture passage in the Gospel of John speaks of to this Truth.

"The Bread That I Shall Give Is My Flesh, Which I Shall Give for the Life of the World"

"I am the living bread which came down from heaven. If anyone eats of this bread, he will live forever; and the bread that I shall give is My flesh, which I shall give for the life of the world" (John 6:51).

It was said that Jesus is the living bread that came down from Heaven. He gave us that bread. It means that He gave us His flesh. Because His flesh was for the life of the world, He had gladly given it to us. By taking on the sins by receiving the baptism onto His flesh, He had all humankind be without any single sin. The Lord has saved us by taking on all your sins as well as mine by giving up His flesh. Those who have faith in this are without any sin, no matter how lacking they might be. Jesus has made us perfectly sinless by taking on all the sins of the world. Dear fellow believers, do you believe this? Jesus has saved us so by giving His flesh.

Are there sins in your spirit? No, there aren't any. There is no sin in your spirits as well as mine. We are the righteous. No matter how lacking, we are the righteous who has received the grace of God. The righteous people are the princess, princes, as well as kings of the Kingdom of Heaven. We have actually become children of God by faith. Now, laughter comes out from those who have faith in this Truth. The laughter comes from deep within their hearts. "Hallelujah! I am said to have no sin. It is said that the Lord gave His flesh and all my sins were completely taken on by His flesh! That's what happened! Yes." As we think more and more, our hearts feel refreshed, and even while we are asleep, laughter comes out from deep within our hearts.

In the Gospel of John chapter 6 verse 53, the Lord has firmly said, *"Unless you eat the flesh of the Son of Man and drink His blood, you have no life in you."* Yet, why do people not eat the flesh of the Son of Man? Why do people not believe in the fact that the Lord has taken on all the sins of whole humankind? The Lord came to this earth to save us and took on all our sins completely by giving us His immaculate flesh. Yet, why do people not believe in such grateful love? Why do they resist? Please, eat by faith. If people were to resist, the Lord think of it as regrettable. And the Lord's life cannot come inside such people. The Lord wants to give us life, but if we were to resist that, life cannot come inside us. Because the Holy Spirit cannot reside inside the hearts of those with sin, the Lord wants us to receive the remission of sin and obtain new life. We must believe in the fact that the Lord has taken on all the sins of humankind by receiving the baptism for you and for me.

"Most assuredly, I say to you, unless you eat the flesh of the Son of Man and drink His blood, you have no life in you" *(John 6:53).* The Lord gave up His flesh to us in order to save us. He gave up His flesh to us so that you and I, including all the people in this world, not missing any single person, could be saved. By giving us His flesh at the Jordan River, that is, by taking all the sins of the world onto His body, the Lord had us eat His flesh by faith What is said to happen if we were to not eat His flesh into which He had taken on all the sins of humankind completely? It is said, *"No life in you" (John 6:53).* It is said that no matter how hard one believes, the Holy Spirit does not come inside.

Is the Holy Spirit inside you? How does the divine Spirit, namely, the Holy Spirit, come inside your hearts? The Lord seals our hearts with the Holy Spirit when we believe in the righteous work done by the Lord as is. The Lord had those who believe receive the remission of sin by giving them the gospel of the water and the Spirit. And to those who have received the remission of sin, He gave the Holy Spirit inside their hearts. It is the case that we have come to receive the Holy Spirit by believing in the gospel of the water and the Spirit with our hearts.

The Lord took on all my sins completely by receiving the baptism at the Jordan River. He took all our sins completely with His flesh, and by shedding blood on the Cross, He has given us life. We must believe in our hearts the work of terminating all our sins and the judgment that the Lord has done. People who believe in the fact that the Lord had taken on all our sins completely at the Jordan River have no sin in their hearts. If sinners were to realize and believe this fact, there would be no sin in their hearts, no matter who they are. The Holy Spirit smacks down a seal on those who are without sin, and dwells insides their hearts. The Lord stays inside us as the Spirit, and I enter inside the Lord by faith; this is how the Lord and I become one. The fact is that the Lord stays as the Holy Spirit inside those who have received the remission of sin by believing in the fact that the Lord has redeemed them through His Son.

It is said, *"Unless you eat the flesh of the Son of Man and drink His blood, you have no life in you" (John 6:53)*. We must believe in both of them. Jesus received the baptism and died on the Cross, and so we must realize that the death of the Lord is your death as well as mine. And, we must believe. That Jesus received the baptism at the Jordan River was to save you and me from sins. We must believe in the fact that God had received the baptism so as to realize His love for us and to save us, and we must also believe in the fact that it was the proper way to our salvation. Only when we believe in these two things, the flesh and blood of Jesus, does the salvation become perfectly realized. Also, only then does life come inside the hearts of those who have received salvation, and does the Holy Spirit come inside. If one were to deny any one of these two, one can never be able to receive salvation.

When our Lord said He would give His flesh, the Jews said, "What do You mean? We just can't understand it." Dear fellow believers, are these words of the Truth difficult also for you? For Jesus is the good Shepherd, He has saved His sheep by giving His flesh and blood for them. The Lord is our good Shepherd. Isn't it too easy? The gospel of the water and the Spirit is easy, but because it is something so very important, we must spread it, listen to it, and so on everyday. Between the flesh and the blood that were given by Jesus, if either one were to be left out, there can never be salvation.

I saw a sign that read, "Are you sinners despite having

faith," posted on some church. Actually, most Christians believe in Jesus in their own way, but sin is still in their hearts. Despite having faith in Jesus, why are the Christians of the world sinners? Do you know why they are sinners despite having faith? It is because they drank only the Lord-given drink. Because they only believe in the Cross, they still have sins even though they profess, "Lord Jesus, I believe. I believe You have died vicariously for me. I believe You have blotted out all my sins. Hallelujah." No matter how fervently they believe, the fact is that the Holy Spirit isn't in their hearts. Because they do not have the Word witnessing the fact that their sins have been transferred, as they sin again, it is the case that sin still remains in their hearts. They wonder, "Oh, how strange. I have faith in Jesus, but there still are sins in my heart. The Lord took away the original sins as well as those committed sins. Yet, why are there sins? Strange! It is strange!" If you are in a case like that, you must accurately examine anything that's strange. If you were to examine, you will come to the conclusion that you have sins despite having faith in Jesus due to the fact that you do not know the way by which the Lord has saved you.

Having come to know about the fact that the Lord has saved us by giving His flesh at the Jordan River, what would happen to you? Even while you were sleeping, you would say, "Lord, I didn't know very well. Yet, Lord, You had done so. Yes, it is true. That is why so many Scripture passages all speak of the flesh and blood. Thank You, Lord. I am truly thankful to You for having saved me in these two ways, the flesh and the blood."

Dear fellow believers, I hope for you to believe in the gospel of the water and the Spirit. The Lord has saved us thus. We have become sinless because the Lord had come in the flesh of man, because the Lord had taken on our sins with that flesh, and because He died on the Cross after having done so. If it were the case that the Lord had come to this earth not in a flesh and did not receive the baptism even though He had come, you and I would be sinners despite our faith.

Christianity isn't a religion. It is faith. It came from above. Faith is to uphold and believe in the fact that the Lord has blotted all our sins. We look up to the work that the Lord has done and receive the remission of sin by having faith in it. This is what faith is. Religion is something that I hold on to and rely on by making a determination. If you were to take a hold on your own saying, "Oh, Lord. I believe in You," it would be useless. You ought to look at the work that the Lord has done and say, "Alas! Lord, You have thus blotted out all my sins. Hallelujah. I believe in this Truth." Only then does the Lord give you a passing grade.

Dear fellow believers, do you have sin? No, you do not. Jesus took on all our sins by giving us His flesh at the Jordan River. *"Behold! The Lamb of God who takes away the sin of the world" (John 1:29)* Jesus, by going to the Cross bearing the sins of the world, has perfectly ended once and for all the punishment for all our sins. The Lord has saved us perfectly so that we may receive the remission of sin by believing it with our hearts. The Lord has made it so that we would be able to receive salvation only by faith, without the need for any virtuous deeds or effort.

Our Lord has saved us. The Lord is our Savior. For 33 years, in order to save us, the Lord was patient with those who disgusted Him, and we can't imagine how patient He was. The Jews, Pharisees, and scribes challenged Jesus, and they tried to strike and to capture Him to kill. If I were the Creator like Jesus, I would have crushed them in an instant, but because our

Lord is merciful, He came to save them, instead. Because He wanted to take on such people's sins also and to have them acquire everlasting life, He was patient like a sheep that is silent before its shearers (Isaiah 53:7). How noble and marvelous love of the Truth is that love? Because our Lord is too compassionate, He even wanted all those who had nailed Him to the Cross to receive the salvation. That is why, even as He were nailed to the Cross, begged the Father, *"Father, forgive them, for they do not know what they do" (Luke 23:34).*

Our Lord came to this earth and gave us His flesh and His blood in order to save you and me. This is what salvation is. Having done so, He has allowed us to breathe. Our Lord made our hearts without sin so that our hearts, which have been oppressed by sins, could breathe. The Lord gave us His flesh, and He gave us His blood. And now, sitting on the right side of the throne of God, He hopes for many people to acquire salvation by eating and drinking His flesh and blood by faith. He desires it so much so that we cannot even imagine it. "I have received the baptism for you and taken away all your sins. I have saved you by giving you everything that is Mine for you. I have blotted out the sins of all you people of flesh. I have saved you with My flesh and My blood." We must realize how the Lord wants us to receive the remission of sin by believing in this. And, we must realize how the Lord longs for us to enter the Kingdom where God resides by acquiring the everlasting life by faith. Are you able to see the heart of God?

Why did God come to this earth in human flesh and suffered all those indignities? Why did our Lord give up His flesh? As our Lord was praying in the garden of Gethsemane, how great was the pain Jesus was about to go through that He said, *"Abba, Father, all things are possible for You. Take this cup away from Me" (Mark 14:36)*? It was the cup of blood.

Because He had taken on all our sins with the flesh, which He had given up, He had to die on the Cross, and it meant drinking the cup of tremendously horrific pain. That is why Jesus, if it were possible, had wanted to avoid that cup. But, Jesus, after having prayed in earnest three times, bowed down before God saying, *"Nevertheless, not what I will, but what You will" (Mark 14:36)*. He said, "Father, do as You will," and gave Himself up to crucified. Though He Himself was without sin, because He had taken on all the sins of the world by receiving the baptism with His flesh in order to save all humankind from sin, the Lord had to pay for the price of all those sins. Truly, although our Lord did not like being blamed for sins since He dislikes sins, the fact is that He had endured all those work in order to save us.

By having faith in Jesus, we must receive the remission of sin and enter the Kingdom of Heaven. And even on this earth, we should be able to live in peace as those without sin. This was the will of our Lord toward us. Dear fellow believers, do you believe? Our Lord has saved us by giving us His flesh. Though this is the Truth, why do people not believe it? When we say this to Christians, most of them tend not to believe in this, saying, "Well, how can there be such a thing?" And, whenever this happens, the Lord feels pain. All the works that the Lord had done by coming to this earth in order to save us are the footprints toward our salvation. Yet, why do they have faith in only some of the works that He had done, and not others? Why do they nullify just some of His atoning works? Why do they put forth only the doctrine of their denominations? What Jesus says is the first essential. We must eat and drink by faith the flesh and blood that Jesus has given us.

Religious sect isn't important. I do not have a religious

sect. Prior to being born-again by believing in the gospel of the water and the Spirit, I studied theology from the *Kosin* denomination, one of the most conservative Presbyterian denominations in Korea. My family had a strong background in the *Kosin* denomination. But now, I am no longer working with such a sect. The fact is that I believe in the Lord because I want to follow Him, and because He has blotted out all my sins, I love Him by faith and do the work of spreading this gospel, which He wishes and finds joy in. It isn't the case that I am working to build and expand my own sect. Are we spreading the gospel of the water and the Spirit all over the world to show off ourselves? No, we aren't. We are not trying to boast that we are better than others. For He has blotted out the sins of all people, the Lord wants all people to receive the remission of sin and He wants those of us who have received it first to become tools for the spreading of the gospel of the Lord.

Some People Ignore the Baptism of Jesus from the Gospel of the Water and the Spirit

What does the Scripture say would happen if we were to ignore the baptism of Jesus? It is clearly written, *"Unless you eat the flesh of the Son of Man and drink His blood, you have no life in you" (John 6:53).* If one does not believe in the gospel of the water and the Spirit, the fact is that the person will go to hell despite having faith in Jesus. There would be no life.

Is the Holy Spirit inside you? There isn't any sin inside the heart of those who have the Holy Spirit. Those who do not have the Holy Spirit do believe in Jesus, but once they commit a wrongdoing, they get tied up again by sin. Because they get tied up by sin again and again, they make a commitment saying, "I must not sin. I shouldn't commit sin." But, for they are human beings, how could they not commit sin again? Also, when they do commit sin again, they become fearful, saying, "Alas, I sinned again. What shall I do?" Why would someone who has faith in Jesus be fearful of the judgment? It is because they hadn't received the salvation since they did believe in the gospel of the water and the Spirit.

If God had told us to pay the price for sin whenever we commit sin, then you would have gone through mourning much more than ten thousand times. Just for the sins that we had committed for a week, we should already have been beaten to death a hundred times over and more. If it were the case that the judgment would be made over sins carried in the heart as well as those of deeds, there wouldn't be a single person left on this world. What did our Lord say? He said, *"But go and learn what this means: 'I desire mercy and not sacrifice.' For I did not come to call the righteous, but sinners, to repentance"* *(Matthew 9:13).*

Dear fellow believers, this 'mercy' refers to the fact that the Lord has blotted out all our sins for He had taken pity on us. And, the passage, *"I desire mercy and not sacrifice,"* means that the Lord does not want us offering prayers of repentance, offering services and acting out things, just as the people of Israel during the Old Testament era had done, coming forth to a priest carrying a sacrificial offering and saying, "I have sinned. Please forgive me. I will be requited." He just wants us to receive the remission of sin by believing the gospel of the water and the Spirit.

Do you eat the flesh of the Son of Man by faith? Please, eat the flesh of the Son of Man. In the Gospel of John chapter 6 verses 54-55, the Lord said, *"Whoever eats My flesh and drinks*

*My blood has eternal life, and I will raise him up at the last
day. For My flesh is food indeed, and My blood is drink
indeed."* The flesh of the Lord is food indeed. The fact that our
Lord has taken on all our sins with His flesh is a true sign of
our salvation. Dear fellow believers, do you believe this? It is
the case that we obtain food of our hearts by our spirits
ruminating, "Ah, yes. The Lord took on the sins of the world
through the baptism. Yes, that's right." Thus, the gospel of the
water and the Spirit is the food that gives life for all eternity
and it does not perish even if we were to keep it for a long,
long time and eat it.

The Lord perfected all the righteousness for me by taking
on all my sins at the Jordan River. Through His baptism, Jesus
completely took on the sins of all people. Jesus came as the
Lamb of God, and went away bearing all the sins of the world.
If we were to remind ourselves of that fact everyday, our hearts
would be without sin. Jesus has taken away sins that we had
committed from birth until the age of thirty by the baptism, and
even if we were to live until the age of seventy, He has taken
away the sins that we would be committing up until then.
Having faith in the fact that He has taken away not only our
sins but also the sins of our fathers and mothers as well as the
sins of our children, that is, the sins of all people starting from
Adam until those at the end of this world becomes the food to
our hearts.

One's spirit cannot bear the sin when it commits the sin.
Yet, how can our spirits be in peace while going through these
sinful lives? It is only possible for our Lord to give us our true
food. What is the true food to the spirits of us human beings?
The true food to our spirits is His flesh. The fact that our Lord
gave us His flesh at the Jordan River is the food to our spirits.
Our Lord's flesh is our true food. And the true drink is the

blood of the Lord. The fact that the Lord had received all the judgment that we were supposed to receive is the true drink. Our spirits feel refreshed due to the fact that all our sins have been atoned for.

If we were to perhaps fall weak and worry about receiving the judgment again by having committed sins, not matter how good the food may be, we would not be able to digest and gain strength from it. What refreshes our hearts and calms us? It is the blood of Jesus. The blood of Jesus refers to none other than the judgment. We have nothing to be judged for because Jesus has received every judgment vicariously. It was something that was done by our Lord who has saved us. That is why the Lord is our Savior.

How can we live refreshingly and peacefully in our hearts? We can enjoy such grace by having the true food and the true drink that the Lord has given us. We are able to live always in our spirits filled with peace and strength because He has given us His flesh and blood. By having faith in the work of His flesh and blood, we are able to live in this world having gained strength with refreshed and peaceful hearts, and we will be able to live forever in comfort even in the world to come. This is our salvation. This is the salvation that has blotted out the sins of us humankind. Dear fellow believers, do you believe? I also believe in the Lord. We don't know how good the Lord is.

For 10 years, after having started to believe in Jesus for the first time, I lived as a Christian sinner. So, for the 10 years, I was very, very anguished. Prior to having faith in Jesus, I believed Buddhism, but because of the illness of my body, I started to believe Jesus. Thus, I came to believe in Jesus and came to know the Law and sin. At first, I had gained peace in my heart, knowing that Jesus had died on the Cross. I believed like that, and for the first five years, I spoke in tongue well, was fervent with love, and was first in helping others. Whenever money was in my pocket, I gave away all of it to people who were in hardship. Whenever I walked down a street filled with beggars, my pockets became empty. A certain missionary said he had given away everything except for a piece of attire and thus, had lived with no possession, and for 10 years, I endeavored to live like that, also.

But, as I tried harder and harder to live uprightly, I came to realize the fact that I had so much lacking in me. Sins started to accumulate inside my heart. I was so afflicted by sins, and I felt as though I was going to die. When I realized the fact that my spirit was in suffocation by sins, I could not even see the faces of people. Not only people, I could not even look up to the sky and I could not even call out the Lord. After having sinned, I could not even say a word when I tried to pray to God. Only the word, "Lord" came out of my mouth, and I did not know what to say next. It was so agonizing. At first, I prayed well, but as time passed by, strangely, more difficult it became for me to pray. As words didn't come out after having called out, "Lord," as I was offering overnight prayers all through the night, I was only repeating, "Lord, Lord," and thus, you could imagine how stifling it must have been for me. I had to go before the Lord and I had to make earnest requests. But, I just could not do so. It wasn't just once or twice that I had to face the morning after dawn, having just called out, "Lord, Lord," all night long.

It lasted for 5 years. It was getting truly tedious. Though such pain cannot be described into words, but the most serious thing was that I felt myself dying due to suffocation of my spirit. "There is no more need for me to go on living. I think I should retire from this world." Only such thought captured my heart, so I could not but always feel suffocated.

Just then, I realized something as I was reading the Gospel of Matthew chapter 3 verses 13 through 15. It was the fact that the Lord has taken on all my sins at the Jordan River. When I realized the fact that the Lord has taken over all my sins by giving me His flesh and receiving the baptism, my spirit that had been suffocating started to breathe in and out immediately. "Now then, I must be without sin. I received salvation without any mishap. I would have died of suffocation despite having faith in Jesus if I hadn't known about the Scripture passage that says the Lord had truly taken on my sins at that moment. Thankfully, I received salvation just in time." I was full of joy and filled with elation. Thus, even when I was in bed, I look at this Scripture passage. Whenever I am board or fall into weaknesses, I take a look at this Scripture passage that tells me how all my sins have passed onto the body of Jesus.

Also, from the Scripture passages, *"Behold! The Lamb of God who takes away the sin of the world!" (John 1:29)* and *"Now where there is remission of these, there is no longer an offering for sin" (Hebrews 10:18),* I obtained a clear proof that the Lord already has perfectly completed my salvation. Furthermore, the Lord said, *"It is finished" (John 19:30),* and by saying, *"There is therefore now no condemnation to those who are in Christ Jesus" (Romans 8:1),* it has become so that there can never be condemnation inside the hearts of those of us who believe in the gospel of the water and the Spirit by which the Lord has perfected all the righteousness.

Dear fellow believers, whenever I fall into weaknesses, I reaffirm these Scripture passages. And, my spirits eats the flesh of the Lord everyday. Now, even if I don't read these passages everyday, I swallow into my heart the fact that the Lord has taken on all my sins with His flesh by ruminating it. I thank the

Lord. I am truly thankful. For me to eat the flesh of the Lord by faith has become the true food. Thus, I am able to laugh, spread the Word, share fellowship, pray for others, and ask God's blessings for them.

Dear fellow believers, our Lord has saved me and you, as well as all the other people, with His flesh and His blood. Do you believe so? Thus, He had made it so that we would never receive the judgment.

I keep myself busy with the gospel works. As I am alone, I realize how lacking and weak I am. I want to march forward spiritually, yet there are so many fleshly thoughts arising inside of me. As I see them, I cannot but recognize myself as is. When I am lying down, I say to myself to stay lying down just a bit longer. Then, I say to myself to doze a little while longer. And then, I say to myself to sleep a little while longer, and it becomes so difficult for me to get up. So, I look at myself and start to grieve, saying, "Lord, how can there be a person like me? Lord, you have saved me. Yet, instead of praying for others, I tell myself to lie down just a bit longer." Despite of it all, I am able to come to my senses and follow the Lord again because the fact remains that there is no sin in my heart. Someone might say, "But, how can you dare say that you are without sin?" Still, the fact remains that my spirit is without sin due to the fact that I have eaten the flesh of the Lord.

The Lord gave us His flesh and blood. Thus, we are able to shake away the fear of sin and the judgment by faith whenever they try to bind us. Even today, not being bound by our weaknesses, we pray, "Lord, I want to help few more spirit receive the remission of sins today," and then go out to the streets or to campuses. As we meet other spirits outside, we start spreading the gospel of the water and the Spirit by asking, "Do you have sins, or do you not? Do you know how Jesus has saved you perfectly?" As we do so, we get to meet numerous people with wrongful faith who say that they believe Jesus but have sins in their hearts, and we start telling them the gospel of the water and the Spirit with elation.

When asked, "Are you righteous?" some people answer, "I am righteous since I have faith in Jesus, but because I commit sins everyday, I am a sinner." How can there be a righteous person who still has sin? To those spirits that are in such confusion, we must widely the gospel of the water and the Spirit in detail. I have seen so many cases where such people receive the remission of sin after only an hour's worth of fellowship in God's Word. After conveying to them the gospel fully, when I ask, "Now, do you have sins?" and they answer back saying that they don't have sin anymore, my heart fills up with joy. You don't realize how joyous they are also, after having seen the Word and confirmed the fact that their hearts are truly without sin. They confess how they could have lived thus far without having known about something so good like this.

Our Lord has given His flesh and blood for you and me, as well as for people of the world, and thus, our hearts become refreshed whenever we eat and drink this food and drink. Because we are without sin, it is the case that we are able to move around honorably, thank God, and praise Him. I always thank the Lord, and because of Him, I am happy. Even though I am so weak, I can always thank the Lord only because the Lord has saved people like me by the gospel of the water and the Spirit. I am thankful for having taken away the judgment by saving people like me with the water and the Spirit. That is why the Apostle Paul had said, *"Rejoice always, pray without ceasing, in everything give thanks; for this is the will of God in Christ Jesus for you" (1 Thessalonians 5:16-18).* Dear fellow believers, we are able to be thankful for all things because our Lord has given us His flesh and blood. Dear fellow believers, is this so, or is it not? Yes, it is.

The flesh of Jesus is His receiving of the baptism, and the blood of Jesus is His receiving of the judgment. Because life lies in the blood, on behalf of those of us who were suppose to receive the curse and die, Jesus received the judgment and the curse at the Cross by having taken on all our sins completely. He has made us not to be judged any more. There is a gospel song in our children's hymn book. " ♪ There is no judgment for me. ♫ The blood of the Lord covers all my sins. ♫ For Jesus has died for me, there is no judgment for me. ♪ " Dear fellow believers, is there any judgment reserved for you? No, there isn't. I can stand before you and give sermons because I have no sin and I have no judgment set aside for me. If I had judgment set aside for me, how would I even be able to raise my face?

Dear fellow believers, please, look up to the Lord and believe in the works that the Lord has done. Please, take in the flesh and the blood of the Lord. That is precisely what having faith is, that is precisely to believe in the Lord, that is precisely what salvation is, and that is precisely what everlasting life is. Praise our Lord! ⊠

You Must Preach the Flesh and the Blood of Jesus to Your Family Members

< John 6:51-56 >

"'I am the living bread which came down from heaven. If anyone eats of this bread, he will live forever; and the bread that I shall give is My flesh, which I shall give for the life of the world.' The Jews therefore quarreled among themselves, saying, 'How can this Man give us His flesh to eat?' Then Jesus said to them, 'Most assuredly, I say to you, unless you eat the flesh of the Son of Man and drink His blood, you have no life in you. Whoever eats My flesh and drinks My blood has eternal life, and I will raise him up at the last day. For My flesh is food indeed, and My blood is drink indeed. He who eats My flesh and drinks My blood abides in Me, and I in him.'"

Our Lord gave eternal life to us who are the righteous. It means that He has given us the everlasting life of living forever under His love and blessing by making us His children. People must eat the gospel of everlasting life, which can have them live forever. Even though we have received such great blessings and are frequently fed on spiritual food, our family members still remain outside His salvation. Therefore, we must feed our family members and brothers and sisters all over the world who have been born again the food of everlasting life, and have them live. To do so, we must eat the food of everlasting life first.

What is the food of everlasting life? Our Lord said that the food of life is none other than the flesh and the blood of Jesus. What must we feed your family members and souls all over the world? We must feed them on the faith of believing in Jesus' flesh and Jesus' blood. If you truly want to save your family as well as souls all over the world from death, the first thing that you must do is for you to feed them on the food of everlasting life that never thirsts. It is because, in having done so, they would also gain salvation from their sins, and everlasting life.

Everyone must eat Jesus' flesh and drink His blood to gain everlasting life. Jesus said, *"The bread that I shall give is My flesh, which I shall give for the life of the world" (John 6:51)*. Jesus said that His flesh is the food of everlasting life. And, that is why we eat the flesh of Jesus as frequently as we can. Those all over the world who haven't been born again can receive salvation from sins and live eternally only if we feed them also the flesh and blood of Jesus. It is the case that you must give your loved ones the gospel of the water and the Spirit, that is, the flesh and blood of Jesus so that they can enjoy the everlasting life, the most priceless gift of God. We should forever engrave in our hearts the word of God, *"Unless you eat the flesh of the Son of Man and drink His blood, you have no life in you" (John 6:53)*.

What is the Food of Life?

The Lord said, *"Whoever eats My flesh and drinks My blood has eternal life" (John 6:54)*. Then, how can you eat the flesh of our Lord? As you well know, Jesus took on all the sins of us people by coming to the Jordan River and receiving the baptism on His body. And believing in this fact is what eating the flesh of Jesus is. Also, to drink the blood of Jesus means to believe in the fact that Jesus has saved us from the judgment for sins by bearing all our sins and dying nailed to the Cross. These are what is meant by eating the flesh and blood of Jesus.

We must eat Jesus' flesh and blood by faith. We shouldn't eat this Truth by ourselves, but rather, we must ceaselessly try hard to feed our family members on the flesh and blood of Jesus. Taking a step further, we must also spread the gospel of the water and the Spirit, by which one can gain everlasting life, to fellow people all over the world.

Rather than Bible knowledge, we must teach Christians all over the world to eat the flesh and blood of Jesus by faith. What they desperately need isn't Bible knowledge. To them, we must first of all preach to them the Word by which they would receive salvation from sins. We must always tell them, "When Jesus received the baptism from John the Baptist, not only did He take on all my sins, but also all your sins. Jesus took on all the sins of everyone in this world by receiving the baptism." It is because that is precisely the faith by which souls all over the world can live eternally, without having to die. "My flesh is food indeed, and it is the food of life for the world." The food of everlasting life is the flesh of Jesus. We must speak of this at all times. Although we cannot do many things, we can spread the gospel of the water and the Spirit to all people of the world. If we were to distribute paper books and electronic books through the Internet everyday, everyone in the world would soon come to know the Truth all.

Do you know that Jesus took on all your sins at the Jordan River? For us to believe in the fact that Jesus took on all the sins of the world by His baptism is precisely to eat the flesh of Jesus by faith. That is why we are delivering this Truth to people everyday while having faith in the fact that Jesus took on all the sins of the world by receiving the baptism from John the Baptist at the Jordan River.

Jesus said, *"I am the living bread which came down from heaven. If anyone eats of this bread, he will live forever" (John 6:51).* Whoever wants to gain everlasting life and to live in happiness forever without ever having to die, they must eat the bread of life which comes down from Heaven. That food of life is precisely the flesh and blood of Jesus. And this food means the gospel of the water and the Spirit. It is the case that anyone who believes in the gospel of the water and the Spirit gains new life.

There is no other true food of life except Jesus. Nothing of this world can become the food of everlasting life, no matter what. Even an anti-aging medicine that is widely known in this world cannot stop people from aging and dying. Even if it's a mountain ginseng, which has a great effect so as to make one wonder if it is the elixir of life that the first emperor of China, Quin Shi Huang (259 BC-210 BC), was looking for, it cannot prevent people from death. Tons of such an elixir cannot prevent you from going to death. However, if you eat the flesh and drink the blood of Jesus, you will never die.

Until the Lord comes, we must therefore feed people all over the world on this food of everlasting life by spreading our faith with allegiance. Even if people of the world do not understand what we are saying very well because of their ignorance of the Scriptures, all we have to do is to spread by faith the fact, "Jesus took on all the sins of human kind once and for by receiving the baptism from John the Baptist at the Jordan River." All we who believed prior to them have to do is to plant the saplings of the gospel of the water and the Spirit inside the thoughts and hearts of people throughout the world. If we were to preach the baptism and the blood of Jesus to people throughout the world, they would also be receiving the remission of sin by believing in the gospel Truth of the water and the Spirit. And, when we get to go before the Lord, we will be commended greatly.

You must know that the food to an everlasting life is the flesh and blood of Jesus and that the flesh and blood of Jesus is the gospel of the water and the Spirit. This truly is the Truth of Heaven and the gospel of secret to life. Jesus said to His disciples, *"Because it has been given to you to know the mysteries of the kingdom of heaven, but to them it has not been given" (Matthew 13:11).* The gospel of the water and the Spirit is the key that unlocks the Kingdom of Heaven. In this world, there can never be any other words that could send people to Heaven, except for these words. As it's been said that if we were to eat Jesus' flesh and blood by faith, we would go to the Kingdom of Heaven, everyone, regardless of who it is, must believe it.

A brother in our church said that, after having received the remission of sins, he spoke about the gospel of the water and the Spirit to his mother whenever there was an opportunity. Having heard the false gospels for a long time, his mother did not believe at first, getting annoyed, refusing, and so on. But, she had heard the genuine gospel so many times that she is now said to have received the remission of sin by having accepted the gospel of the water and the Spirit in her heart purely as it is. And so, when she came to our church for the first time, I asked the man's mother to perhaps give out the testimony of her salvation. And, she said clearly, "I am now without sin because Jesus took on all my sins when He had received the baptism, died on the Cross for me, and resurrected."

The only way for us to receive the remission of sin and live eternally is to eat and drink Jesus' flesh and blood. For people, only Jesus' flesh and blood is the food of everlasting life, and there can be nothing else. This gospel of the water and the Spirit is not just a doctrine of a specific denomination. Jesus' flesh and blood is the bread of life that enables us the people to live forever by eating them. Thus, to eat and drink the flesh and blood of Jesus is to gain everlasting life, but if one were to not eat and drink the flesh and blood of Jesus, there can be no life inside him. We must realize and remember in our hearts the fact that those who do not eat and drink the flesh and blood of Jesus have no life, but those who eat and drink the flesh and blood of Jesus have an everlasting life; we must know that those who eat the flesh of Jesus and drink the blood of Jesus will never die and will come back to life even if they should die.

Our Lord said to us clearly: *"Your fathers ate the manna in the wilderness, and are dead. This is the bread which comes down from Heaven, that one may eat of it and not die" (John 6:49-50)*. He said that if we eat and drink the flesh and blood of our Lord, we will not die and we will live forever having gained everlasting life. By faith, we must therefore eat the flesh and blood of Jesus, which is the bread of everlasting life that comes down from Heaven. Have you become someone who has eaten the flesh and blood of Jesus by believing in the gospel of the water and the Spirit? If so, there is inside you the Holy Spirit that gives you new life.

Jesus said that His blood is drink indeed, but do you know why He said so? A drink refreshes people's body. As such, Jesus cleansed all our sins by shedding blood after having received the baptism from John the Baptist. Put differently, He has vicariously received the judgment for all our sins by shedding blood on the Cross. Thus, the thirst in our hearts was quenched, and our hearts became delighted. That is why the Bible said, *"Repent therefore and be converted, that your sins may be blotted out, so that times of refreshing may come from the presence of the Lord" (Acts 3:19).* Because Jesus took on all our sins by the baptism, His blood is the true drink of faith, which has paid back all our sins.

There is no Life If One Does Not Eat and Drink Jesus' Flesh and Blood

However, isn't there someone among you who believes that only the blood of the Cross of Jesus is essential to your salvation? Those among you who believe only in Jesus' blood can never be cleansed of their sins. One who does not believe in the gospel of the water and the Spirit cannot gain everlasting life, but rather only the eternal punishment in hell awaits the person. You must eat the flesh and blood of Jesus by faith. Only then, can you gain true cleansing of sins and everlasting life.

Do you have the faith of believing in the passage, *"Unless you eat the flesh of the Son of Man and drink His blood, you have no life in you. Whoever eats My flesh and drinks My blood has eternal life, and I will raise him up at the last day" (John 6:53-54),* as it is? God gave people the food of everlasting life by the gospel Truth of the water and the Spirit, and that is none other than the flesh and blood of Jesus, the Son of God. By giving us Jesus' flesh and blood, God gave those who eat and drink by faith the everlasting life, which allows them to live eternally.

The flesh and blood of Jesus is our life. This flesh and blood of Jesus is the true food sent down from Heaven to the faithful. Yet, on this earth, there are many people who do not believe in the gospel Truth of the water and the Spirit. On this earth, there are many people who believe only in Jesus' blood of the Cross. That is a faith that leads people to destruction. We have received salvation from sin by the faith of believing in the flesh and blood of Jesus. And, we will enter the everlasting Kingdom in the future and live there eternally.

Though we are those who have gained everlasting life, there isn't that much time left for us to live in this world. Please do not think as though you would live on this earth for tens of thousands of years or million and billions of years. One cannot live that long. We are just vagabonds, living in this world for just a short while. I hope for you to realize that there isn't that much time left for you live in this world. Someone can perhaps say that this is something only the eschatologists would say. But, that is not the case. Now, let's figure out the remaining days of our lives. The Bible says, *"The days of our lives are seventy years; and if by reason of strength they are eighty years, yet their boast is only labor and sorrow; for it is soon cut off, and we fly away" (Psalm 90:10)*. If you are 30, and perhaps you will live until 80, than all the remaining months in your life will merely be 600 months. That's all. If you are 50 now, it will be 420 months. How fast does a month go by?

Dear fellow believers, there isn't that much time left in your personal lifespan. Because there isn't that much time left in my life, even I continue to live contemplating what is the most valuable way to live. I think there is 10 years left in my lifespan, at best. This is the conclusion that I have come to reach after having calculated by myself regardless of whether or not Jesus would come within that time frame. Then, do people who are younger than me live a bit longer? Even younger people cannot be certain that they would live that long. Even though people take the vow, "let us live together until our hairs turn gray," before the officiator in a marriage ceremony, there are many people who die before then. Even from looking at things happening in this world, time isn't left that long for this world.

Also, the time is near when Jesus will be coming down to this world. Just wait it see if it will really happen so. Currently, the world is moving fast, knowledge is swift, transportation is quick, people's hearts are hasty, and sins have become flourishing. It's becoming just like the state God spoke of regarding the end of this world. But, several years ago, even when there was nothing wrong in this world, I have already spoken plentifully about the imminent end of the world as I lectured on the Scripture passages in the Revelations.

Yet, even if the end should come tomorrow, we must do the job at work places, and continue to do God's work. We must not easily be swayed by the fact that the end of this world is coming. Instead, because the end is coming, we must exert more and more effort into the precious work of sharing the food of everlasting life, which is the flesh and blood of Jesus, during this remaining short period. Because the world doesn't have much time left, we must do this work more diligently and with a clearer mind, and we must only do this work. Some people tend to think let us live as things would go since there isn't much time, but that is not the case. If there is a great amount of time left, one could say that we should live with some time to spare. Because the day is soon coming when we can no longer spread the gospel due to the coming of tribulations, we must keep our minds sharp, strengthen our hearts much more with faith, and invest the days into the work of sharing the food of everlasting life.

Dear fellow believers, do you think there is so much time left for this world? Only when natural disasters and world-wide wars occur and only when orders to mark the right hand or the forehead with a sign come out from the world government, will you believe, saying, "Alas, what the pastor at our church said was right." Dear fellow believers, it would be too late by then. If you don't believe now, you won't be able to believe then. Rather, when that time comes, hearts would become more persistently stubborn, and thus, having faith would not even be possible. Such a person is someone who would measure things happening around, and receive "the mark of the beast" in the end. Faith is something that has to be prepared before the time comes.

There isn't much time left until our lives and this earth come to an end. For this reason, we must put our efforts into sharing this flesh and blood of Jesus, which is the food of everlasting life. Speak to your family repeatedly about the gospel of the water and the Spirit. And, unite with the church of God, which is spreading the gospel throughout the world. With a united faith, we must spread the flesh and blood of Jesus. We must shout out far and wide that Jesus took on all your sins with His baptism and that Jesus died on the Cross for you.

Really, during the short period of time left while we get to live in this world, we must live for the gospel of the water and the Spirit. For the food of everlasting life is the flesh and blood of Jesus, while we are living in this world with what little time is left, shouldn't we be His workers who share the food of everlasting life by giving people Jesus' flesh and blood? We shouldn't be thinking only about what could we do so that our body would be well off and what could we do to eat well. And, instead of thinking as if we would live on this earth forever, during our truly little remaining lifetime, we must become someone who shares the food of life, that is, the flesh and blood of Jesus. We who have been born again must do so.

If we were to live for our flesh haphazardly due to the fact that we do not have sins, that would be something very evil. If we who have been born again by believing in the gospel of the water and the Spirit were to live carefree as we wish, not doing the work of spreading the flesh and blood of Jesus, after having received the remission of sins, we would fall into sin and become the most evil people in the world. The Lord said, *"Therefore, to him who knows to do good and does not do it, to him it is sin" (James 4:17),* and also said, *"And that servant who knew his master's will, and did not prepare himself or do according to his will, shall be beaten with many stripes" (Luke 12:47).*

On this earth, there aren't that many people who know the fact that the food of life is the flesh and blood of Jesus. There are even fewer people who believe this. Truly, we do not know how we have come to eat the flesh and blood of Jesus by faith, but it is something to be thankful for before God. Also, before God, we are thankful for having been given the faith that allows us to reside in God by having the flesh and blood of Jesus. Thus, how could we not spread this Truth?

Dear fellow believers, we must believe in the fact that truly, the flesh and blood of Jesus is the food of everlasting life. And, we must give out this food to all people. Until the day when our life ends, we must live for this work. We must live for this work instead of some other works.

Who knows this Word of secret? Who knows that the Word of the flesh and blood of Jesus is the gospel of everlasting life? Other than those who have been born of water and the Spirit (John 3:5), no one knows. It isn't an exaggeration to say that all the Christians throughout the entire world do not know. As Christians carry out the communion service, how do they view the flesh of Jesus while they take a piece of bread? They see it as just a ceremony. In some churches, they bring in bread and claim the doctrine of transubstantiation, which says that the moment when someone eats that bread by faith, it would be as though the person has eaten the flesh of Jesus. It is saying that this bread turns into Jesus' flesh inside the body. This is what transubstantiation is. But, the command, "Eat the flesh of Jesus," as it is said in the Bible, does not mean that.

The faith of eating the flesh of Jesus means that I believe in the fact that Jesus took on all my sins with His flesh when He received the baptism, and to drink the blood of Jesus means that I believe in the fact that the flesh of Jesus, who had taken on our sins, received the judgment for sins by being nailed to the Cross on our behalf and shedding His blood. The faith of believing in the fact that Jesus received the baptism for all my sins and received the judgment vicariously on the Cross for the world is the faith of eating and drinking the flesh and blood of Jesus.

In the Bible, the Word of God, which we believe, there is the gospel of the water and the Spirit. In any other document anywhere on this earth, there isn't such a teaching, which says that one would receive everlasting life if the person were to eat and drink the flesh and blood of Jesus. It is only in the word of God. The Bible clearly states, "We will receive the everlasting life if we believe in the fact that Jesus took on all our sins when He had received the baptism of John the Baptist and saved us from sins with His flesh and blood by having received the judgment vicariously on our behalf." By believing in this, we become children of God.

Thus, we ate the flesh and blood of Jesus by faith. You and I have eaten the food of everlasting life by believing in the gospel of the water and the Spirit. As the ones who have eaten this food of life first, we must do the work of handing out this flesh and blood of Jesus to many people. What this means is the responsibility to carry out such a work lies within us, who are born again by the gospel of the water and the Spirit. I hope for you to believe in the fact that the food of everlasting life lies in Jesus' flesh and blood. To your family members and souls all over the world, whether they believe it or not, all we have to do is to convey the Truth by saying, "Jesus took on all your sins by having received the baptism, and He vicariously received the judgment for your sins by dying on the Cross."

True food of everlasting life lies in Jesus' flesh and blood: It isn't in the flesh of Jesus alone, and it isn't in the blood of Jesus alone. We must eat and drink both the flesh and blood of Jesus by faith. You have to believe in the Truth that Jesus took over the sins of the world by having received the baptism from John the Baptist and He received the judgment for my sins vicariously by being crucified. When people believe in both the baptism of Jesus and the blood of the Cross, they say they feel refreshed. It is because Jesus took on all our sins by the baptism and vicariously received the judgment for them at the Cross. It is so because Jesus' blood of the Cross is for payment of the judgment of our sins.

However, if one were to believe only in the blood of the Cross without eating the flesh of Jesus, there will always be sin inside a person's heart. Having such faith is only trying to feel as though one has received the cleansing of sin emotionally without having cleansed one's sins perfectly by the Word of

Truth in Jesus' baptism. The baptism Jesus received from John
the Baptist isn't something that Jesus received because He was
humble, and neither is it just some ceremony. The important
thing is to know why Jesus had received the baptism. The most
important thing is to have faith with the understanding that
one's own sins were transferred over to Jesus when He had
received the baptism.

Those Who Haven't Been Born Again Do Not Know What "the Flesh of Jesus" Means

Christians perform two types of baptism: baptism by
immersion and baptism by effusion. Those who have received
this baptism by immersion ignore those who have received the
baptism by effusion, and those who have received the baptism
by effusion (sprinkling or pouring), say that a person doesn't
always have to receive the baptism by immersion in water.
Thus, they start arguing over these issues. Like this, people
discuss only the ceremonial aspects of baptism, arguing which
type of baptism is right. But, it just ends there.

While I was resting my mind this afternoon, I watched a
Christian TV-channel, and a certain pastor came on and started
a sermon on the baptism of Jesus. I listened a little to what
exactly he was trying to say, but it was hilarious. He was just
gibbering along without being able to address the issue
according to the Scripture. What he was delivering was merely
a mosaic of all the notions that theologians had said, but he had
absolutely no knowledge of the true meaning of baptism.

In contrast, I hope for you to believe that the flesh and
blood of Jesus is the food of everlasting life. I hope for you to
realize this Truth and for you to believe it. Whoever it may be,

if a person does not eat and drink the flesh and blood of Jesus, there is not life inside. Dear fellow believers, you may not know much about the Bible, but you must at least believe the fact that your sins were transferred over to the flesh of Jesus when He received the baptism. That is what eating the flesh of Jesus is. Because Jesus bore our sins by receiving the baptism, the faith of believing in the fact that He had vicariously received the judgment on our behalf on the Cross is, in turn, exactly the same as drinking the blood of Jesus. By having faith in Jesus' receiving of the baptism and in His shedding of the blood on the Cross, we must eat the flesh and blood of the Lord.

Let us read the Gospel of John chapter 6 verse 53. *"Then Jesus said to them, 'Most assuredly, I say to you, unless you eat the flesh of the Son of Man and drink His blood, you have no life in you.'"* This is not a doctrine of our denomination. Clearly, this is of the Word of the Lord. The sad fact is that, despite all of this, people are not trying to understand properly and believe this passage.

There are many people who drank only the blood of Jesus. They say, "People who drank the blood of Jesus do not have sin." And then, they act as though refreshed, saying that they have nothing for which to be judged because Jesus bore all their sins and vicariously received the judgment on the Cross and that they have received salvation. But inside them, there is no life. I ask them in return, "If so, what does it mean by 'eat the flesh of Jesus,' as it is said here?" And, they get troubled and confused. They stop me from asking more questions by saying that it is a characteristic of heresies to inquire on the Bible in every detail.

As we talk with them, it is possible to see vividly that there is no Holy Spirit inside their hearts. There are many people whose heart does not have the Holy Spirit despite having faith in Jesus. Though they believe that Jesus is the Son of God, that He is God, that He atoned for all their sins by dying on the Cross, that He resurrected, that He ascended to Heaven, and that He will come again, the fact is that there is no life inside of them. The fact that there is no life inside of them means that there is no Spirit inside of them. It is said, *"Now if anyone does not have the Spirit of Christ, he is not His" (Romans 8:9).* If the Spirit of Christ is not in them, then they are those who have been abandoned by God.

Our Lord said, *"Again, the kingdom of heaven is like a dragnet that was cast into the sea and gathered some of every kind, which, when it was full, they drew to shore; and they sat down and gathered the good into vessels, but threw the bad away" (Matthew 13:47-48).* A fisherman casts fishing net into the sea, and after some time, when he raises the fishing net, fish caught in the net come up. After that, he spreads the net wide on the boat deck and starts to separate the fish caught in the net one by one. At the same time, he places the edible fish into a container, while throwing away the inedible fish on the deck, like sticklebacks. Because if he were to put the inedible fish back into the waters, they would get caught again, he chucks them on the ship's floor and leaves them to die. When it dies, he throws them back to sea so that they become food for other fish.

Just as the fisherman keeps the good fish while throwing away the bad ones, it isn't the case that you will go to Heaven just because you believe in Jesus. Only those who ate and drank the flesh and blood of Jesus get to enter the everlasting life of Heaven. When Jesus sees our faith, He knows it as is at once. The Holy Spirit is inside those who have eaten and drunk Jesus' flesh and blood. He places people who have the Holy

Spirit into Heaven. But, people who drank the blood of Jesus only, despite the fact that they do have believed in Jesus, are thrown into hell for they are like the unusable fish. At that moment, it is useless no matter how much one begs the Lord, crying out, "Dear Lord. Oh, Lord." The Lord will say to such a person, "You cannot be in Heaven," and throw away the person in hell. Dear fellow believers, those who do not have life get thrown away. People who believe only in the blood of Jesus are those who do not have the Holy Spirit.

Those who only drank the blood of Jesus cannot but think about only their sins whenever they come before the Lord. "Oh, no. I committed this sort of sin, again. By offering a prayer of repentance this morning, I washed away the sins clean, yet I commit the same sin, again." Because the sins that they commit continue to come across their minds, they are resorting to offering the prayers of repentance. However, those who have received the remission of sin by truly being born again of water and the Spirit do not get distressed due to sins because they are able to and did send over sins quickly by faith, even if they do commit sins. They confess their faith saying, "Jesus has already taken over all my sins by receiving the baptism at Jordan River 3 years prior to getting crucified. Just as Jesus said, *'Permit it to be so now, for thus it is fitting for us to fulfill all righteousness' (Matthew 3:15),* by a way of receiving the baptism, Jesus took on all the sins of the world completely, and saved me from sins. Soon after, He saved me from the judgment for my sins by going to Cross, shedding blood, and vicariously dying." Like this, a person who can easily associate with this Truth of salvation and believe in this Truth is someone who has received true salvation.

Do you come across the desire to chase after the trends of the world? Despite having become the righteous without sin by believing in the gospel of the water and the Spirit, instead of living for the gospel, do you have the desire to be the pioneer who leads the new trend of fashion of the world? It is because you haven't realized that we are the ones who are true forerunners in the world. Because we believed in the flesh and blood of Jesus like so, we received the salvation and became the ones that have everlasting life. That is why we must lead a spiritual life. We must live for the gospel of the water and the Spirit and for our Lord who has saved us. If we were to benefit others by spreading the gospel of the water and the Spirit and also, if we were to raise up a wave of the Truth all over the world, then that is the life of leading the most priceless fashion.

People who are born again of water and the Spirit must not follow the evils of this world. God hates you who are born-again to be swept by sinful cultures of the world. The righteous should create a new trend, instead of following the trend of the world. It is necessary for the righteous to create a new trend. Dear fellow believers, when everyone else is in hip-hop fashion, try putting on a suite. Would you be most noticeable? When everyone is muddled up in same fashion and in uniformity without any individual character, if someone who looks different appears, eyes will be drawn on the person, and people will be chasing after that. When everyone else is living like crazy, try living uprightly. That person would look most wonderful. Such a person is the true trend leader. I hope for you to know that to do things like others do is being absent of personal character.

People who have received the remission of sins mustn't follow the world. They should lead the world. The righteous must steer this world. When I see dramas written by TV drama writers, they seem just too puerile. It is so puerile that I wonder how such a story could be so popular. So, I wonder if I should also do some writing. Dear fellow believers, do you think I can write if I want to or not? If I write, I write a masterpiece. But, I chose not to write. I choose not to write dramas because I won't have the time for spreading the gospel if I were to do so. I choose not to do so not because I don't have the skills but because there is no need to do so.

Truly, those of us who are born again must live this wonderful life of sharing the food of everlasting life, the flesh and blood of Jesus. No matter how deeply we indulge ourselves in the pleasures of the world, there is no fun. It is said, *"But she who lives in pleasure is dead while she lives" (1 Timothy 5:6).* You should live for the everlasting life instead of chasing after pleasures of the world. You and I should meet our Lord after having done this wonderful work of giving eternal life to others and having them gain everlasting life.

Do you believe that the food of life is the flesh and blood of Jesus? If you do, you are doing very well. But, the fact is that most Christians still do not know it, even though 2,000 years have passed since the realization of this Word of the Truth. As for the people who do not know this Word of secret even now, please be awakened and take the food of everlasting life by believing in the gospel of the water and the Spirit and then eating and drinking the flesh and blood of Jesus. If a person dies without having consumed the food of life, then it would mean hell, without exception. It would mean getting separated from God.

On the last day, our Lord will bring the bodies of those who have been born again by the gospel of the water and the Spirit back to life, and He will give them the everlasting life. If you don't want to be someone who had been discarded in that moment by the Lord, you should eat the food of everlasting life, which is the flesh and blood of Jesus, more so than ever. It doesn't end with you eating alone, but rather, we must feed our family members, people around us, and also all the people throughout this world, on the food of everlasting life. ⊠

For What Should We Live?

< John 6:63-69 >
"'It is the Spirit who gives life; the flesh profits nothing. The words that I speak to you are spirit, and they are life. But there are some of you who do not believe.' For Jesus knew from the beginning who they were who did not believe, and who would betray Him. And He said, 'Therefore I have said to you that no one can come to Me unless it has been granted to him by My Father.' From that time many of His disciples went back and walked with Him no more. Then Jesus said to the twelve, 'Do you also want to go away?' But Simon Peter answered Him, 'Lord, to whom shall we go? You have the words of eternal life. Also we have come to believe and know that You are the Christ, the Son of the living God.'"

For what are you and I now living? We are now working not for something that will perish away, but for something everlasting that will never perish. In other words, we are laboring to save the lost souls all over the world, and we are living to revive people's hearts. We are doing what is only proper.

Are you now really living for what is everlasting? Of 24 hours in a day, how many hours are we living for the imperishable? It may very well be the case that we are in fact working a few hours for what is everlasting. Far from it, aren't we actually spending more hours for what will perish away? Except for what we do for the purpose of living for the imperishable, everything else is of the flesh. If you are laboring hard for your own flesh that will rot away, then you are indeed wasting your time.

Of course, we sometimes seek what may seem to be of the flesh, as we need them to support the gospel ministry. But if it's needed for the gospel, then nothing is of the flesh. Whatever profits the gospel is what is truly spiritual. My fellow believers, unless we live for the gospel, we cannot call ourselves the disciples of Jesus. If we are indeed Jesus' disciples who believe in the righteous acts that the Lord had done on this earth, then we must now know clearly how we should lead our lives. Even though we are in a body of corruption, we can still carry out incorruptible work with this corruptible body.

I often contemplate how much of my life is really devoted to what is everlasting, to what will never perish. So out of 24 hours a day, when I examine myself to see how many hours I spend for the imperishable work, and how many hours I spend for the perishable work, I come to discover that I am not spending that many hours for the work that will not perish. A certain minister from our Mission counted how many hours he was working for the gospel, setting aside the time spent in bed, having meals, using the bathroom, and so forth, and he found out that there were actually very few hours. The hours that people spend to live for the imperishable are very few indeed. Even if we were to live the whole day for what will not perish, it would still not be enough. Even if we were to devote all our lives, we would still not spend enough hours to live for the imperishable. In other words, very few hours are actually spent to live for what is everlasting.

Are You Spreading the Gospel of the Water and the Spirit?

Our Lord says that it is the Spirit that gives life. We need to ponder here how many souls we are really saving. Is there any soul that has received the remission of his sins because of you, as you preached the gospel of the water and the Spirit to him? Only this work that saves souls can be described as an everlasting and spiritual work. The Lord is saying that spreading the gospel of the water and the Spirit to others, so that they may also receive the remission of sin, is the only everlasting work that does not perish.

In John 6:51, the Lord said, *"I am the living bread which came down from heaven. If anyone eats of this bread, he will live forever."* He then went on to say: *"Most assuredly, I say to you, unless you eat the flesh of the Son of Man and drink His blood, you have no life in you. Whoever eats My flesh and drinks My blood has eternal life, and I will raise him up at the last day. For My flesh is food indeed, and My blood is drink indeed. He who eats My flesh and drinks My blood abides in Me, and I in him. As the living Father sent Me, and I live because of the Father, so he who feeds on Me will live because of Me. This is the bread which came down from heaven—not as your fathers ate the manna, and are dead. He who eats this bread will live forever"* (John 6:53-58).

Like this, John chapter six speaks about how the Lord came as the bread of life and has given us eternal life. In other words, this chapter explains that whoever eats the flesh of Jesus and drinks His blood will receive everlasting life. Those of us who first knew this Truth and believed in it prior to others must spread this gospel of salvation to everyone else. Only then do we actually carry out the everlasting work. If we spread the things of our own, they will all perish away. Only when we preach what the Lord has done for us—that is, His flesh and blood—do we labor for what will not perish forever, doing the work that saves souls. To spread what the Lord has done for us is to labor for the food that does not perish.

Just because we spread our knowledge systematically, this does not necessarily mean that souls are saved. Only when we preach the Lord does the work of salvation arise. Therefore, doing only what the Lord has asked us to do is carrying out His everlasting work. In other words, spreading our own message means nothing.

When the Lord said, *"I am the living bread which came down from heaven. If anyone eats of this bread, he will live forever; and the bread that I shall give is My flesh, which I shall give for the life of the world,"* the Jews gathered around Him could not understand this, and so they murmured among themselves, saying, "How can this Man give us His flesh to eat?" During the age of the Early Church also, Christians were profoundly misunderstood by the unbelievers because of this passage. At that time, as Christians were persecuted, they hid in underground caverns called the Catacombs to worship God, and the people who first came to Church were shocked to hear when a preacher said in his sermon, "Whoever eats the flesh of the Lord and drinks His blood will receive everlasting life." Some of them misunderstood this and thought, "Are these people cannibals? How can they devour each other, no matter how starved they may be?" As such misunderstandings were magnified, countless Christians were put to death during the Early Church period.

The Catholic Church performs Holy Communion at every Mass. Its followers eat the wafer distributed by the priest. They believe that when a priest blesses the wafer, this piece of bread actually turns into the body of Jesus. They also believe that when the priest prays over the cup of wine, the wine is actually transformed into the blood of Jesus. This doctrine is called "Transubstantiation." So Catholics believe that they can receive everlasting life if they participate in Holy Communion to eat the wafer and drink the wine, and this is how they practice their religion.

This, however, is completely unfounded. To believe that Jesus came to this earth incarnated in the flesh, shouldered our sins by being baptized, died on the Cross, and has thereby saved us from all our sins—this is to really eat the flesh of Jesus and drink His blood. Jesus has saved us from our sins through the gospel of the water and the Spirit, and He has given us God's life. For us to accept the God-given gospel of the water and the Spirit into our hearts is to eat the flesh of Jesus and drink His blood. None other than this gospel is the very bread that saves our souls.

Let Us Examine Ourselves to See How Much of Our Present Lives We Are Indeed Living for the Lord

Why do you live in this world? Are you living only for material prosperity? No, you are not. It is to work to save other souls that we are living on this earth. The Bible says, *"Therefore, whether you eat or drink, or whatever you do, do all to the glory of God" (1 Corinthians 10:31)*. This passage means that we should live for the work that saves souls. In other words, rather than living on this earth for what will only perish away, we should live for the work that saves dead souls.

My fellow believers, what is it that makes us keep on

living? If your life is completely meaningless, then this can only mean that you are dong something wrong. You have to know why are you living, realizing exactly for what purpose you are carrying on with your life. Only then does your life have a meaning. You must set your mind, knowing that the purpose of your life is to obey the Word of God and carry out the work He has entrusted to you, and you must live by faith according to the will of God. There is nothing more meaningless and tiresome than working without any purpose, not knowing why you are doing what you are doing now.

For our sisters, are you living just to take care of your children so that they would grow up to be successful? But what happens if you live for such a purpose? After looking after your children all this time, you will only die, and your own children will also end up repeating after you, taking care of their children only to perish away like yourself. What is this? This is not the kind of life that is truly lived for what is everlasting. While you are still alive, you must first meet Jesus and receive the remission of your sins. And then you must labor to save other souls. You must charge toward the goal, to the everlasting work. If you don't know why you are now living—that is, if your life is purposeless—then you life is a completely worthless life.

Yet despite this, most people in this world do not know why they live. So many people fall into alcoholism or drug addictions, as their hearts are empty. Precisely because they do not know why they should live, they spend meaningless days on the treadmill going round and round endlessly until the day they die. The Bible says that such a purposeless life is like that of the beasts that perish (Psalm 49:20).

What about you then? Why do you live? Do you live just because you can still breathe and your heart is still beating?

You must have a clear direction in your life, as to why you live, and for what you should live. Our lives are different from that of a beast not just in how we eat, reproduce, and sleep. We don't live only to accumulate more wealth to live the good life, nor do we live just to take good care of our own children. If these were our purpose in life, just how hollow would our lives be? When we nurture our children to grow up to be successful, they all think that they grew up on their own. It's so empty and meaningless.

From the very moment you are born, your life is nothing more than a series of steps taken toward your own tomb. How futile is this? What hope do you have in such a life? Our Lord said, *"Do not labor for the food which perishes, but for the food which endures to everlasting life" (John 6:27).* In other word, He told us to labor for what is everlasting. He also said, *"It is the Spirit who gives life; the flesh profits nothing."* Our Lord came to this earth to save us and give us eternal life. And He told us to live for what lasts forever. He is saying to us, "You should also live like Me. Live for the gospel, proclaim My name, and carry out the work of the Father that enables everyone to receive the remission of sin. And after you have done all these things, come to Me."

As Jesus healed the sick and fed the hungry by performing the miracle of five loaves and two fish, tens of thousands of people gathered around Him immediately like a cloud and followed Him everywhere. Although they were following the Lord out of a carnal motivation, Jesus actually wanted to give them spiritual blessings. That is why Jesus said to them, *"My flesh is food indeed, and My blood is drink indeed,"* telling them that they had to receive everlasting life by believing in His work. He also said, *"It is the Spirit who gives life; the flesh profits nothing,"* but when the people heard His Word, they all went away. Even many of His disciples left Him then, as it is written, *"From that time many of His disciples went back and walked with Him no more" (John 6:66).*

In other words, although countless people had received the food of the flesh and were healed from their illnesses while following Jesus around, with His last few Words, Jesus threw cold water on their hearts, who were seeking only the things of the flesh. He said to them, "It is the Spirit who gives life; the flesh profits nothing. I did not come to this earth just to give you bread. I will not give you bread again in the days to come. My desire is to save your souls and give you everlasting life; I am not working just to fill your bellies." When the people heard this, they left Jesus, thinking, "Well, I guess that's it; I won't get any more benefit from Him again."

Among today's Christians also, there are many who believe in Jesus only to prosper in their flesh. In other words, many Christians believe in Jesus hoping that their family would be in harmony, their spouses would succeed, and their children would go to a good college—in short, they believe in Jesus only to prosper on this earth materially. However, Jesus came to this earth to save people's spirits, not to bring prosperity to their flesh. Right now, countless Christians are completely disoriented in their belief.

It is to blot out people's sins that Jesus came to this earth. He came to revive people's hearts that were bound in sin. Therefore, if you believe in Jesus just to satisfy your worldly desires, you are committing a grave sin now. It's a serious sin to misbelieve in Jesus (John 16:9). So, if you believe in Jesus just to prosper on this earth, then you should pack your everything now and leave Jesus right away. You would be better off to just live out in the world industriously and diligently. If you live like this all your life, you will then at least be able to buy a house to put a roof over your head and save enough money to last to your retirement.

Let's assume here that you make about $2,000 a month from your job. Even if you only spend $1,000 on living expenses and save the remaining $1,000 every month, to purchase a decent apartment in any metropolitan area, you would have to save for at least 30 years. Moreover, if you get sick or injured, then you will end up spending all the money that you had saved for several years. Even if you save for your entire lifetime, all that you will have to pass down to your children as an inheritance would be no more than a house and a car. After dying and leaving this inheritance to your children, what will you then have to show to God? You will have nothing to show to Him. Would you be able to say to the Lord, "Well, I made half a million dollars while on earth"? No, you won't have anything to show to Him.

The Lord said, *"For whoever gives you a cup of water to drink in My name, because you belong to Christ, assuredly, I say to you, he will by no means lose his reward" (Mark 9:41).* The Lord will remember how you labored for Him. Few people actually do the everlasting work that does not perish. Among the countless pastors in this world, it's rare to see anyone who leads even one person to be born again. The vast majority of them do nothing in their entire lifetime. Because these pastors themselves live for the perishable, and make others live for the things that perish as well, when they die, they all will be sent to hell to rot away forever. I admonish you to remember what our Lord said, that "it is the Spirit who gives life." He has entrusted us with this work that gives life.

Let us together turn to John 6:67-68: *"Then Jesus said to the twelve, 'Do you also want to go away?' But Simon Peter answered Him, 'Lord, to whom shall we go? You have the words of eternal life.'"* Jesus said to the disciples, "If you want to go also, then go. It is the Spirit who gives life. I've come to save everyone's soul, not to heal your illnesses." We can see here that Peter was born again. When Peter said, "Lord, to whom shall we go? You have the words of eternal life," he was confessing the following: "Your Word is the very Word of everlasting life, the Word that saves us. Your Word is none other the Word of God. It is according to Your Word that we have come to live forever, and it is according to Your Word that we have received the remission of our sins. Our happiness and eternal prosperity are all because of Your Word." That is why Peter confessed, *"We have come to believe and know that You are the Christ, the Son of the living God" (John 6:69).* What Peter believed in was the very Word of eternal life.

We must know and believe in what our Lord has told us, and we must live properly according to it. I ask you not to waste away your life in vain, living like a pig obsessed with what to eat and drink, only to die meaninglessly. Of course, before we were born again through the gospel of the water and the Spirit, we could not but live such a life. Why? Because we did not know what was the right life. However, now that we have become born-again people, we know that the Lord has placed us on this earth so that we would live for what is worthwhile, for what is everlasting, and for what saves people from their sins. This is why God has given us His Church, our families, and our jobs as well. I admonish you all to believe that God has permitted all our circumstances to make us carry out the work that saves souls. We must indeed have the right spiritual understanding of this issue and live by faith.

Are you still spiritually too immature that your mind is set on the things of the flesh? "How could I succeed and live well on this earth? Now that I have no sin, what should I do to live happily with my family?" Is this not what you want by any chance? I beseech you to realize that we are not on this earth for such perishable things. We exist on this earth for the work that saves other people's souls, for the work of testifying the Word of God, and for the work of spreading the gospel. You must grasp that it is to entrust us with the Great Commission called the spreading of the gospel that God has made us be born again and placed us on this earth. We must live for the work of saving people's souls. And we must know that the flesh profits nothing. Apart from the work of proclaiming the gospel of God, everything else will all disappear. It is our spirits that are saved by believing in Jesus. Even though our outward beings are perishing, our inner beings are renewed day by day (2 Corinthians 4:16). We must live for the work that saves other souls. We must live the rest of our lives for the treasure that will never disappear forever. Whether at work or at home, we must do everything for the work of saving other souls, and we must concentrate our everything on this purpose. Whatever we do, we must do the work of the Spirit. My fellow believers, whether you eat or drink, I want you to live for the work that the Lord has entrusted to us.

Why did God save you and me? If all that you want from your life of faith is to become rich in the flesh, then leave the Church quietly. If, on the other hand, you want to live all your life spreading the gospel and helped by God, then you should unite with the Church. If someone who has been born again by believing in the gospel of the water and the Spirit lives only for his own flesh, his heart will never find any satisfaction. Nor will God leave him alone to live like this. If any of God's beloved ones ends up falling in love with the world, God will infallibly make him return to Him by whatever means necessary.

My fellow believers, our Church is not a worldly church. If you want to live happily in the Lord, then you must live your entire lifetime carrying out the work that saves souls. If this is what you want, then you should stay with us, but if this is not what you want, then you should pack up all your belongings and just leave.

Of course, it's true that we sometimes find ourselves pursuing worldly things. However, our purpose must still be clear. Even though we cannot always live according to the will of God, let us at least know what the right goal is in our lives. The fact that we still have some insufficiencies is completely different from not knowing the purpose for our lives. It is to save souls that we are praying, preaching the gospel, and expanding the Kingdom of God. We have no other purpose than this. The just must believe only in the righteousness of God, and they must live for this righteousness alone. ✉

We Must Have the Proper Knowledge of the Truth

< John 6:60-71 >

"Therefore many of His disciples, when they heard this, said, 'This is a hard saying; who can understand it?' When Jesus knew in Himself that His disciples complained about this, He said to them, 'Does this offend you? What then if you should see the Son of Man ascend where He was before? It is the Spirit who gives life; the flesh profits nothing. The words that I speak to you are spirit, and they are life. But there are some of you who do not believe.' For Jesus knew from the beginning who they were who did not believe, and who would betray Him. And He said, 'Therefore I have said to you that no one can come to Me unless it has been granted to him by My Father.' From that time many of His disciples went back and walked with Him no more. Then Jesus said to the twelve, 'Do you also want to go away?' But Simon Peter answered Him, 'Lord, to whom shall we go? You have the words of eternal life. Also we have come to believe and know that You are the Christ, the Son of the living God.' Jesus answered them, 'Did I not choose you, the twelve, and one of you is a devil?' He spoke of Judas Iscariot, the son of Simon, for it was he who would betray Him, being one of the twelve."

What Are You Grumbling About?

John chapter six is difficult to understand for today's Christians also. So even pastors rarely give any sermons on this passage. They usually interpret the message of this chapter as the following: "That Jesus gave us His body means that He has saved us by being crucified to death." However, they make reference only to the blood of Jesus, not His flesh. The flesh of Jesus refers to the fact that Jesus took upon our sins once for all by being baptized and suffered on the Cross, and so unless one knows the gospel of the water and the Spirit, he cannot understand this passage.

That is why today's Christians who have not been born again simply cannot understand the passage from John chapter six, and as a result, their hearts end up leaving Jesus to pursue the things of the world. In other words, if people do not know the gospel of the water and the Spirit, then while they may at first come to believe in Jesus as their Savior, they will eventually leave Him. At the time when Jesus spoke this passage, there were over 5,000 people who had witnessed His miracles and were following Him, but when Jesus told them to eat His flesh and drink His blood, they all left Him, as they couldn't understand Him. Even worse, many of the very disciples who identified themselves as Jesus' followers also left Him, saying, "This is a hard saying; who can understand it?"

For Christians in this age also, that Jesus told them to eat His flesh and drink His blood is a very difficult truth. However, because the gospel of the water and the Spirit is the definitive Truth, if you know this gospel and believe in it, then it's very easy for you to have the flesh and blood of Jesus spiritually, and if you believe in this Word with your heart, then you will receive everlasting life.

Jesus Himself knew that His disciples were complaining about what He said, and so He told them, *"Does this offend you? What then if you should see the Son of Man ascend where He was before?"* Put differently, our Lord was saying, "Does this confuse you? You seek to follow Me, but do you now find yourselves unable to follow Me and want to leave Me, all because of what I said?" Then the Lord spoke even more clearly that He Himself was the bread that came down from Heaven, saying to them, "I am the bread that came down from Heaven, but what will you do when you see Me ascending back to Heaven? Will you then believe in Me? I've explained Myself to you, that I have come from Heaven. Should you see Me ascending to Heaven again, will you then stop complaining and believe in Me?" The Lord is the bread that came down from Heaven. He has fed us with this bread of life, and having ascended back to Heaven, He is now sitting at the right hand of the throne of God the Father; and He will return to this earth again to take us away.

Just as the people at that time could not understand what Jesus was saying, today's Christians are equally ignorant of the gospel of Truth, and therefore few actually understand what the Lord meant when He told us to eat His flesh. Even worse, few actually want to understand it. In other words, many Christians do not understand what the Bible is saying precisely because they believe in Jesus only as a matter of religion. If we believe in the Word of the Scriptures without even understanding it, then this can only mean that we don't believe in Jesus properly, but instead we have reified Him on our own and believe in this reified Jesus.

The Lord said, *"It is the Spirit who gives life; the flesh profits nothing. The words that I speak to you are spirit, and they are life" (John 6:63).* He made it clear here that it is the

Spirit who gives life. Put differently, this is what He was saying: "You must believe in what God has done for you with your heart. You shouldn't believe in Me motivated only to gain great benefits for your own flesh. What I am now saying to you is life. I have blotted out your sins and given you everlasting life, and on the last day, I will bring your body back to life also. If you receive new life by faith, then your body will also live again. The blessings that I give are the blessings of eternal life that belong to Heaven. And you can attain these blessings by believing in My Word. Therefore you should not believe in Me just to gain carnal benefits."

In other words, we should reach our salvation by believing in what the Lord has done for us with our hearts, rather than believing in Him just to fulfill our own carnal purposes, thinking that we would somehow be healed from our illnesses, succeed in our businesses, or become rich if we believe in Jesus. Today's Christianity is oriented toward healing physical illnesses, succeeding in the world, and moving up the ladder, but this is a very wrong orientation.

The Apostle John said to the people of God, *"Beloved, I pray that you may prosper in all things and be in health, just as your soul prospers" (3 John 1:2)*. Quoting this passage, many pastors preach that if one believes in Jesus, he would be blessed to be healthy and prosper in all things, as much as his soul would prosper. They call this teaching as the precept of "three-fold blessings in Christ." As people struggling in the world are told that they would become rich and successful if they believe in Jesus, they are only too happy to hear this, and so there is a pronounced trend in today's Christianity where people devote themselves to their own churches and revere their pastors even more, all to gain blessings and benefits for their own flesh.

In particularly, the followers of the Pentecostal Church in Korea are apt to believe that their children would be admitted to the college of their choice if they pray hard, but be rejected if they don't pray enough. They think that all their problems can be solved just by praying to Jesus, but this is a very mistaken notion. Of course, to the born-again, God does bestow His grace, and if they are sick, the Lord does open the way for them to be healed. However, for those who have not received the remission of their sins, just because they believe in Jesus, this does not mean that they would be blessed in their flesh. The notion that you can be healed from your illnesses and become rich if you believe in Jesus is a complete fraud.

I once watched on a Christian channel a world-renowned Korean revivalist named Rev. Cho holding a revival meeting. Quoting this passage from 3 John 1:2, he said from the pulpit, "Put your hands on where it hurts. God will heal your physical illnesses immediately." So the people gathered there prayed putting their hands on different parts of their own bodies, and then among the multitudes, some of them began to stand up testifying that they were healed from their sicknesses. The wave of joy swept across the whole congregation. The pastor then ended his sermon by concluding, "If you believe in Jesus, you will be healed from your illnesses, you will drive away demons, your poverty will go away, your family will be in harmony, and all such blessings will be yours." The congregation were so rejoiced to hear him that they said, "I've never heard such a great sermon!" However, this kind of faith is a superstitious faith, called Christian shamanism. It is extremely wrong to believe like this.

Are demons driven out just by believing in Jesus blindly? Those who have not been born again sometimes claim that they drove out demons by believing in Jesus, but it's actually nothing more than a show, with the demons pretending to have left. If you believe in Jesus, does your flesh prosper unconditionally? If you really believe in Jesus and follow Him, there is so much suffering that you must bear because of your faith. So how can anyone say that his flesh will prosper?

Jesus said, *"It is the Spirit who gives life; the flesh profits nothing."* Our Lord wants to give us new life by saving our souls from sin, not to bring prosperity to our flesh. He came to this earth to blot out our sins, to give us new life, to make us God's children, and to bestow us with the eternal blessings of the next world. We must grasp this clearly.

The core message of 3 John 1:2 is that above all, our souls must prosper. That is the key premise. What, then, does it mean by the prosperity of the soul? First of all, for our souls to prosper, we must believe in what the Lord has done for us with our hearts, and thereby receive the remission of our sins, attain eternal life, and become God's children. It is after then that we can see how the Lord helps us and blesses us in our everyday life. This is what the above passage means. Jesus never said that we can be healed from our illnesses and become rich just by believing in Him, without first receiving the remission of our sins.

The Lord made it clear here that pursuing the prosperity of our flesh profits nothing. If you want to believe in Jesus as your Savior, you must first receive the remission of your sins by believing in the gospel of the water and the Spirit. And once you receive the remission of your sins, it is fitting for you to carry out God's work. However, if you believe in Jesus just to prosper in your flesh, then your faith is completely wrong. Any pastor that teaches like this is utterly wrong. As countless Christians are deceived by false pastors, they sell their houses and offer the money to their churches, thinking that if they donate a house they would gain two houses. In a similar vein, they even take out loans to give their tithes, thinking that they would be blessed far more if they offer more tithes. They think, "My income is $1,000, and so I should offer $100 for my tithe, but I actually gave $1,000. So I am sure that God will reward me with $10,000." If you believe in Jesus based on such a calculation, then you are being defrauded spiritually. However, unfortunately enough, countless pastors are swindling their congregations out of their money with such a lie. To believe like this is nothing more than believing in Christianity only as one of the many religions of the world.

Of course, the born-again are able to offer even their entire possessions to the Lord if this is necessary. Our workers are actually living such a life. To serve the gospel, they only spend about one-tenth of their hard-earned money for themselves on what they absolutely need, and they offer the rest, 90 percent of their income, to the ministry of spreading the gospel. However, they don't do this just to receive more material blessings by offering more to God. Rather, they do this out of their thankful and willing hearts, because they want to serve more the precious gospel that the Lord has given to mankind.

Christians who have not been born again also dedicate themselves to their churches, but it is to achieve their own carnal desires. This is simply wrong. For instance, many of them think that if they carry on with their lives of faith and eventually become elders, God would somehow bless them. But this is all nothing more than a lie. Yet because they think that God would bless them and make them rich if they become elders, they try everything in their means to be appointed as elders, devoting themselves to their churches and being slavishly loyal to their pastors. They do this precisely because they have been deceived by the false teachings of their pastors. So, when you visit a prison, you will be surprised to see that quite a few inmates had actually been elders or pastors in worldly churches. What is the explanation for this? As they tried to serve their churches beyond their means, they couldn't help but resort to swindling.

The pastors who have not really been born again exalt those who are powerful and rich in this world onto elevated positions in their churches. When such people attend their churches, they appoint them to eldership in a short time. In doing so, they deceive the rest of the congregation into thinking, "That man's business is prospering so much, now that he has become an elder. I should become an elder as well." However, you should also remember the fact that there are many Christians who, ensnared by such a trap of deception, end up going broke or even imprisoned, despite becoming elders.

Our Lord said, *"The flesh profits nothing."* This Word is the Truth. The flesh is indeed profitless. If God brings prosperity to some aspects of your life after you are born again, it's all because this is related to the Lord's spiritual work. Do you think that even if you pray according to your own carnal desires for something that has nothing to do with the Lord's work, He would still answer such prayers? No, that is not the case. All those who believe so and preach so are completely foolish.

The Lord is the bread that came down from Heaven. He is the only Son of God the Father. He is God Himself who created the world in the beginning. So He knows everything. Would our Lord not have known that Judas would betray Him? Of course He knew this. As John 6:64 says, *"'But there are some of you who do not believe.' For Jesus knew from the beginning who they were who did not believe, and who would betray Him."* Jesus had twelve disciples following Him, but one of them did not believe in Him as the Savior. Our Lord knew beforehand that Judas would betray Him. He knew very well that for Him to be crucified and bear all the condemnation of sin, Judas had to betray Him.

With Judas in His mind, the Lord said, *"Therefore I have said to you that no one can come to Me unless it has been granted to him by My Father" (John 6:65).* This means that no one can believe in Jesus properly unless the Father leads him. In other words, not just anyone is allowed to recognize and believe in Jesus, who came by the water and the Spirit.

The Lord said, *"Blessed are the poor in spirit, For theirs is the kingdom of heaven" (Matthew 5:3).* If anyone wants to believe in Jesus properly, then he must first admit himself as a completely helpless sinner. In other words, he must confess that he cannot avoid but commit sin and be cast into hell, and he must demonstrate his helplessness by asking for God's mercy. Only when such a humble heart is relayed to God the Father does He have mercy on him when He sees him, saying, "I will save you through My Son." It is such people whom God the Father leads to His Son, and it is such people to whom Jesus gives His flesh and blood, allowing them to receive the remission of sin and everlasting life. They will then be remitted from all their sins and attain eternal life by believing in Jesus with their hearts.

No One Believes in Jesus as His Savior Just Because He Wants to Believe So

Judas always called Jesus *"rabbi,"* not *"Lord."* This

means that he did not believe in Jesus as His Savior who came down from Heaven. The title rabbi, which means teacher, may seem good in the secular realm, but in the born-again realm, it is not a good title. In God's Church, some other titles, such as "Mister" or "Miss," are not honorable titles either. If our servants of God call you "Mister so-and-so," then this is the evidence of the fact that they consider you as someone who has not been saved. In Jesus' sight, Judas was an offspring of the Devil. God cannot bestow His mercy on such people. God the Father does not lead such people to His Son Jesus.

Some of our brothers and sisters say, "I recognized and believed in Jesus who came by the water and the Spirit. When I first heard this gospel, I was so happy to hear it that I couldn't help but believe in it. But my friends did not believe. I don't understand why they wouldn't believe, when all that they have to is just believe." When we see people who don't believe in this wonderful gospel, we just can't understand them. So we think, "Why won't they believe, when that's all that they have to do? They must be so foolish!" However, when God sees them, they are utterly evil, and therefore He cannot have mercy on them. In other words, it is only too fitting for them to just live like this and end up in hell.

God extends His helping hands and gives the blessing of the remission of sin to someone who comes before His presence and asks Him for His mercy, not to anyone who shamelessly stands against God even in His presence. Such ungrateful people think, "Why did God make me like this only to suffer so much? Why did He allow me to be born in such a destitute family? If there is God, how could He have done this to me? Is this who God is?" Those whose hearts stand against God like this, who do not mourn for themselves, whose hearts are hardened, and who are satisfied only by the things of the world and not by the things of God—all these people are rejected by God. In other words, the Lord does not lead such people to the Father.

That is why it is absolutely indispensable for everyone to be humble before God. Even if the wickedness of the flesh arises, one should wake up, admit himself in all honesty, "I am such a worthless person," and ask God for His help. It is only such people whom God the Father leads to Jesus to be saved. Put differently, it is these people whom Jesus teaches His Word, thus enabling them to recognize their sins, as well as to receive the remission of their sins through the gospel of the water and the Spirit, and thereby making them God's children.

Today, even though there are countless Christians on this earth professing to believe in Jesus, they do not believe in the gospel of the water and the Spirit. What explains this? The answer to this puzzling question is found in today's Scripture passage. The Lord said, *"No one can come to Me unless it has been granted to him by My Father."* No one can reach his true salvation unless God the Father leads him, whether he is your friend or your own family member. That is precisely why we must pray to God on behalf of our beloved ones, asking Him, "Father, please lead my family. Please save them all." On their part too, they must also lower their hearts and ask God for His help, saying to Him, "God, please save me, for I am an evil person." Otherwise they will never believe in Jesus no matter how often they hear us explaining how He came by the water and the Spirit. On the contrary, their hearts will only be hardened to say, "I don't want to see you ever again if this is all you want to talk about."

Even though the gospel of the water and the Spirit is the real Truth, there are so many Christians who stubbornly refuse to believe in it until the very end. Yet despite this, I still preach this gospel of the water and the Spirit time after time, thousands and tens of thousands of times. These Christians must also put on God's mercy. We must pray for them so that God would have pity on them. We have to pray, "Lord, please have compassion on these souls and save them." That's because they are saved only if God the Father has mercy on them. Yet even after all this, if their souls still remain too hardened to deserve any compassion from God, then they will be cast into hell in the end. How could God the Father save such people, when they continue to stand against Him even as He wants to bestow His mercy on them? There is no other option but to cast them all into hell.

Even though more than 5,000 people were following Jesus in today's Scripture passage, when the Lord said to them, *"No one can come to Me unless it has been granted to him by My Father,"* most of them simply left. All those people in the crowd had followed Him around, saying, "Jesus, my Lord," but almost all of them went away like tidal ebb. The crowd was so large that it had over 5,000 men alone, who had followed Jesus around and said to Him, "Rabbi, You are our King and our hope," but they all left. So, it is written in John 6:66, *"From that time many of His disciples went back and walked with Him no more."* In other words, when the Lord said, "I give you My flesh and blood. Eat My flesh and drink My blood. You will then attain everlasting life and receive the remission of your sins," many of His followers could not understand this, and so they turned against Him and left, saying to themselves, "It's so hard to understand. He doesn't give us any more bread, but only says that the flesh profits nothing. It'll be all in vain to follow Him any longer. I guess He is not who I thought He was."

The Bible says that many of the disciples of Jesus went

away and walked with Him no more. The Lord then asked the twelve disciples, "Do you also want to go away?" Of more than 5,000 people, it appears that all of them had left except for the twelve disciples of Jesus. So the Lord asked them, "Do you also want to leave Me?" Then Simon Peter answered Him, *"Lord, to whom shall we go? You have the words of eternal life. Also we have come to believe and know that You are the Christ, the Son of the living God" (John 6:68-69).*

It is written in the Bible, *"For God so loved the world that He gave His only begotten Son, that whoever believes in Him should not perish but have everlasting life" (John 3:16).* God the Father sent His Son to this world, and this Son, coming incarnated in the flesh, took upon all our sins by being baptized, was crucified to death, arose from the dead, and has thereby become our Savior. If God says that this is how He has saved us from our sins, then we should grasp it and believe in it with a yes. How can anyone know the Truth unless he believes in God? If we don't realize from the Bible that God has spoken like this, or if we don't believe in it even when we realize it, then how would we be able to know that Jesus is God Himself and our Savior?

Peter answered Jesus by saying, "Lord, to whom shall we go? You have the words of eternal life. Also we have come to believe and know that You are the Christ, the Son of the living God." Jesus' disciples knew and believed that He was God Himself. And they understood what He said. However, those who did not understand the Word of the Lord all left Him. The Word of our Lord is the Word of eternal life. Because the Word of Truth that saves us is with the Lord, we can never depart from Jesus. Therefore, no matter what persecutions and temptations might come on our way, we can never forsake our faith in the Lord, nor ever leave His Church.

Given the fact that the Word of everlasting life resides inside God's Church, where would we go by turning away from it? Would you leave God's Church to pursue money? If you leave the Church, it's only because you don't believe in the Word; if you really believe in the Word, you can never bring yourself to leave. Would you be able to hear the Word of eternal life if you were to leave the Church? No, you won't hear it anywhere else. Would you be able to worship properly at this hour then? Do you think, "Well, I'll just establish my own church; I don't see why I shouldn't be able to worship"? Not just anyone can establish a church and minister. God said,

"Unless the LORD builds the house,
They labor in vain who build it;
Unless the LORD guards the city,
The watchman stays awake in vain" (Psalm 127:1).

You can plant a church and minister only if God is with you, works on you, and gives you His Word and faith; it is not the case that anyone can minister at a church just with his own determination. While anyone can preach the gospel, not anyone can establish a church and lead other souls.

When the Lord said, "Do you also want to go away?" Peter had the following answer: "When You have the Word of eternal life, where will we go, and where will we look for the Word of everlasting life?" While the other disciples remained quiet, Peter answered like this. Peter was the first among the disciples, a true pioneer of faith.

What the Lord said is the Truth. Today, people keep translating the Bible into new versions. There is a load of money to be made with every new Bible publication, and so targeting this, they continue to translate the Bible into new versions. But could they really come up with a better translation of the Bible than what we have now, even if they were to live for 5,000 years to research and translate the Scriptures all that time? There is a saying in Korea that an ignorant man is a brave man—like such a fool, these people plow ahead recklessly to translate the Bible all on their own without even knowing the gospel of Truth that would enable them be really born again, but once they are finished, their translation is actually full of mistakes.

Even if one considers himself to be a man of great learning with impeccable writing skills, once he tries to express his convictions in writing, he will likely hit a dead end after writing only a few pages. Perhaps that's why we respect novelists. We respect them because while their stories are fictional, it's never so easy to observe our physical surroundings and human relationships to such a penetrating depth, reconstruct them all, and put them together into a book. However, human ability is nothing in the realm of the Spirit of God. So, we must humble our hearts before God and listen carefully to what He is saying through His Word.

The Word of eternal life is with the Lord. That is why we listen to His Word, and why we believe in it upon realization. Our Lord is the bread that came down from Heaven, and He is the One who, having ascended to Heaven, will return to this earth one day. The day when the Lord returns is the day when the history of this planet earth will end. When war and famine break out everywhere, you should realize that that this very day has come near.

When the Lord returns to this earth, He will raise our bodies back to life again. This is the Word of Truth. Jesus Himself said, *"For assuredly, I say to you, till heaven and earth pass away, one jot or one tittle will by no means pass from the law till all is fulfilled"* (Matthew 5:18). The salvation that our Lord has brought to you and me through the gospel of the water and the Sprit is forever effective. It will remain effective even when we are in the Kingdom of Heaven.

I thank God for giving us His Word of eternal life. ⊠

HAVE YOU TRULY BEEN BORN AGAIN OF WATER AND THE SPIRIT?

HAVE YOU TRULY BEEN BORN AGAIN OF WATER AND THE SPIRIT?

PAUL C. JONG

Among many Christian books written about being born again, this is the first book of our time to preach the gospel of the water and the Spirit in strict accordance with the Scriptures. Man can't enter the Kingdom of Heaven without being born again of water and the Spirit. To be born again means that a sinner is saved from all his lifelong sins by believing in the baptism of Jesus and His blood of the Cross. Let's believe in the gospel of the water and the Spirit and enter the Kingdom of Heaven as the righteous who have no sin.

RETURN TO THE GOSPEL OF THE WATER AND THE SPIRIT

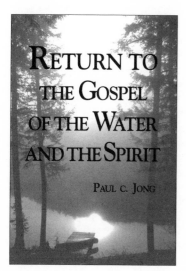

RETURN TO THE GOSPEL OF THE WATER AND THE SPIRIT

PAUL C. JONG

Let's return to the gospel of the water and the Spirit. Theology and doctrines themselves can't save us. However, many Christians still follow them, and consequently have not been born again yet. This book clearly tells us what mistakes theology and doctrines have made and how to believe in Jesus in the most proper way.

The Fail-safe Way for You to Receive the Holy Spirit

In Christianity, the most significantly discussed issue is salvation from sins and the indwelling of the Holy Spirit. However, few people have the exact knowledge of these two topics. Nevertheless, in reality people say that they believe in Jesus Christ while they are ignorant of true redemption and the Holy Spirit.

Do you know the true gospel that makes you receive the Holy Spirit? If you want to ask God for the indwelling of the Holy Spirit, then you must first know the gospel of the water and the Spirit and have faith in it. This book will certainly lead all Christians worldwide to receive the Holy Spirit through the remission of all their sins.

Our LORD Who Becomes the Righteousness of God (I) & (II)

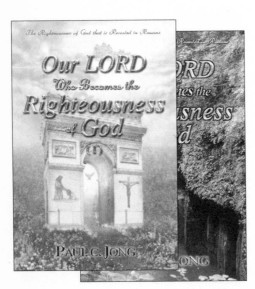

The teachings in these books will satisfy the thirst in your heart. Today's Christians continue to live while not knowing the true solution to the personal sins that they are committing daily. Do you know what God's righteousness is? The author hopes that you will ask yourself this question and believe in God's righteousness, which is dealt in detail in these books.

The Doctrines of Predestination, Justification, and Incremental Sanctification are the major Christian doctrines, which brought only confusion and emptiness into the souls of believers. But, dear Christians, now is the time when you must continue in the Truth which you have learned and been assured of.

These books will provide your soul with a great understanding and lead it to peace. The author wants you to possess the blessing of knowing God's righteousness.

IS THE AGE OF THE ANTICHRIST, MARTYRDOM, RAPTURE AND THE MILLENNIAL KINGDOM COMING? (I)

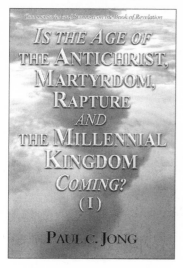

After the 9/11 terrorist attacks, traffic to "www.raptureready.com," an Internet site providing information on the end times, is reported to have increased to over 8 million hits, and according to a joint survey by CNN and TIME, over 59% of the Americans now believe in apocalyptic eschatology.

Responding to such demands of the time, the author provides a clear exposition of the key themes of the Book of Revelation, including the coming Antichrist, the martyrdom of the saints and their rapture, the Millennial Kingdom, and the New Heaven and Earth-all in the context of the whole Scripture and under the guidance of the Holy Spirit.

This book provides verse-by-verse commentaries on the Book of Revelation supplemented by the author's inspired sermons. Anyone who reads this book will come to grasp all the plans that God has in store for this world.

IS THE AGE OF THE ANTICHRIST, MARTYRDOM, RAPTURE AND THE MILLENNIAL KINGDOM COMING? (II)

Most Christians today believe in the theory of pre-tribulation rapture. Because they believe in this false doctrine teaching them that they would be lifted before the coming of the Great Tribulation of seven years, they are leading idle religious lives steeped in complacency.

But the rapture of the saints will occur only after the plagues of the seven trumpets run their course until the sixth plague is all poured-that is, the rapture will happen after the Antichrist emerges amidst global chaos and the born-again saints are martyred, and when the seventh trumpet is blown. It is at this time that Jesus would descend from Heaven, and the resurrection and rapture of the born-again saints would occur (1 Thessalonians 4:16-17).

The righteous who were born again by believing in "the gospel of the water and the Spirit" will be resurrected and take part in the Rapture, and thus become heirs to the Millennial Kingdom and the eternal Kingdom of Heaven, but the sinners who were unable to participate in this first resurrection will face the great punishment of the seven bowls poured by God and be cast into the eternal fire of hell.

The TABERNACLE: A Detailed Portrait of Jesus Christ (I)

How can we find out the truth hidden in the Tabernacle? Only by knowing the gospel of the water and the Spirit, the real substance of the Tabernacle, can we correctly understand and know the answer to this question.

In fact, the blue, purple, and scarlet thread and the fine woven linen manifested in the gate of the Tabernacle's court show us the works of Jesus Christ in the New Testament's time that have saved the mankind. In this way, the Old Testament's Word of the Tabernacle and the Word of the New Testament are closely and definitely related to each other, like fine woven linen. But, unfortunately, this truth has been hidden for a long time to every truth seeker in Christianity.

Coming to this earth, Jesus Christ was baptized by John and shed His blood on the Cross. Without understanding and believing in the gospel of the water and the Spirit, none of us can ever find out the truth revealed in the Tabernacle. We must now learn this truth of the Tabernacle and believe in it. We all need to realize and believe in the truth manifested in the blue, purple, and scarlet thread and the fine woven linen of the gate of the Tabernacle's court.

The TABERNACLE: A Detailed Portrait of Jesus Christ (II)

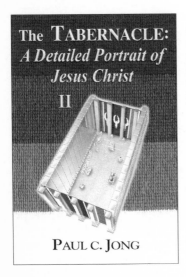

As God had commanded Moses to build the Tabernacle in the Old Testament, in the New Testament, God wants us to also build a Sanctuary in each of our hearts so that He may dwell in us. The material of faith with which we can build this Sanctuary in our hearts is the Word of the gospel of the water and the Spirit. With this gospel of the water and the Spirit, we must wash away all our sins and be cleansed. By telling us to build Him a Sanctuary, God is telling us to empty our hearts and believe in the gospel of the water and the Spirit. We must all cleanse our hearts by believing in the gospel of the water and the Spirit.

When we cleanse away all the sins of our hearts by believing in this gospel Truth, God then comes to dwell in them. It is by believing in this true gospel that you can build the holy Temples in your hearts. It is highly likely that until now, at least some of you have probably been offering your prayers of repentance to cleanse your hearts, trying to build the Temples by yourselves. But now is the time for you to abandon this false faith and be transformed by the renewing of your minds by believing in the gospel of the water and the Spirit.

The Elementary Principles of CHRIST

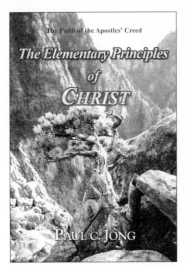

We must have the faith that the Apostles had and believe as they did, for their faith and beliefs came from the Holy Spirit. The Apostles believed in Jesus Christ, His Father, and the Holy Spirit as their God.

The Apostle Paul confessed that he died with Christ and was brought to new life with Him. He became an instrument of God by believing that he was baptized into Jesus Christ (Galatians 3:27). In God's gospel are found the baptism that Jesus received, the blood that He shed on the Cross, and the gift of the Holy Spirit that He has bestowed on everyone who believes in this true gospel of the water and the Spirit.

Do you know and believe in this original gospel? This is the very gospel that the Apostles had also believed. We, too, must therefore all believe in the gospel of the water and the Spirit.

The Gospel of Matthew (I) & (II)

There are countless new Christians throughout the world, who have just been born again by believing in the gospel of the water and the Spirit that we have been spreading. We are indeed yearning to feed on the bread of life to them. But it is difficult for them to have fellowship with us in the true gospel, for they are all far away from us.

Therefore, to meet the spiritual needs of these people of Jesus Christ, the King of kings, The author proclaims that those who have received the remission of their sins by believing in the Word of Jesus Christ, must feed on His pure Word in order to defend their faith and sustain their spiritual lives. The sermons in these books have been prepared as new bread of life that will nourish the born-again to edify their spiritual growth.

Through His Church and servants, God will continue to provide you with this bread of life. May God's blessings be on all those who have been born again of water and the Spirit, who desires to have true spiritual fellowship with us in Jesus Christ.

The First Epistle of John (I) & (II)

He who believes that Jesus, who is God and the Savior, came by the gospel of the water and the Spirit to deliver all sinners from their sins, is saved from all his sins, and becomes a child of God the Father.

The First Epistle of John states that Jesus, who is God, came to us by the gospel of the water and the Spirit, and that He is the Son of God the Father. The Book, in other words, mostly emphasizes that Jesus is God (1 John 5:20), and concretely testifies the gospel of the water and the Spirit in chapter 5.

We must not hesitate to believe that Jesus Christ is God and to follow Him.

Sermons on Galatians: From Physical Circumcision to the Doctrine of Repentance (I) & (II)

Today's Christianity has turned into merely a world religion. Most Christians nowadays live in a situation of being sinners because they haven't been born again by spiritual faith. It is because they have only relied on Christian doctrines without being aware of the gospel of the water and the Spirit until now.

Therefore, now is the time for you to know the spiritual fallacies of the circumcisionists and keep distance from such faith. You have to know the contradictoriness of the prayers of repentance. Now is the time for you to stand firmer than ever on the gospel of the water and the Spirit.

If you haven't believed in this true gospel so far, you have to believe in our Savior who came to us by the gospel of the water and the Spirit even now. Now, you have to be complete Christians with the faith of believing in the gospel Truth of the water and the Spirit.

The Love of God Revealed through Jesus, The Only Begotten Son

It is written, "No one has seen God at any time. The only begotten Son, who is in the bosom of the Father, He has declared Him" (John 1:18).

How perfectly did Jesus reveal the love of God to us! How perfectly did Jesus deliver us! What perfect Truth of salvation is the gospel of the water and the Spirit! We have never regretted receiving our salvation through our faith in Jesus, who came by water and blood (1 John 5:6).

Now, we have become His sinless people. Whoever believes in the gospel of the water and the Spirit can receive the eternal remission of sins and earn eternal life.

THE WILL OF THE HOLY TRINITY FOR HUMAN BEINGS

Through the Book of Genesis, God wants us to realize His good intentions toward us. Where is God's will for us revealed? It is revealed in the gospel Truth of the water and the Spirit that God accomplished through Jesus Christ. We must come into this good intention of God by faith, manifested in the gospel of the water and the Spirit. To do so, when we consider God's Word, we need to cast aside our existing carnal thoughts we have had, and believe in God's Word exactly as it is. All of us must throw away our mistaken knowledge accumulated until now, and open our spiritual eyes by placing our faith in the righteousness of God.

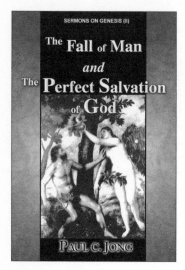

In the Book of Genesis, the purpose for which God created us is contained. When architects design a building or artists draw a painting, they first conceive the work that would be completed in their minds before they actually begin working on their project. Just like this, our God also had our salvation of mankind in His mind even before He created the heavens and the earth, and He made Adam and Eve with this purpose in mind. And God needed to explain to us the domain of Heaven, which is not seen by our eyes of the flesh, by drawing an analogy to the domain of the earth that we can all see and understand.

Even before the foundation of the world, God wanted to save mankind perfectly by giving the gospel of the water and the Spirit to everyone's heart. So although all human beings were made out of dust, they must learn and know the gospel Truth of the water and the Spirit to benefit their own souls. If people continue to live without knowing the dominion of Heaven, they will lose not only the things of the earth, but also everything that belongs to Heaven.

Paul C. Jong's Christian books have been translated into 51 major languages at this point: Albanian, Arabic, Bengali, Bulgarian, Burmese, Chichewa, Chinese, Croatian, Czech, Danish, Dutch, English, French, Georgian, German, Greek, Gujarati, Hebrew, Hindi, Hungarian, Indonesian, Iranian, Italian, Japanese, Javanese, Kannada, Khmer, Latvian, Malagasy, Marathi, Mongolian, Nepali, Polish, Portuguese, Romanian, Russian, Serbian, Slovak, Slovene, Spanish, Swahili, Swedish, Tagalog, Taiwanese, Tamil, Telugu, Thai, Turkish, Ukrainian, Urdu, and Vietnamese. They are also available now through our free e-book service.

E-book is digital book designed for you to feel a printed book on screen. You can read it easily on your PC monitor in your native language after downloading the viewer software and a text file. Feel free to visit our web site at http://www.nlmission.com   http://www.bjnewlife.org   to download our e-books, and you will get the most remarkable Christian e-books absolutely for free.

And, would you like to take part in having our free Christian books known to more people worldwide? We would be very thankful if you link your website to ours so that many people get an opportunity to meet Jesus Christ through our inspired Christian books. Please visit our site at http://www.bjnewlife.org/english/about/take_banners.php to take our banners to your website. In addition, we would be also very thankful if you introduce our website to the webmasters around you for adding our link.

The New Life Mission
Contact: John Shin, General Secretary
E-mail: newlife@bjnewlife.org

Memo

Memo

 Memo

Memo

Memo